Iron Dads

Critical Issues in Sport and Society

Michael Messner and Douglas Hartmann, Series Editors

Critical Issues in Sport and Society features scholarly books that help expand our understanding of the new and myriad ways in which sport is intertwined with social life in the contemporary world. Using the tools of various scholarly disciplines, including sociology, anthropology, history, media studies and others, books in this series investigate the growing impact of sport and sports-related activities on various aspects of social life as well as key developments and changes in the sporting world and emerging sporting practices. Series authors produce groundbreaking research that brings empirical and applied work together with cultural critique and historical perspectives written in an engaging, accessible format.

Jules Boykoff, *Activism and the Olympics: Dissent at the Games in Vancouver and London*

Diana Tracy Cohen, *Iron Dads: Managing Family, Work, and Endurance Sport Identities*

Jennifer Guiliano, *Indian Spectacle: College Mascots and the Anxiety of Modern America*

Kathryn Henne, *Testing for Athlete Citizenship: The Regulation of Doping and Sex in Sport*

Michael A. Messner and Michela Musto, eds., *Child's Play: Sport in Kid's Worlds*

Jeffrey Montez de Oca, *Discipline and Indulgence: College Football, Media, and the American Way of Life during the Cold War*

Stephen C. Poulson, *Why Would Anyone Do That? Lifestyle Sport in the Twenty-First Century*

Iron Dads

MANAGING FAMILY, WORK, AND ENDURANCE SPORT IDENTITIES

Diana Tracy Cohen

RUTGERS UNIVERSITY PRESS

New Brunswick, New Jersey, and London

Library of Congress Cataloging-in-Publication Data

Names: Cohen, Diana Tracy, 1981– author.
Title: Iron dads : managing family, work, and endurance sport identities / Diana Tracy
Cohen.
Description: New Brunswick, New Jersey : Rutgers University Press, [2016] | Series: Critical
issues in sport and society | Includes bibliographical references and index.
Identifiers: LCCN 2015032496| ISBN 9780813570952 (hardcover : alk. paper) |
ISBN 9780813570945 (pbk. : alk. paper) | ISBN 9780813570969 (web pdf) |
ISBN 9780813573748 (epub)
Subjects: LCSH: Triathletes—Psychology. | Triathletes—Family relationships. |
Fathers—Psychology. | Fathers—Family relationships. | Triathlon—Psychological aspects. |
Endurance sports—Psychological aspects.
Classification: LCC GV1060.73.C59   2016 | DDC 796.42/57—dc23
LC record available at http://lccn.loc.gov/2015032496

A British Cataloging-in-Publication record for this book is available from the
British Library.

Visit our website: http://rutgerspress.rutgers.edu

Manufactured in the United States of America

To my parents, Loreen and David, and my husband, Dan

CONTENTS

Acknowledgments   *ix*

Abbreviations and Definitions   *xiii*

1   Taking the First Step   1

2   Inside Triathlon Culture   26

3   To Tri or Not to Try   41

4   The Juggling Act   61

5   Why Class Matters   87

6   Faith Meets 140.6   109

7   Throwing in the Towel   121

8   The Road Ahead   133

Appendix: Methodological Reflections   153

Notes   169

References   173

Index   187

ACKNOWLEDGMENTS

Even though an iron-distance triathlon looks like a solo event on its face, competing is really a team effort. Family, friends, coaches, training partners, medical professionals, bike mechanics, massage therapists, and others all work feverishly to help an athlete reach the finish line. Like most endurance sport endeavors, the experience of preparing this manuscript was made possible thanks to the effort of a dedicated team of individuals. While the road was not always paved with endless bike lanes or brightened by sunny skies, I am thankful to the many people who made this journey possible. In particular, I would like to thank the fifty men who shared their stories with me. I continue to be humbled by their generosity. Thanks go out to these incredible Iron Dads for giving me their time, for speaking candidly, and for making this project possible.

I thank Central Connecticut State University for supporting my research in various ways. The Carol A. Ammon College of Liberal Arts and Social Sciences provided me with both financial resources and valuable course release opportunities. A special acknowledgment is extended to Dean Susan Pease and Associate Dean Richard Roth for seeing merit in this work. The talented and passionate faculty members in my department help to make CCSU a wonderful place to work. Thanks to Jerold Duquette for reading sections of my manuscript and taking an interest in my progress. Paul Petterson supported me at every turn in this project, as he has since I joined the faculty in 2008. I was eternally grateful to have Paul at the helm of our humble department for so many years. This project was enhanced by the efforts of two talented undergraduate research assistants, Jonathan Salomone and Ryan Baldassario.

I would like to thank Rutgers University Press for bringing this book to life. As a first-time author, knowing that I could turn to senior editor Peter Mickulas for prompt and candid advice was invaluable as the book took form. Copyeditor Molan Goldstein, prepress department director Marilyn Campbell, and production editor Carrie Hudak all offered critical feedback that improved the quality of my writing. Kevin Young from the University of Calgary and Fayne Linda Wachs from California State Polytechnic

University, Pomona, both gave the book a meticulous reading. Their investment in my research, evident in their highly insightful and incredibly thorough reviews, was greatly appreciated. Finally, I extend my gratitude to Critical Issues in Sport and Society series editors Douglas Hartmann and Michael Messner for welcoming my work to this exciting collection of groundbreaking research.

My sociology dissertation committee members—William Marsiglio, Kendal Broad, Charles Gattone, Tamir Sorek, and Jim Leary—were vital enablers of this project. Thanks for welcoming me back to Gainesville. Working with this talented and caring group helped fuel my passion for interdisciplinary thinking. William Marsiglio, my committee chairperson, was the driving force in helping this book take form. He pushed my work ethic to a new level of excellence and inspired my sociological imagination. His patience and selflessness is something that I seek to emulate when mentoring my own students. Returning to the University of Florida to pursue my sociological interests was the most rewarding experience of my life. I grew immensely in both the personal and professional realms. I am thankful to all who enabled that life-changing opportunity. I also extend a special acknowledgment to members of my University of Florida political science dissertation committee—Beth Rosenson, Daniel A. Smith, Lawrence C. Dodd, David Hedge, and Kendal Broad—for teaching me the skills to become successful in academia. It was an honor to be mentored by such passionate scholars who take a sincere interest in bettering the lives of their students.

It was not that long ago when I got my first exposure to triathlon. Prior to 2007, I was just a casual runner. My life changed when, while working as a student intern for the Hartford Marathon Foundation in 2006, I met Barry Stoner. Barry and I have become great friends and training partners. I remember the day that we went down to Lake Terramugus in Marlborough, Connecticut. It was there where I learned how to swim. Thanks to the one and only "Hillman" for introducing me to this wonderful lifestyle and for giving me memories that I look upon with great fondness. Thanks also go out to the people who have helped keep me on the race course. I have the best team of professionals standing by me in Daniel Veltri and Scott Gregorc. A special thank you goes out to my friends Steven S. Smith, Phillip P. Smith, Hans Franzen, and Jonathan Wright. The world needs more people like them. I also extend my eternal gratitude to Grandmaster Moo Yong Lee and the United Tae Kwon Do family. Grandmaster Lee's teaching philosophies have had a profound impact on my life. His classes are poetry in motion.

Finally, I want to acknowledge my family. My love goes out to Grandmas Nana and Nono. I know that Nono is talking politics with someone up above right now. She is probably taking out her frustrations on some unsuspecting conservative as I write. I miss our talks dearly. My love also goes out to the Wertz family and the Howard Beach branch of the Cohen clan. Thanks to Uncle Ash, Aunt Sandra, and cousins Lisa, Aaron, Alison, and Christal. Next, I want to acknowledge my mother and father, Loreen and David. They have been my biggest fans. I love them both very much and wish them health and happiness each and every day. Unfortunately, Dad has to deal with the fact that I like the Tampa Bay Rays. As a Yankees fan, he probably wonders if we can even be friends. Yes, we can still be friends—except when our teams play one another. Then all bets are off. Finally, thanks to my partner, Dan. Dan's continual stream of selfless encouragement is a gift that I treasure. His sense of humor and willingness to try new things keeps life fun. I thank him for being my partner in crime. I look forward to a lifetime of unpredictable adventures with him by my side.

Columbia, Connecticut
June 2015

ABBREVIATIONS AND DEFINITIONS

70.3	The numerical abbreviation for a half iron (or IRONMAN 70.3) triathlon. The figure represents the number of miles competitors travel over the course of said event—1.2-mile swim, 56-mile bike, 13.1-mile run.
140.6	The numerical abbreviation for a full iron (or IRONMAN) triathlon. The figure represents the number of miles competitors travel over the course of said event—2.4-mile swim, 112-mile bike, 26.2-mile run.
BT	Beginnertriathlete.com, an online triathlon forum.
DNF	Did not finish. This is when a competitor starts a race but drops out prior to reaching the finish line.
DNS	Did not start. This is when a competitor intends to race, usually indicated by advance event registration, but does not start.
IM	IRONMAN, a corporate brand name owned by World Triathlon Corporation. It also refers to a distance, with "IRONMAN" corresponding to a race of 140.6 miles and "IRONMAN 70.3" corresponding to a race of 70.3 miles.
Non-branded	Non-branded triathlon events. These are general iron-distance (140.6) or half-iron-distance (70.3) events that are put on by a company other than World Triathlon Corporation. "Non-branded" is synonymous with the term "independent" race.
ST	Slowtwitch.com, an online triathlon forum.
T1	The first transition in a triathlon. Competitors transition from swim to bike.
T2	The second transition in a triathlon. Competitors transition from bike to run.
Transition	A space where competitors advance from one discipline to another. There are two transitions in a typical triathlon.
Tri	Triathlon, a sport consisting of swim, bike, and run segments.

WTC   World Triathlon Corporation. This corporation owns the IRONMAN brand.

XC   Executive Challenge, a program designed by World Triathlon Corporation exclusively for top-end executives participating in one of their 70.3 or 140.6 events.

Iron Dads

1

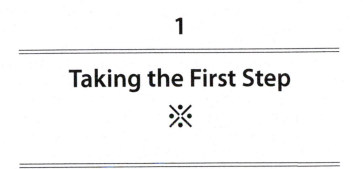

Taking the First Step

A record-setting 2,701 athletes stand on the beach of Lake Winnipesaukee, a picturesque race venue located in the mountains of New Hampshire. The IRONMAN Timberman 70.3 triathlon is about to begin. Nervous energy flows throughout the crowd. Athletes wrapped in neoprene wetsuits and race-issued swim caps engage in last-minute mental gymnastics to prepare for their journey. Being in one of the later swim waves, I stand on the edge of the beach taking in the scene. This view never gets old. The athletes are hard to distinguish from one another save the variety of swim cap colors that decorate the crowd. The scene is busy. Some competitors are in the water warming up while others stand on the side of the beach and stretch. A number of athletes are talking with friends and family members on the water's edge. Others stand pensively looking out at the bright orange buoys that line the swim course. Among the crowd of black rubber, one athlete stands out to me. He is a tall, thin man waiting on the shore. He stands smiling, lifting his daughter out of her carriage. He raises her up above his head, down to his knees, then back up again. The father and daughter duo share a smile.

The father is about to embark on a difficult athletic undertaking. IRON-MAN Timberman 70.3, as the name implies, will require the man to travel 70.3 miles under his own locomotion. He will swim 1.2 miles, bike 56 miles, and then run 13.1 miles, all in an attempt to beat the eight-hour and thirty-minute event cutoff. In addition to the distance, the father may be quick to point out that not all race venues offer similar terrain. Today's event takes place in New Hampshire, a locale that features challenging hills in the bike segment. The task ahead is not for the faint of heart.

The race start requires athletes to line up according to their respective swim waves. Each wave consists of people sharing common age and sex demographics. In an attempt to spread out the number of people heading off on the course at one time, the waves are staggered in five-minute increments. As one wave begins the race, each successive group moves up in line and holds at the start. There are twenty waves in all this morning. We are now approaching the start of the first group, the professional men. The scene is one of controlled chaos, with people shuffling in all different directions. Despite this seemingly panicked atmosphere, the father still stands on the edge of the water caught in a moment of joy with his daughter. The man reaches in the carriage and tickles his baby girl. They are inside their own world. The father is seemingly oblivious to the fact that the first wave has gone off and that most athletes have taken their place in their respective holding areas. I watch as the duo embrace each other for the final time. After a few more moments of play, a woman, seemingly the mother of the child, approaches the carriage. She shares a few quiet words with the triathlete, gives him a kiss on the cheek, and begins to wheel the carriage toward the swim exit. It is there where they will wait for their Iron Dad to emerge from the crisp waters of Lake Winnipesaukee.

With the father now standing alone, I felt compelled to better understand the background of this intriguing competitor. Who is he? What does he do for a living? What inspired him to race this morning? How does he balance being an athlete and a father? When does he have time to train? Excited to learn the details of his story, I approach the man as he looks for his respective holding area. His name is Mark. He works as a patent attorney in Massachusetts where he lives with his wife, Francie, and one-year-old daughter, Michelle. He trains for half and full iron-distance events in his fleeting spare time. Today he is hoping to complete IRONMAN Timberman 70.3 in under five hours. He expresses concerns that lack of training opportunities may slow him down, but he is dedicated to competing as hard as he can. All of his hard work will be on display as he moves from discipline to discipline.

It is not uncommon to overhear triathletes talking about very elaborate race schedules. For athletes living in New England, as Mark does, this typically means filling the calendar with events from May through early October. I was interested to know how IRONMAN Timberman 70.3 fit into Mark's competitive season. Was this his "A" race, the biggest race of his season? Was he training for something bigger, such a full iron-distance triathlon? Based on his composure at the race start, my own racing experience led me to suspect that Mark was not a first-time competitor. Wanting to learn more about these details of his training, Mark and I continued chatting as the various swim waves went off. I knew that our opportunity to talk was dwindling so I pushed the conversation as long as I could.

As I had suspected, Mark is a seasoned iron-distance competitor with six years of endurance sport training and racing under his belt. His race today is part of a long triathlon season that will conclude with IRON-MAN Florida in early November. In that event, Mark will seek to travel 140.6 miles. An iron-distance triathlon consists of a 2.4-mile swim, 112-mile bike, and 26.2-mile run, all performed consecutively. He will have seventeen hours to complete the event, needing to beat intermittent time cutoffs along the way. As Mark and I slowly inch closer to our respective swim starts, he briefly outlines his training regimen with me. The schedule closely resembles a full-time job. It includes early-morning spins before work, swimming during his lunch hour, and running on the treadmill after everyone has gone to bed. This type of training is necessary, he assures me. Mark will train for twenty hours a week at the peak of his workout schedule. It is all done in hopes of setting a personal record in Florida later this year, with a long-term eye toward qualifying for the IRONMAN World Championship race in Kona.

Mark's story resonated with me. In 2009, I trained for IRONMAN Wisconsin, my first full-distance triathlon, while balancing the roles of wife, junior faculty member, friend, daughter, and athlete in other sports. I have been competing in half and iron-distance triathlon races ever since. I often find that there is not enough time in the day to pay attention to all of my responsibilities. Life becomes a daily juggling act—an act that becomes particularly pronounced during my more intense training periods. I am constantly assessing what my priorities are at any given moment. Over the years, I have also come to realize just how selfish an activity endurance sport can often be. Thankfully, I am privileged to have a spouse that is supportive of my activities. Tolerating a partner who goes on five-hour training rides on the weekend, scatters bike parts throughout every room in the house, and talks about triathlon at every meal is not easy. In realizing how lucky I was, I began to wonder how other families handled the training burden. My husband and I operate in the context of a childless marriage. Once a couple decides to have a child, managing responsibilities becomes exponentially more complex. Children consume energy, resources, and time. So does long-course triathlon. Given the complexities of mixing parenthood and iron-distance training, one has to wonder why parents decide to compete in the first place, as well as how positions of social privilege shape that choice.

As an active triathlon competitor and social scientist, I have an interest in how people fit endurance sport training into their daily lives. The scene with Mark and his daughter Michelle brought human faces to this seemingly abstract sociological puzzle. Mark is a living, breathing Iron Dad—a man who actively juggles work, family, and endurance sport identities.

Listening to his story brought a lot of questions to mind. How do fathers with families, full-time jobs, and other responsibilities fit a high level of endurance training into their lives? What happens at this nexus of work, family, and sport? What sacrifices are made both in the workplace and in the home to reach the goal of crossing an iron-distance finish line? How do Iron Dads construct their image of good fathering? Is it possible for fathers to meet their own parenting expectations while working toward that elusive finish? How does the experience of privilege engender the desire to test oneself in a long-course triathlon? At what point does "sport" become "work"? Finally, how does training for and competing in 140.6-mile triathlon events influence one's fathering identity, and vice versa? After hearing Mark's story, I decided to investigate this exciting line of research. It was there on the beach of Lake Winnipesaukee that the concept for this study was born.

Why Iron Dads?

This research focuses on a population that I call Iron Dads—men like Mark who negotiate work, family, and endurance sport identities. One question that will undoubtedly arise to readers is why the focus on fathers. As one colleague tried to convince me at the inception of this project, "Iron Moms are the more interesting story." I argue that Iron Dads and Iron Moms share equally interesting yet subtly distinct stories. It is in exploring these subtle distinctions that a major project focusing exclusively on fathers is warranted. A future study focusing on mothers is similarly called for. Through exploring the narratives of my study participants, I uncover the details of their lived experiences as fathers, endurance athletes, workers, and men.

People may be quick to assert that Iron Moms are the more interesting story because of the perceived dedication that they have toward being parents. Society expects mothers to be engaged, nurturing caretakers. Common cultural dialogue suggests that family commitments come before work. For example, we commonly hear that a woman's natural sphere is in the private domain (Milestone and Meyer 2012). The term "housework" is, for the most part, socially constructed as the work of a woman (Ryle 2015). Thus, society has seemingly prioritized roles for mothers already—you are a parent first, a triathlete second. At the same time, people may perceive a parallel yet slightly distinct social narrative for fathers. This narrative expects fathers to be engaged and nurturing parents, but offers them more forgiveness when they neglect their parental responsibilities. So, when conflicts arise between family and sport, people may *perceive* that fathers have more flexibility to choose between the two roles. This is because, at the core, common societal discourse still situates mothers at the center of child-rearing activities. These common discourses, in my opinion, are inconsistent with how many men and women experience their worlds.

It is valuable to reflect on the changing expectations and behaviors of both men and women. First, while fathers' family engagement has not risen to the same level of mothers', the reality is that resident fathers are spending more time with their children (Kaufman 2013; Lamb 2010; Pleck and Masciadrelli 2004). A 2009 study found that on average, employed fathers spend approximately three hours per workday with children under the age of thirteen (Galinsky, Aumann, and Bond 2009). This is up from two hours per workday in the preceding decade (Yeung et al. 2001). The degree of contact, including both emotional and physical involvement with their children, is something that is of increasing importance to many fathers (Eggebeen and Knoester 2001). Second, fathers are also embracing more child-centered approaches to parenting (Coakley 2006). Gayle Kaufman (2013) coined the term "superdads," referring to a new and growing cohort of men. "Old" dads subscribe to more old-fashioned views of parenting. They see their role as being the breadwinner of the family. Kaufman suggests that these individuals "make little change to their work lives upon becoming parents" (6). "New" dads embrace a more progressive view of fatherhood, altering some of their work practices. "Superdads," Kaufman offers, "deliberately adjust their work lives to fit their family lives" (7). These dads enter the private domain, spheres traditionally reserved for women, with great enthusiasm (Kaufman 2013). This suggests that the behaviors of some fathers are changing.

Despite these encouraging trends, larger questions loom in the minds of many men. Parenthood is in a time of flux, and, consequently, expectations for fatherly involvement are unclear. This is in part because there is no single model of fathering (Flouri 2005; Kaufman 2013). This is also because we see changing norms regarding men, women, and their roles in both the home and workplace. More women are entering the workforce. A few trends are notable in this regard. First, for many families, economic challenges have necessitated women's presence in the workplace. Second, a sizable percentage of women are financially responsible for their families— a figure that is growing exponentially. A 2013 Pew Research Center study found that 40 percent of households with at least one child under the age of eighteen had a "breadwinning mom," defined as a solo or primary female income earner (Wang, Parker, and Taylor 2013). This same statistic was 11 percent in 1960, demonstrating a clear increasing pressure for mothers to provide income for their families. New trends are also emerging in the context of dual-earning households, with an increasing number of these women making more than their male partners. In 2008, 26 percent of all dual-earning households saw the wife earning at least 10 percent more than her husband (Galinsky, Aumann, and Bond 2009; US Census Bureau 2010). These trends present a serious challenge to traditional parenting roles and the social perception of who should be the breadwinner of the family.

Strong contradictory messages surrounding fatherhood have consequences at both the micro and macro levels (Kay 2006). Fathers still face a constant tension between needing to be the breadwinner and being a nurturing parent (Kay 2009; Marsiglio and Roy 2012). Society often projects a "more is better" approach when it comes to spending time with children (Kaufman 2013). At the same time, the desire to be the breadwinner is closely interwoven with contemporary definitions of hegemonic masculinity, common societal norms of what it means to be a man. While these narratives of masculinity are not the only ones in existence, they are dominant in society. This means that many men regard income as an important component of their vision of the masculine self. While their children are young, and potentially even well after that, fathers internalize the burden of keeping the family financially stable (Christiansen and Palkovitz 2001). Seeking financial rewards in the workplace may mean dedicating oneself more to the job, effectively taking the man away from his family. Fathers tend to have greater attachment to their jobs than they did before having a child. The inverse is true for women who become mothers (Kay 2009). Employed fathers are also more likely to report feelings of time deficit with their children compared to mothers (Bianchi 2011). This leads to distinct challenges for men when attempting to negotiate multiple identities. If fathers are investing more time in their employment, how can they be involved parents?

Sport and leisure activities serve as powerful mediums for fathers to be active with their children. Andrea Doucet (2006) found that many fathers see themselves as being less competent caretakers than their child's mother. With society emphasizing the connection between sport and masculinity, physical activity becomes an attractive context for fathers to engage and even nurture their children. Some men feel a heightened sense of caretaking competence in these situations. Physical activities may also present opportunities to make unique connections with their children (Kay 2009). For example, Ralph LaRossa (2009) argues that the game of catch is "meant to symbolize paternal bonding" between father and son (36). Due to the physical proximity required in the game of catch, this athletic context allows for fathers and their children to converse in meaningful ways. Is it possible that endurance sport training, such as running or biking together, may provide similar opportunities for father-child engagement?

Some observers may perceive a sharp division between parenting opportunities and engaging in endurance sport training. Their perception stems from the view that participation in endurance sport is a selfish activity. This study's participants confirm that there is a substantial degree of truth to that statement. If they permit it, long-course triathlon training can consume competitors emotionally, physically, and financially. I am not suggesting, however, that parenting and endurance sport cannot and do not coexist. To the contrary, many of the men I interviewed went out of their way to involve their child in training opportunities. This included activities such as swimming with their child during pool workouts, riding an indoor bike trainer while watching movies with the family, and running outdoors as their child biked alongside them. Like Iron Moms, Iron Dads face the challenging puzzle of balancing the demands of being a nurturing parent with the demands of training. However, Iron Dads also face additional societal standards, stressful tensions, and physiological realities that may be unique to their positions as fathers and men. When we explore these nuanced complexities, we start to see the real identity conflicts unfold.

The Role of Women

Women play a critical role in informing and influencing the Iron Dad identity. All but two of the fathers who participated in this research were involved in heterosexual marriages. One of the two single fathers interviewed was seeing a girlfriend. The other was not in a romantic relationship. When asked to explain how they juggle their multiple roles, most of the married participants immediately cited their spouses, describing them as important enablers in the process. Almost universally, the men studied expressed the importance of involving, consulting, and listening to their wives as keys to maintaining a self-perceived healthy and well-balanced lifestyle. In most instances, spouses not only gave their consent to introducing the complexity of iron-distance triathlon into their lives, but also greatly extended themselves to help make the situation workable.

While this may sound like a positive development, in reality there are some interesting inconsistencies that emerge from spouses taking on the enabler role. As a number of dads rightfully pointed out, enabling comes at an expense. This often manifested itself in the wives taking on more housework and watching the kids for longer periods of time. Personal and emotional space was chipped away. For example, family vacation time for many of these families revolved around an event. The term "race-cation" was used on numerous occasions to describe this phenomenon. Aspects that one typically associates with vacation time, such as making more liberal decisions about meals or abandoning regular sleep patterns, were not on the agenda in the days leading up to the event. Further muddying the water, most iron-distance triathlons require numerous responsibilities prior to the event. Athletes must pick up their race materials, rack their bikes the day before the race, and work to keep their bodies sharp. This is not to suggest that a family cannot have fun on a race-cation. Some fathers went out of their way to pick event venues near popular family attractions, such as races in proximity to Disney World. However, contradictions were evident in how some of these race-cations were ultimately described. One woman interjected when her husband was being interviewed, suggesting that her trip to IRONMAN Florida 70.3 "was not the vacation that she was hoping for." She complained about the amount of time focused on the race itself. The man being interviewed expressed that after the event, he lacked energy to walk around Disney's theme parks. Put simply, orchestrating a race-cation is not a simple task.

Many of my study participants described themselves as having a well-balanced marriage, but as they dug deeper into discussions regarding division of labor, the reality that emerged was less than egalitarian. This important finding really materialized while I was conducting interviews on location at IRONMAN Texas. It was not my initial objective to collect data from spouses for this project. However, as the research evolved to include a more comprehensive sampling procedure, opportunities to get spousal input became more pronounced. I got to see—in the flesh—how the wife of an Iron Dad responded to her spouse's answers. These reactions proved to be a rather unexpected yet extremely rich data source. These data are interspersed throughout, providing a unique glimpse into how the wives of Iron Dads experience the iron-distance triathlon.

A Grounded Theory Approach

Based on in-depth interviews with forty-eight Iron Dads and two men embedded in the endurance-sport industry, as well as textual analysis of triathlon blog postings made by fathers, this study interprets firsthand accounts of how endurance sport training influences parenting, family, employment, and the self. Analysis of the in-depth interviews and blog threads utilized a grounded theory approach (LaRossa 2005). As opposed to exploring specific hypotheses, grounded theory allows researchers to investigate topics without any preconceptions (Glaser 1992; Strauss and Corbin 1994). This process revealed the key themes, which are presented in the analysis. They include new theoretical insights about how individuals manage their athletic identities. Readers seeking a more in-depth explanation of the study may consult the appendix for details of my methodological approach.

Interviews

This study required all participants to meet four criteria: (1) be a father, either biological or adoptive, (2) have at least one child under the age of twelve, (3) have a full-time job while iron-distance training and racing was occurring, and (4) be currently training for a 140.6-mile event, or have completed one within the past year. Each of these four requirements was based on careful consideration of who would best be able to best inform this study. I focused on fathers of children under twelve because, at or around that age, children start to become more self-sufficient. Negotiating childcare becomes more of a central consideration in planning out one's training when children are young. Participants included both resident and non-resident fathers. More specifically, two non-resident fathers were interviewed for this project. Given the growing number of non-resident fathers in the United States, studying both groups of men is important. A separate interview guide was used for these two individuals.

Study participants were recruited in one of two ways. To start, Iron Dads were recruited via two popular triathlon blogs, Slowtwitch.com and Beginnertriathlete.com. These two websites feature a diverse mixture of bloggers that include age-group and elite triathletes, coaches, and race directors. A recruitment posting was issued making a call for participants. Men then expressed their interest in participating in the study either by sending me a personal message via the website or by posting a response to the original discussion thread for me to view. The fact that I have been a longstanding contributing member on both websites made the Internet a rich recruiting source. As a second strategy, participants were recruited on location at the 2012 IRONMAN Texas exposition. Held in The Woodlands, a suburb just north of Houston, the event draws approximately 2,700 competitors annually. Each competitor must pick up his or her registration materials at the event exposition prior to the competition, also making this a rich recruiting source. I met a mixture of competitive and noncompetitive athletes.

Out of the forty-seven Iron Dad study participants meeting the recruitment parameters, thirty-one men were recruited via the Internet. Sixteen more were recruited on location at IRONMAN Texas. An additional three men were recruited specifically for their longstanding positions in the sport, for a total of fifty study participants. Two of these particular men did not meet any of the recruitment parameters but, due to their vast knowledge of and experience with iron-distance triathlon, were seen as valuable resources for the project. The first of these individuals was involved with an independent race organization brand that produces Olympic, half-iron, and full-iron triathlons. The brand advertised itself as embracing a family-oriented perspective on the racing experience. In doing so, their races offered some distinct features from other triathlon events. The second individual is Mike Reilly, known in the triathlon community as the "voice of IRONMAN." While Mike has never competed in a 140.6-mile event, he has had a front-row seat for hundreds of races. He calls races live over the microphone and is famous for shouting "you are an IRONMAN" as participants cross the finish line. A participant who did not meet all of the recruitment criteria, Dick Hoyt, was interviewed because of his status as a pioneering Iron Dad. Thanks largely in part to the efforts of Team Hoyt, a father-and-son team, there is now a physically challenged division in the IRONMAN World Championship. Interestingly, Dick Hoyt and Mike Reilly share a special bond. When asked what were some of the more memorable moments in working race finish lines, Reilly pointed to Dick and Rick Hoyt's historic 1989 IRONMAN World Championship finish. It was there that Rick became the first physically challenged athlete to cross the finish line in Kona.

Textual Analysis

To better examine the lives of busy triathlete fathers, this study also analyzed online threads and discussion postings pertaining to the intersection of sport, work, and family. Using textual analysis with a grounded theory approach, I uncovered valuable patterns in how Iron Dads talk about their lives on two of the most popular triathlon blogs: Beginnertriathlete.com (BT) and Slowtwitch.com (ST). These websites offer moderated forums where contributors make posts via digital accounts. Each account is identified by a unique screen name. The two sites allow users to start new discussion threads on a specific topic. The creator of the thread crafts a title; forum users can then click on that title and read the entire discussion. People interested in contributing to that specific discussion make posts, or individual contributions to the thread. When a forum user clicks on a thread title, posts will appear in chronological order. Both Slowtwitch.com and Beginnertriatlete.com feature outstanding search functions. Threads containing different permutations of key words were sought. Some examples of identified threads included:

"How does a 'regular' person find the time for HIM [IRONMAN 70.3] or IM [IRONMAN] training?"
"Balancing Family"
"Things you have bought and hidden from your significant other and their reaction when busted."
"The essence of the IRONMAN experience?"
"Open letter to unsupportive SO [significant other] of triathletes."

"IMNY [IRONMAN New York]—Looks like my family will miss the start . . . unreal."

"Rev3 vs IRONMAN branded . . . Rev3 wins hands down." [a thread that talks about families and finish-line chute policy—a controversial issue to some within the triathlon community]

I confirmed that all individual posts included in this study were made by men who met the recruitment criteria.[1] If I could not infer this information from the post itself, the user's prior forum history, or from my knowledge of the member's background, I used the private message function on each site to make this confirmation. Each post was coded in NVivo utilizing a grounded theory approach similar to that utilized for analyzing the interviews. I identified sensitizing concepts—main themes that emerged from the research—and discuss them throughout this book. Discussion posts were grammatically and semantically corrected for enhanced readability. These corrections do not alter the substance of the material in any way. When referring to the trademarked brand name, IRONMAN has been capitalized, as stipulated by World Triathlon Corporation.

The main purpose of supplementing my interviews with textual analysis of blog postings was twofold. First, this search gave me valuable insight into what fathers are talking about regarding the intersection of family, work, and sport. I also got a sense of how they are talking about these topics. A great example of this is a thread called "you know you're a triathlete dad when—." This thread is a useful lens to see how triathlete fathers balance their time, money, and emotional energy. At the onset of the project, these types of threads helped to inform my interview guide. Second, as my research progressed, they assisted in illuminating trends among Iron Dads. Besides simple discussion, some of these threads include polls, Iron Dads seeking advice from other Iron Dads, and other valuable insights. I discerned patterns in how these fathers balance their time and demands.

Observations

Finally, this study is supplemented by personal observations. The in-depth interviews conducted on location at IRONMAN Texas provided an opportunity to see competitors and their families operating in the endurance sport context. Many Iron Dads stopped by with their spouse and children, which gave me the chance to observe family dynamics as they unfolded. At times, spouses would jump in and answer questions, making the interview a collaborative effort between the husband and wife. Other wives shared their perspective after the interview was over. Of equal importance was seeing the body language of the family members. Some spouses offered supportive nonverbal cues such as affirmative nods or smiles when their husband answered a particular question. Other times, wives would offer disapproving stances such as crossing their arms, rolling their eyes, or shaking their heads. Children also provided useful visual cues. I could see the child reacting to the IRONMAN environment. Some were clearly overcome with excitement, grabbing at artifacts on booth tables. Many had drawn signs for their father at a nearby booth, a signal of the children's involvement in the race experience.

My own participation in the sport has also provided ample opportunity to observe Iron Dads and their families. I have participated in more than ten full-distance IRONMAN events at seven different venues. These venues include St. George, Utah; Coeur d'Alene, Idaho; Panama City Beach, Florida; The Woodlands, Texas; Mont-Tremblant, Canada; Chattanooga, Tennessee; and Madison, Wisconsin. As a competitor, I am exposed to the IRONMAN race experience from beginning to end—training, going to the expo to pick up my materials, shopping at the event merchandise store, attending pre-race meetings and practice swims, and of course, traversing the course itself. While these opportunities for observation may not have been approached as systematically or scientifically as the other methods utilized for this research, they still served as a meaningful resource for the project.

As researchers, we often take an outsider's view to studying a population. We stand as passive observers trying to learn about a particular phenomenon. More cutting-edge and sometimes controversial approaches call for a researcher to actually get involved in the lives of his or her participants. A prime example of this is Sudhir Venkatesh's *Gang Leader for a Day* (2008).[2] Venkatesh, a professor of sociology at Columbia University, recounts his experience as a graduate student at the University of Chicago. After entering an abandoned housing project to administer a survey, he discovered a world he never knew existed. Through personal interactions with gang members and other people in the neighborhood, he provides readers with a unique look at the crack epidemic in inner-city Chicago. His book is bold, captivating, and accessible to a non-academic audience. While participating in long-course triathlon hardly resembles the physical danger that Venkatesh subjected himself to in the name of research, it does provide a useful lens through which to view Iron Dads in action. It also provides a ripe opportunity to see fathers interact with their spouses and children, as well as to understand the inner workings of endurance sport culture.

Insider Status

At the onset of my research, I debated the extent to which I would reveal my identity as an active endurance sport athlete. Giving due diligence to the process of reflexivity, I tried to anticipate the positives and negatives of presenting myself as an "insider." Ultimately, I believe that exposing my identity as a competitor provided me with a number of notable advantages. First, it likely assisted with cooperation, a key dimension of successful interviewing practice (Marshall and Rossman 1999). While I cannot measure cooperation in absolute terms, none of the participants I contacted over the telephone cut the interview short. To the contrary, many of these men chatted with me well after the interview had concluded. As it turned out, I was scheduled to compete in the same events as some of the participants. Second, revealing my identity as an active competitor allowed me to establish a rapport with the Iron Dads. This was apparent in the participants' language. Men used terms, acronyms, and phrases that are unique to the triathlon world. They used abbreviations such as CDA (Coeur d'Alene, a popular race venue in Idaho), DNS (did not start), and ST (Slowtwitch). The localized knowledge of this long-course triathlon racing "code" hit me when I got back one of my early transcripts from my transcriber. The transcriber had a hard time deciphering the word Coeur d'Alene; the document contained a series of question marks in places where the name was cited. While this little town in Idaho may be obscure to some, it is known to many competitors within the iron-distance racing community. IRONMAN Coeur d'Alene takes place every summer, drawing approximately 2,500 triathletes to this quaint town. Still, the code remains evident. Even the abbreviation of this popular brand name—IM (for IRONMAN)—would seem foreign to most people outside of the triathlon world.

While it was impossible for me to measure the extent to which my participants opened up as a result of talking to an iron-distance insider, I did notice a number of other verbal cues signifying that the men recognized our common bond. At points, participants would use phrases such as "you know what I mean," suggesting that we share a common frame of reference. One such example came when I talked to a father about safety on the race course. He was commenting on the physicality of a mass-start swim. He relayed an experience where he was kicked in the face by a fellow competitor. The father reflected, "It was just brutal with no space, all the way past the first turn buoy. You know what I mean." While I have experienced similar contact in the swim portion of events, I knew that I had to be careful in proceeding with my questioning. I wanted to understand how *he* experienced the swim. I replied to this father's story by saying, "Yes, I have an idea of what you mean, but tell me exactly what you experienced as you approached the turn buoy."

While I am an insider to the iron-distance racing community, I am not an insider to every dimension of the Iron Dad world. I am a woman—a reality that was easily ascertained by participants upon hearing my voice on the telephone or seeing me at the expo. Would participants have been more forthcoming with a male interviewer? It is hard to say definitively in this particular situation. Given this possibility, I asked two male research assistants to conduct a handful of interviews with Iron Dads. We then compared results and ultimately concluded that no systematic differences emerged between their interviews and my own. Participants may have also regarded me as being in a relative position of authority. The bottom line is that complicated dynamics are at play, and it is, to some extent, hard to understand how those dynamics affected the information I received. Being sensitive to interview dynamics and addressing possible biases when possible are constant challenges scholars face when conducting qualitative research.

The methods described above come together to illuminate the complex web of life activities for Iron Dads. Issues related to childcare, finances, time with a spouse/partner, time alone, employment, and fitness all come together when one decides to train for a 140.6-mile event. Tough choices have to be made and priorities have to be set on a daily basis. The result is often a tug of war between contending responsibilities. What identity should take priority, and when? How does one make time to complete necessary daily activities? This research helps us understand how Iron Dads manage their competing identities by introducing a variety of new concepts, including sporting guilt, the athletic visibility continuum, and balancing mechanisms. Sporting guilt is the guilt that arises from the prioritization of sport or leisure over other life responsibilities. The way that Iron Dads manage this guilt is by utilizing balancing mechanisms—tactics that an individual employs in an attempt to reach a self-perceived state of balance. Iron Dads also address sporting guilt by managing their placement on the athletic visibility continuum. The athletic visibility continuum suggests that an athlete's sporting identity, and all activities connected to that identity, can take on varying degrees of visibility in the eyes of others. Collectively, engaging in these processes speak to ways that Iron Dads conceptualize time, space, and role commitment. This book also explores how faith and class inform these sensitizing concepts. Before we get into a detailed discussion of how these ideas apply to Iron Dads, it is useful to consider the uniqueness of the iron-distance racing context.

Setting the Context: The Universality of Sport

Sport is one of the most powerful institutions in the world. It serves as a "regulatory agency that channel[s] behavior in culturally prescribed ways" (Eitzen and Sage 2009, 8). Sport reflects societal norms, values, and statuses, meaning that things we value in society are evident in the sporting arena. Sport also serves as a powerful institution for the construction and maintenance of gender ideology (Coakley 2009). While Michael Jordan is a household name, very few people are familiar with Chrissy Wellington. She is a recently retired professional triathlete who has won every single full-distance event that she had registered for, including multiple IRONMAN World Championship titles. Despite this dominance, she is routinely announced after the men's pro field at races. She has never been given the honor of wearing the number "1" bib for a 140.6-mile race. That honor typically goes to the defending men's champion. While some long-course events have let the defending female pro wear the number 1, the IRONMAN World Championship—viewed by many as the biggest stage in triathlon—has yet to follow suit. This is a signal that even seemingly progressive sports still uphold the traditional gender hierarchy in subtle yet meaningful ways.

Like society at large, many sporting environments are landscapes of privilege and oppression. People have social statuses within society. Holding a particular status means being subject to various societal constraints and behavioral expectations. These constraints and expectations are affirmed and reaffirmed in the sporting world. For example, individuals do not enjoy equal access to sport. Factors such as race, gender, sexuality, ethnicity, and social class can limit, if not completely close, one's access to particular sporting environments. These factors also inform how a person can participate in sport. This includes the position/role that the individual will play, and where that individual can play. Even now, in the twenty-first century, numerous famous golf courses around the world still prohibit female and African American members. The famed Augusta National Golf Club once required all caddies to be African American. At the same time, African Americans were prohibited from playing on the greens. This is a prime example of individuals being forced into certain roles in sporting environments, including that of a servant. Todd Crosset's (1995) insightful study on the world of female professional golfers shows how these athletes struggle for recognition in this white, upper-class, male-dominated sport landscape. Like golf, the iron-distance triathlon landscape is a place of privilege and oppression.

In addition to access, privilege underlies participation in sport in other key ways. Pierre Bourdieu noted that "economic barriers—however great they may be in the case of golf, skiing, sailing, or even riding and tennis—are not sufficient to explain the class distribution of these activities" (Bourdieu 1984, 217). There is also a strong influence of a middle-class "habitus," or particular way of being, in iron-distance culture (Bourdieu 1984). A rich literature suggests that self-empowerment, a value firmly reflective of middle-class ideals, can be found in a myriad of sporting contexts

(Atenico and Wright 2009; Cole, Giardina, and Andrews 2004; Hanold 2010; Wheaton 2004). My study participants discuss how middle-class values are normalized in the triathlon environment. Similar to Maylon Hanold's (2010) findings on ultrarunners, long-course triathletes value self-empowerment and success. Participation in the sport is a powerful mechanism for competitors to feel better about themselves. Throughout this book, we will see how middle-class values serve as a "disciplining discourse" (Hanold 2010, 174) in the way Iron Dads approach their training and racing. Middle-classness not only influences the desire to participate in the sport itself, but also shapes how study participants compete in the event. It critically informs their identities as triathletes. As I will discuss later, the habitus that emerges in long-course environments also works to signal distinction from other socio-economic and athletic groups (Bourdieu 1984).

Beyond class divide, there are other key ways in which sport can be viewed as a microcosm of society. As an institution, sport both reflects and perpetuates the competitive ethos that is evident in today's society (Eitzen and Sage 2009; Hartmann 2015). Some people who register for long-course triathlon events speak about "winning their age group" or "qualifying for Kona," important performance benchmarks during the race experience. However, as many of the Iron Dads explained, training and racing with a desire to be highly competitive can be a very difficult tightrope to walk. This is in part because amateur athletes do not get paid for their efforts. Further, obligations associated with work and family can serve as practical barriers to achieving athletic goals

Another way that sport reflects social values is in its emphasis on materialism. Looking at the bike racks in a 140.6-mile event will give you a sense of how materialism manifests itself in long-course triathlon. The racks are filled with high-end Cervelo, Trek, and Specialized bikes. These tricked-out machines do not even represent the sum of one's ownership in the bike world. Some triathletes have a fleet of bikes and high-end carbon wheelsets. Drawing on triathlon humor, a few participants joked that the ideal number of bikes you should possess is N+1, meaning one more than the number that you currently own. This sport-driven emphasis on materialism can be a great source of anxiety for Iron Dads. How do you justify a $2,000 carbon wheelset and $5,000 bike to your wife? As chapter 5 reveals, spending this type of money on triathlon gear creates a perceived obligation to "give back" to the family in some way. While many people outside the triathlon world would quickly dismiss the idea of spending $5,000 on a bicycle—finding the very concept absurd—this is the sporting context in which Iron Dads operate. I shared a laugh with numerous study participants over the idea that our race bikes are worth more than our cars. I had the following exchange with Eli at the IRONMAN Texas Expo:

> ELI: Something tells me most of the people here make money. I look at the bikes and, you know, they're probably more expensive than most people's cars.
>
> INTERVIEWER: So do you fall in that category? Do you have money to spend on the sport?
>
> ELI: Well, I don't know if I fall in that category, but I have money to do the job. I make enough.

This exchange with Eli reminds us that we must give recognition to the unique culture that inevitably evolves in each sporting microcosm. Individual sports are defined by a distinct set of rules, language, players, interactions, and hierarchies. Triathlon—especially long-course endurance racing—is no different. Economic and social class are on display.

What Is Triathlon?

Triathlon is an athletic event consisting of consecutive swimming, cycling, and running segments, referred to casually as "swim, bike, run." Athletes must transition from one discipline to the next in designated areas called transition zones. The event's time clock reflects the time it takes an athlete to get from the start line to the finish line, including the swim, bike, and run portions of the race, as well as two transitions, referred to as "T1" (swim to bike) and "T2" (bike to run). While some events have evolved to include other disciplines—sometimes referred to as adventure racing—swimming, biking, and running represent the core of a traditional triathlon.

There are different race distances in triathlon ranging from the sprint distance to full 140.6-mile competitions. Sprint distances typically consist of a 400- to 700-yard swim, 12-mile bike, and 3.1-mile run. The next widely recognized distance is the Olympic. Unlike the sprint distance, the Olympic distance does not offer flexibility in the distance of each respective segment. As the name implies, Olympic distance races mirror the exact course requirements at the Olympic Games. This race consists of a .93-mile swim, 24.8-mile bike, and 6.2-mile run. Olympic races are sometimes referred to as the standard or international distance due to their widespread recognition and popularity. Next up the distance ladder is the half-iron, or 70.3, consisting of a 1.2-mile swim, 56-mile bike, and 13.1-mile run. Finally, one can take on the challenge of the full-iron, or 140.6 distance. This event consists of a 2.4-mile swim, 112-mile bike, and 26.2-mile run. The word

"IRONMAN" is trademarked and refers to branded events put on by World Triathlon Corporation (WTC). The brand is well known for its 70.3-mile (IRONMAN 70.3) and 140.6-mile (IRONMAN, no numeric reference) races. The more generic phrases "iron-distance" or "full-distance" are often used to describe participation in a non-branded 140.6 event, while "half-iron distance" or "half-distance" serve as the 70.3 equivalent. While the brand names may differ, barring any course measurement inaccuracies, the distance at branded and non-branded 70.3 and 140.6 races are identical. For this reason, my study does not distinguish between participants of branded versus non-branded events. Notably, all study participants had attempted at least one half or full IRONMAN branded event. In recognition of market diversity in event-management companies, the terms full-iron or full-distance (140.6), and half-iron or half-distance (70.3), are used throughout. Exceptions are if a specific race venue is being referenced or if a quoted study participant uses a different word or brand name.

Due to the nature of the time and financial commitment associated with a 140.6-mile event, I focused my research exclusively on iron-distance competitors. In doing so, I answer Matthew Lamont and Millicent Kennelly's (2012) call for more focused research on athletes participating in specific triathlon distances. For a variety of reasons that I will explore later, full-distance racing represents a unique sporting environment. Its culture and rules are distinct from any other sporting activity. Its culture is also distinct from triathlons of shorter distances. By focusing exclusively on iron-distance triathletes, this research is able to tease out a more detailed understanding about the lives of these unique competitors.

The Growing Popularity of Endurance Sport

The first triathlon was held in 1974 when a track club attempted to find a new way to pique interest in the club's training events. The sport remained a mystery to most people for a number of years after that event. In 1982, the United States Triathlon Association and the American Triathlon Association merged to create one unified governing body: the United States Triathlon Association. At the time, the organization had 1,500 members. Interest in triathlon remained relatively low for over a decade. In 1994, at the International Olympic Committee Congress meeting in Paris, it was decided that triathlon would become a full medal sport in the Olympics. The United States sent its first-ever Olympic triathlon team of three men and three women to the 2000 games in Sydney, Australia.

Since its inclusion in the 2000 Olympic Games, participation in triathlon has increased exponentially. It is one of the most rapidly growing sports worldwide (Drummond 2010; Hadzipetros 2009). One of the best measures of interest in the sport can be gathered by looking at year-long license subscriptions to the domestic governing body, USA Triathlon (USAT). This is a meaningful measure of participation because most triathlons require participants to be members of USAT prior to competing. While some athletes elect to purchase one-day licenses, many become year-long members. Annual USAT membership rates notched an all-time high in 2013. In 2000, membership was 21,341 individuals. This figure grew to 68,986 in 2005; 95,018 in 2006; 134,276 in 2010, and surpassed 174,000 annual members in 2013 (USA Triathlon 2014b; USA Triathlon 2015). That means that in the span of thirteen years, one-year memberships increased by more than 715 percent. Notably, 358,461 one-day licenses were purchased in 2013. While organizational growth is clearly evident, what these membership figures do not illuminate is what distances athletes are competing at. Theoretically, these USAT members could be competing exclusively at the sprint and Olympic distances. How do we know if the 140.6-race distance is popular in America today? Is it an event completed by only a very small fringe of the membership? Is the distance becoming more popular as time goes on? To answer these questions, we can look at the abundance of iron-distance events worldwide, as well as registration trends for these races.

Some World Triathlon Corporation–branded races in North America sell out within minutes of registration becoming available online, a testament to the 140.6 racing distance's growing popularity in contemporary endurance sport culture. For example, the inaugural running of the IRONMAN U.S. Championship, a race that took place in New York and New Jersey in August 2012, sold out to general entry in eleven minutes (Fineman and Buteau 2011). General online registration for IRONMAN Florida 2013 sold out in less than one minute (World Triathlon Corporation 2013), and 2014 IRONMAN Chattanooga closed in under three (Falkenrath 2013). Particularly for IRONMAN-branded events, online registration has become a race to the computer. It is a pre-event competition where eager participants must wait until a specific time for the registration website to become available. The online system is typically so flooded with requests that it is very difficult for people to progress though the successive screens. One can easily find many blog postings from frustrated triathletes who tried to register for an IRONMAN-branded race but were either shut out or had technical difficulties. This is a strong indication that there is much more demand than supply for the brand's most popular venues. We also see that World Triathlon Corporation is continually adding races to its domestic and international circuits. As of June 2015, the World Triathlon Corporation produces forty-one full-distance and eighty-eight half-distance events worldwide. They also host a range of shorter events.

So who, exactly, are full-distance competitors? In 2008, USA Triathlon commissioned a study called "Mind of the Triathlete" (TribeGroup 2009). The study surveyed 15,000 triathletes with the objective of finding out what types of people participate in multi-sport events. The results showed that 17 percent of all individuals surveyed had competed in an iron-distance event in the past year. More than six in ten (63%) of all triathlon competitors were married. Unfortunately, the study did not collect data on the number of children that respondents had. What the survey did uncover, however, was the gender disparities found at the longer distances of triathlon. According to the study, men made up the majority (60%) of all triathlon competition fields. The gender gap widened substantially at the 140.6 distance, with men making up 75 to 82 percent of a typical race field. At the 2011 running of IRONMAN Florida, a course that features a notoriously flat bike and run, men made up 78 percent of the field. At the 2012 running of IRONMAN St. George, an event that features an extremely hilly bike course by comparison, men made up 82 percent of the competition field. It is valuable for us to question the reason for such notable gender discrepancies at the longer distances. This is particularly true given research highlighting women's ability to excel at ultra-distance events (Speechley, Taylor, and Rogers 1996).[3] Is it something about the distance itself, or are there other social-psychological factors at play? For example, are there societal realities that empower men to participate more than women? I argue that some of the resources that men draw upon to integrate endurance training into their lives are deeply embedded in gendered practices and institutions. These include family and work environments. As I discuss at length in chapter 5, men also draw upon financial and social capital as a means of integrating training into their lives.

Fatherhood through the Lens of Sport and Leisure

Sport and leisure offer a variety of unique contexts for family bonding. A sizable amount of literature discusses the role of sport and leisure in family life. Taking a life-course perspective, Rhona Rapoport and Robert Rapoport (1975) show that in addition to family and work, leisure is one of the three main institutions in our lives. Applying the symbolic interactionist perspective to parenting, we see that moms and dads engage in "purposive leisure" as a way of demonstrating and instilling values in family members (Shaw and Dawson 2001). Within this body of literature, however, rests a "marked imbalance" in the academic coverage of mothers' and fathers' experiences with sport and leisure (Kay 2006). Fortunately, this area of research has benefited from increased attention over the past decade.

In 2006, *Leisure Studies* came out with a special edition dedicated to fathering in various sport and leisure contexts, work that was later published as an edited volume (Kay 2009). Collectively, the contributing authors shed light on the centrality of sport and leisure in the fathering process (Kay 2009). From the evolution of father-daughter relationships (Willms 2009) to the importance of sport and leisure in non-resident father-child relationships (Jenkins 2009), the authors talk about how the complex, ever-changing evolution of fathering expectations play out in various sport and leisure contexts. By focusing on iron-distance triathletes, my research seeks to add a new context to this growing understanding.

As Tess Kay's edited volume reminds us, not all sport and leisure contexts are identical. There are unique structural and cultural properties associated with each that may impact the fathering process. Triathlon represents a unique context because it takes place in multiple landscapes, both on land and in water. It challenges competitors to gain proficiency in three separate sport disciplines—swimming, biking, and running. Finally, specific to iron-distance training, it crosses into a territory that may be best described for many as "serious leisure" (Stebbins 2007). Amateurs, referred to as age-group athletes, participate for personal satisfaction. Although they are not getting paid, they aim to build enough endurance to travel 140.6 miles under their own power. The dedication required to build to this level of endurance is substantial (Lamont and Kennelly 2011). It takes time, money, and an understanding family. This research investigates how men shape environments and use the resources around them to construct their life as a father, athlete, employee, and man.

While sports are a positive family experience for many men, physical activity can also be a vehicle for abuse. Some fathers, seeking to live vicariously through their offspring, push their children too hard. Rationality can easily be muted by the desire to win. Further, there can often be a fine line between engaged parenting and pushing beyond reasonable limits. This is what makes sport a particularly tricky parenting environment. A father who pushes his son to tears in swim practice can argue that he is just trying to help his child progress as an athlete. Since sport is founded on the principle of pushing physical and emotional limits, it is difficult for onlookers to argue otherwise. This means that abuse, being masked as a byproduct of engaged parenting in a sporting context, can easily go undetected or unchallenged. I did not detect evidence of abuse being perpetrated by any of my study participants. However, it is important to acknowledge that abuse can and does happen through sport.

Contributions of the Book

Endurance sport is a hot topic in today's society. An increasing number of people are taking on the challenge of incorporating endurance sport into their lives (USA Triathlon 2011). In triathlon, men who are forty and older comprise one of the largest growing cohorts (Gardner 2010). As sociologists, we need to understand how this increased participation in sport relates to and affects critical institutions such as work and the family. Understanding how sport influences one's experiences as a parent, and vice versa, is something we have yet to fully understand. While iron-distance triathlon races may not be on the radar screen of many parents, it is possible to liken such training to other hobbies and activities. Many people are highly dedicated to activities outside of work and family. Social scientists have much to learn by studying how these individuals balance time, finances, and responsibilities in conjunction with these hobbies. For instance, scholars can develop a better understanding of role salience and how people manage competing identities within a sporting context.

World Triathlon Corporation, the largest full-distance event management company, is becoming increasingly visible in today's culture. The IRONMAN trademark has extended its name recognition well beyond the confines of the triathlon race course. Many people who do not compete—or have never given any consideration to competing—own something bearing the brand logo. One of the most prominent examples of this is the Timex series of IRONMAN watches, sold at popular retail outlets such as Walmart and Sports Authority. Perhaps you own one yourself. We also see IRONMAN-branded strollers, shoe inserts, beds, body composition scales, and even perfume. Trade books about IRONMAN have become more frequent in publication. While some insiders have pointed to this branding of common items as a dilution of the iron-distance race, it certainly raises the event's visibility within the mainstream society—particularly among outsiders. As endurance sport becomes more visible, so does the desire to be associated with the IRONMAN brand. As I discuss in chapter 5, this is particularly evident when observing behavior at the IRONMAN race store. The morning after competing in a 140.6-mile event, some athletes stand in line for hours just for the privilege of shopping for branded finisher gear.

This book discusses a number of topics that extend well beyond the iron-distance context. It addresses the grey continuum connecting sport and work. Some would argue that getting up at 4:00 A.M. to run in the dark sides more with work than it does sport. This is particularly true for amateur athletes who are not getting paid for their athletic efforts. The book also explores contradictions in health. The concept of a "healthy body" is a contested, socially constructed ideal (Bridel 2013; Cronan and Scott 2008). While many observers would agree that iron-distance triathletes are extremely fit individuals, the extent to which a competitor may beat up his or her body—especially on race day—leads us to question how healthy the activity actually is. Are these competitors who are willing to put their body through extreme tests of endurance, to the point of collapsing on the course, truly engaging in healthy sport? A 2012 article from the *Wall Street Journal*, "One Running Shoe in the Grave," reports that "a fast-emerging body of scientific evidence points to a conclusion that's unsettling, to say the least, for a lot of older athletes: running can take a toll on the heart that essentially eliminates the benefits of exercise" (Helliker 2012). Looking out at an iron-distance course, you can't help but wonder about the bodily stress that the athletes are experiencing. Even some professionals stumble across the finish line, legs wobbly or totally giving out on them.

However ironic it may seem initially, when considering the notion of athletes competing in pain, we must also consider the concept of pleasure. Pain and pleasure share a strong interconnectedness (Atkinson 2008; Bridel 2010; Pringle, Rinehart, and Caudwell 2015). This book further untangles that complicated relationship. Chapter 3 suggests that exploring the boundaries of pleasure and pain is a reason why some Iron Dads register for an iron-distance event in the first place.

This research primes us to consider the life complexities that are unique to endurance sport athletes. Very few activities require participants to compete for ten to seventeen hours. When I tell people that I have taken over sixteen hours to finish a number of my IRONMAN races, I receive one common response: "I have never done anything in my life for that length of time—not even sleep!" People struggle to find a context that they can relate to. The very idea of preparing for a course of that length takes a huge emotional, physical, and financial toll on event participants. Many of these repercussions are easily anticipated—lack of sleep, relationship stress, and so on. This study explores the more subtle, perhaps less predictable consequences of training for an event of that magnitude.

This work is written for academic and non-academic audiences alike. For scholars, I have developed new theoretical concepts that can be transported to other areas of research in family, sport, and leisure studies. For current or aspiring Iron Dads and Iron Moms, I offer pragmatic advice on how to live a more healthy, well-balanced life. This advice emerged after assimilating content provided by people just like them—adults who seek to juggle work, family, and endurance-sport training. My research participants live that life and have learned through trial and error. I hope other athletes can identify useful concepts to apply to their own lives. For current and future race directors, I offer suggestions on how to construct family-friendly events. Finally, for those just interested in learning more about endurance sport, this book draws out interesting nuances about the iron-distance culture.

Looking Ahead

Drawing on narratives surrounding the training and racing experiences, chapter 2 investigates the complex landscape of the Iron Dad identity. The Iron Dad identity represents the nexus of multiple dimensions of the self— father, partner, athlete, friend, sibling, and employee, among others. I set the theoretical groundwork for understanding the various roles that Iron Dads embrace, providing a critical foundation for understanding how different identity maintenance processes work.

Chapter 3, "To Tri or Not to Try," discusses the complex and diverse reasons why Iron Dads choose to embrace the difficult undertaking of becoming an iron-distance finisher. Given the varied responsibilities that these men take on, why would they even consider racing 140.6 miles? I discuss the seven most commonly cited reasons for participation: (1) using iron-distance racing as a catalyst for bodily change; (2) being a role model; (3) using iron-distance racing as a means for doing the extraordinary; (4) coming to iron-distance racing through media influence; (5) being attracted by the event's proximity; (6) racing for something larger than the self; and (7) exploring the extremes of the pleasure/pain dichotomy. Supplementing these seven themes, I assess the significance that influencing future generations has for Iron Dads—a concept known as generative fathering (Dollahite and Hawkins 1998; Dollahite, Hawkins, and Brotherson 1997; Snarey 1993).

Once Iron Dads decide to take on the challenge of a full-distance event, how do they fit training and racing into their lives? Chapter 4, "The Juggling Act," uncovers various social and psychological processes associated with identity construction and maintenance. I introduce three new concepts: managing sporting guilt, managing one's status on the athletic visibility continuum, and adopting balancing mechanisms. Using these new concepts as a guide, I uncover the details of how current competitors find success in multiple areas of their lives. Collectively, these three processes reveal how they craft their existence as athletic competitors, fathers, and men.

Chapter 5, "Why Class Matters," examines how work and social class, particularly middle-class ideals, influence the construction and maintenance of the Iron Dad identity. I explore how social privilege shapes opportunities to negotiate competing identities. Through the narratives of Iron Dads, I also examine how class resources enable individuals to more readily meet their personal fathering and workplace expectations while training for an iron-distance event. I reveal key processes in which men activate class resources to help achieve their personal goals. Resources associated with a higher class standing, including social capital networks, money, and education, all help Iron Dads manage their social and physical environments.

Chapter 6, "Faith Meets 140.6," investigates how religion and spirituality shape the construction and maintenance of the Iron Dad identity. I uncover how faith in a higher power creates a moral compass to help negotiate competing identities. I explore three processes that are unique to Iron Dads of faith, including (1) internalizing a connection between faith and sport; (2) sharing this connection; and (3) using faith to help inform one's placement on the athletic visibility continuum. I also situate the place of prayer and fellowship within the larger iron-distance community. In doing so, I draw upon literature surrounding sport landscapes to make connections between physical environment and religion. This chapter also assesses the significance of religious-based endurance sport communities, highlighting the influence of the Fellowship of Christian Athletes as an example of one such organization.

Sometimes athletes conclude that it is time to "throw in the towel" on their training. Chapter 7 identifies when and how Iron Dads come to that conclusion. I tease out what this decision means for these individuals as both athletes and men. I explore the dynamics of two types of situations: (1) instances when an Iron Dad quits mid-training cycle and (2) instances when an Iron Dad decides to hang up iron-distance racing after the event at hand is completed. Both of these situations present unique circumstances. I show how these situations arise and how fathers adjust their athletic goals accordingly. Iron Dads share insights on the decisions that enabled them to find a better self-perceived life balance, a balance that sometimes required putting off the iron-distance goal until later in life.

At the conclusion of each interview, I asked Iron Dads to answer the question: What advice would you give to a father who was considering registering for a 140.6-mile event? In the final chapter, "The Road Ahead," Iron Dads offer commonsense advice to both current and prospective iron-distance competitors. Taking a holistic look at the long-course racing landscape, I also offer practical advice to event management teams for creating a more family-friendly environment. Drawing on some of the more progressive policies seen throughout the racing industry, including pre-race festivities and friendly finish-line policies, I suggest how events can be more sensitive to athletes with families. I also offer methodological and theoretical suggestions for future research on family, sport, and fathering.

2

Inside Triathlon Culture

The clock is nearing midnight at the 2012 running of IRONMAN Texas. I have been out on this course for much longer than anticipated. We are now in the sixteenth hour of the competition and a mere sixty minutes remain before the finish line closes. Why am I still out here at this late hour? The heat and humidity started taking its toll on me early on in the bike course. I will admit—I went out too aggressively for the first fifty miles. As a result, I was not able to consume the calories I needed to sustain a good race. I am now very lightheaded and forced to walk the majority of the marathon. It is a long way, but I continue on. I walk past the stunning mansions bordering Lake Woodlands. Sounds of footsteps surround me as complete darkness takes over the course. Glow sticks hang on trees to light the path. Slowly but judiciously, I make my way toward the final miles of this 140.6-mile journey. I can hear a faint sound in the background. As the noise gets louder, I know the finish line is getting closer. Before too long, Mike Reilly, "the Voice of IRONMAN," will be calling my name.

I now approach a place that I have been two times before—a fork in the course. Bear left for loops 2 and 3 of the run, bear right for the finish line. Finally, after feeling the torture of bearing left two previous times, it is my moment to take that coveted right. "Less than half a mile to go," a course marshal shouts in my direction. *Thank God.* In a burst of excitement, I sprint up a short path, up the street, and toward the finish line. The finish chute wraps around in a U-shape design. I slow down to take in the moment, high-fiving spectators along the way. I scream in excitement, but my voice is drowned out by the roar of the crowd surrounding me. After a grueling sixteen hours and thirty minutes, I hear the words that I have been eagerly anticipating since I signed up for the event a year ago: *you are an IRONMAN!*

Within IRONMAN culture, for many, the sound of Mike Reilly calling your name as you cross the finish line is the ultimate dream. As a competitor approaches the finish chute, he announces his or her name, followed by a very distinct phrase: you *are* an IRONMAN. The semantics of this iconic phrase are notable. It suggests that IRONMAN is something you are, not just something you do. This is a subtle yet very distinct difference. We all have the capability to do things in our lives. The extent to which we embody the identity and lifestyle of those activities, however, speaks to a much different level of significance that activity may take on for any given individual. My own experience has revealed to me that to say that IRONMAN is something that you *are*, as opposed to something you *do*, suggests that iron-distance triathlon is deeply integrated into your sense of self. It is a significant part of your overall identity as a person.

The Iron Dad identity, the focus of this work, represents the nexus of multiple dimensions of the self. These men are fathers, partners, friends, siblings, employees, and, of course, endurance athletes. What is an Iron Dad identity? If there are numerous Iron Dads in the world, does that suggest that there is no single Iron Dad identity? The answer is yes. The Iron Dad identity formation process not only differs between individuals, but can also change over time within an individual as he moves throughout his life course.

Defining the Self, Creating an Identity

What Is Identity?

Imagine that you were asked to describe yourself. What would you say? Perhaps you would talk about your physical features—characteristics such as height, weight, or hair color. Alternatively, perhaps you would talk about some of the roles that you take on—parent, sibling, athlete, spouse, or employee. An identity reflects the various traits and meanings that we attach both to ourselves and to the people around us (Stryker 1980). Identities are socially constructed entities that operate in the context of shared cultural meaning (Mead 1934). We as individuals are engaged in an ongoing dialogue with our identities. As we interpret and synthesize new experiences and cultural norms, we refine existing identities and establish new ones. In essence, identity represents the culmination of various social and psychological experiences that one has had over a lifetime. Collectively, these experiences make up the self.

On the broadest level, this research defines an Iron Dad as an individual who juggles work, family, and iron-distance training and competition. While this definition is useful in helping us identify the population that we are talking about, it does not address what it actually means to be an Iron Dad. How do fathers embrace, display, and negotiate their identity? What does being an Iron Dad mean to each individual person? Exploring these types of nuanced questions calls for uncovering the deep-rooted cultural symbolism and social expectations associated with the various capacities that make up the self. As one dives into these deeper levels of analysis, it becomes apparent that there is no rigid way that Iron Dads try to balance their multiple roles. This is because identity is not a fixed concept; it is fluid and ever-changing (Harris and Parker 2009). This is demonstrated in the following exchange with Colton, a financial analyst and stepfather of two:

> INTERVIEWER: How central is being an IRONMAN to your overall identity as a person?
> COLTON: It's one piece of it, but it's not the essential aspect.
> INTERVIEWER: Is it high on your priority list?
> COLTON: Uh, this year, it's been very high on my priority list, yes.

The use of the term "this year" is notable. It suggests that specific identities may become more pronounced at certain points in time. This makes sense given that people are not one-dimensional. We as individuals represent a collection of identities which stem from the numerous roles that we embrace (Stryker 1968, Stryker and Burke 2000). In essence, the self is a structure that exists in the context of a larger web of relationships.

The concept of multiple identities applies to the Iron Dad population. This is because, fundamentally, these men tend to occupy multiple roles in society. With each role that is embraced, individuals create meaning that they apply to themselves in that context. At the same time, individuals are also subjected to cultural expectations surrounding those roles. This leaves a person engaged in a give-and-take with society. In other words, the construction of an identity is a two-way process. A fundamental part of engaging in this two-way process means making daily decisions about priorities. Many Iron Dads go through daily self-assessments of their priorities. Men in this study recognized that they were the confluence of multiple identities. Frank, a father of two, relates, "I'm a business owner, and I'm a father, and I'm a husband, and I'm an entrepreneur, and I'm a well-known figure in our community. But yeah, the IRONMAN label is part of my identity. It is, absolutely." Ian, a former marine, recalls how "IRONMAN" was his military call sign. "Being an IRONMAN is who I am, pretty much. Not that it identifies me, but people know that I push myself. People know that I rely on my faith and I get through it. But, you know, when I was in the Marine Corps, it was my call sign. That's what they called me over the radio. It's who I've been, you know? It's been attached to me since I was sixteen or seventeen years old in some way or form."

Isaac, a father of two and restaurant owner, describes how his athletic identity wanes after an event is over:

> During the time when you're training, it certainly becomes a part of your identity. I felt that for myself, and I felt that others felt that way around me. But it's such a fleeting kind of feeling that as soon as it's done, as soon as the event is over and you're over the soreness, you don't know if you're even capable of doing it again. So, to feel like you still are an IRONMAN, it's more surreal to not even do it. I remember stuff, so I suppose I am [an IRONMAN], but if you don't keep up the training for even a couple of months, then you don't feel like doing it anymore. So that identity of feeling like that's you, it's suddenly not.

Isaac reminds us that identities take positions relative to one another. After an event is over, he finds that his identity as an IRONMAN becomes less prominent. How does one define which role will be most prominent at any moment in time? The concept of "role salience" helps determine which daily activities are prioritized. Sheldon Stryker (1968) discusses this salience as being hierarchical in nature, meaning that the most significant role will take priority in a social situation. At times, a "structural overlap" exists in that more than one identity is pertinent at a specific point in time (Stryker 1968, 560). In these circumstances, the most salient role should prevail (Burke and Reitzes 1981; Stryker 1968). The concepts of structural overlap and role salience are particularly valuable in the context of this research. Isaac goes on to point out the emotional difficulty that structural overlap can present. "I think that the commitment to IRONMAN requires so much training that you're sacrificing. There is a sacrifice to be made. Being married and having kids, there is a price that's going to be paid to find the time to train. So, yes, there are times, of course, where I thought that I should be doing this or that instead of riding my bike, but I would ride my bike anyways."

Iron Dads are constantly balancing the roles of father, athlete, worker, and other varied capacities. Which role identity is most salient at various points in time? If on the morning of a big race a participant's son wants to play, will the father take time to engage in activities with his child? Will an Iron Dad compromise or disrupt his pre-race rituals on a day where playing the role of athlete is so clearly important? When is being a father, worker, and athlete most salient, respectively? Before we answer these questions, we must gain a better understanding of how full-distance triathlon as a social context shapes the identity formation process.

Iron-Distance Triathlon as a Context for Identity Formation

Sport creates a ripe context for individuals to construct social and psychological identities. Belinda Wheaton (2004) reminds us that inhabitants of a sport develop a unique social identity surrounding that activity. Given this, what does it mean to be an IRONMAN? My work is not the first to suggest that there is an "IRONMAN identity."[1] William Bridel (2010) defines the concept as "something that is produced as an athlete crosses the finish line" (8). He emphasizes the "transformative possibility of the sport associated with the finishing of one or more events" (8). In evaluating Bridel's work, we see the murkiness in defining precisely what it means to be an IRONMAN and to embrace an accompanying identity. While I believe that Bridel gives us an excellent starting place, I expand on this conceptualization in a few key ways.

First, my study participants remind us that we should not be too focused on an outcome while neglecting process. In other words, while the finish line most certainly represents a critical turning point in the formation of an IRONMAN identity, the process of acquiring said identity does not begin at the finish. Data from my Iron Dads suggest this is a fluid process that begins as early as when a person officially registers for the event. Second, we should give consideration to how critical institutions such as the family and work shape the formation of the self. Bridel does an outstanding job of explaining how cultural depictions of health influence the construction of the IRONMAN. This is firm recognition that other socially constructed institutions matter. My research seeks to expand on Bridel's work by considering the role that other key institutions take in shaping the full-distance racing experience.

Bridel suggests that the IRONMAN identity exemplifies core principles valued in the triathlon event itself—namely, challenge, toughness, achievement, and discipline (8). To be sure, these are important cultural conditions that define the context in which the Iron Dad identity is shaped. At the same time, though, they are realities that some Iron Dads (albeit a small cohort) challenge in subtle yet meaningful ways. For example, a few of my study participants stressed the importance of training as a means of bringing the family together in a positive athletic environment. The focus was not on giving everything to reach the finish line but, instead, on showing their children that athletics can be a valuable way to connect with nature or faith. Herein rests an interesting interplay. Is it really all about the finish line, or can the IRONMAN identity be fostered well before reaching that treasured space?

My study reveals that there are numerous permutations of race outcomes that can have a meaningful effect on one's athletic self. After a person registers for a 140.6 event, there are three potential outcomes: not starting (referred to as a "DNS," or "did not start"), starting the race but not making it to the finish line ("DNF," or "did not finish"), or finishing. Not finishing a race, as well as not starting a race, can be important turning points in the IRONMAN identity formation process. I argue in chapter 7 that these events could be just as powerful in their transformative possibilities as crossing a finish line. While none of the Iron Dads that I interviewed for this project had this particular outcome, some competitors cross the finish line seconds after official race time expires. Technically, these individuals are not recognized as official finishers and their official race outcome is noted as a DNF; however, these moments are often the most precious and memorable for finish-line observers. In IRONMAN Coeur d'Alene 2012, Cathy Stephens crossed the finish line at 17:00:20, a mere twenty seconds after the midnight cutoff. Mike Reilly, the finish-line announcer, narrated the experience over the event loudspeaker:

MIKE: I wish I could say that she's an official finisher, but she's not. But I'm going to tell you what. She's an IRONMAN in our hearts. Let's hear it for her. Tell her [facing the crowd] . . .
CROWD AND MIKE TOGETHER: You are an IRONMAN!
MIKE: [spoken as he walks down the finisher chute and stops before a man extending his medal] We have a finisher right here. He will give his medal to her. [Mike high-fives man and gives him a hug.] I am going to put this medal around her neck. [. . .] Hey, go get her. Bring her back. Bring her back. [. . .] Now, I was going to give her this medal from this fellow competitor [. . .] this is the guy that gave her the medal [fellow competitor who gave medal hugs Cathy].[2]

What transpired next is simply amazing. Cathy comes back down the finish chute holding a big sign that reads "Dear asthma: I WIN." She holds the sign proudly above her head as she takes a final victory lap back down to the start of the chute. A fellow competitor who finished the event earlier in the day gives her his finisher's hat. Hundreds of people lining the finish area are cheering and clapping. Notably, they are cheering and clapping just for her. By coming in barely after midnight, Cathy is able to enjoy recognition that is unique to a 17:00:20 finisher. With the exception of professionals, competitors do not typically go back out onto the course for recognition. Doing so would pose a safety risk to finishers charging down the chute. By finishing after the event had officially concluded, remaining competitors were not of concern. Cathy was the only competitor in the "field of play" during this special moment. Her experience made it to You-Tube. Within a span of eight months, the video received over 5,700 views. It has subsequently received thousands more. While she did not cross the line before midnight and thus would not be recognized in the race results as an official finisher, Cathy certainly carries an IRONMAN identity. The same can be said of the thousands of people who toe the line at full-distance races each year as first-time participants. These athletes have yet to cross the finish line, but to varying degrees, they already embrace and display their IRONMAN identity as they move throughout the course.

With that said, the finish line is most certainly a revered place in the 140.6 racing experience. It is a place of celebration. Competitors cry, jump for joy, roll across the finish line, and do push-ups in the chute. The array of finish-line antics never ceases to amaze even the most seasoned competitors. This raises the question: why is crossing the finish line such an important juncture in the IRONMAN identity formation process for Iron Dads? The answer, in part, is because men negotiate sporting identity through contemporary understandings of masculinity. These understandings stress the idea of finishing what you start. They also stress the ability to endure pain and to "conquer" obstacles. To do anything less is not "manly" (Messner 1995).

Iron-Distance Triathlon as a Privileged Masculine Landscape

Earlier in the chapter, I mentioned that there is no strict way that men do, or perform, an Iron Dad identity. However, to suggest that there is no rigid definition of what it means to be an Iron Dad does not imply that we have no common ground on the subject. To the contrary, shared cultural symbolism plays a key role in how Iron Dads express and negotiate their presentation of self. These men operate in a landscape where they are continually subjected to shared social expectations. Iron Dads are not just fathers, athletes, and workers; they are men who operate in a larger social context that values a certain definition of what it means to serve in those various capacities. These cultural values influence the way that men do fathering, sport, and work. Cultural values also influence the way that men do masculinity, a key consideration when considering their lives. Masculinity is also a central element of sporting environments. This elevates the importance of obtaining certain goals, particularly reaching the finish line. One could argue that the act of crossing the finish line represents a unique manhood act (Schrock and Schwalbe 2009). Bringing due attention to the study of "practices and processes" associated with men's actions, manhood acts help men to reaffirm their status as a biological male (289).

Crossing the iron-distance finish line brings distinct and exclusive credibility to the presentation of a masculine self.

Michael Kimmel defines masculinity as "the social roles, behaviors, and meanings prescribed for men in any given society at one time" (2004, 503). Masculine identities are constructed through our daily interactions within the larger context of complex societal institutions. Iron Dads consider social norms regarding masculinity, on both the conscious and subconscious level, when creating and re-creating their multiple identities. Some of the men in this study describe masculinity as being a central part of their fathering and sporting identities. R. W. Connell (1995) informs us not only that is masculinity context-based, but also that multiple masculinities can exist simultaneously. These definitions can vary across cultures, within one country across time, over a person's lifespan, or within one country at the same time (Kimmel 2004). For this reason, I argue that the relationship between triathlon, fatherhood, and masculinity is uniquely different for each Iron Dad. Further, I argue that within the iron-distance racing environment rests a subtle yet distinctly unique masculine culture. We can think of this environment as a masculine "sportscape," or landscape with particular values and cultural paradigms.

Gender in the Iron-Distance Sportscape

Institutions represent gendered spaces that reflect hegemonic gendered standards, logic, and values (Kimmel 2004). Sport exemplifies this institutional power, projecting images of what body, attitude, and actions should optimally be (Atencio, Beal, and Wilson 2009; Birrell 2007; Ford and Brown 2006; Laurendeau and Sharara 2008; Thorpe 2005, 2008; Waitt 2008). Sport presents a ripe arena for men to demonstrate masculine practices. It encourages the hegemonic masculine standards of violence, aggression, wealth, and physical dominance (Coakley 2009). Many sporting competitors internalize these normative images and definitions. Competitors who embrace hegemonic standards of masculinity are idolized (Dworkin and Wachs 2000). Iron-distance race courses represent a unique sporting context, or sportscape, in which to demonstrate gendered practices (Bale 1993, 1994). The outdoor sportscape that iron-distance racing resides in provides an opportunity for nature and human habitat to collide (Stoddart 2011). It is also in this sportscape where power gender relations are displayed and reaffirmed (Fusco 2005; Stoddart 2011). Performances of hegemonic masculinity are rewarded and celebrated (Stoddart 2011; van Ingen 2003; Vertinsky 2004; Waitt 2008).

I argue that that Iron Dads operate from a socially privileged standpoint in sport culture. Full-distance triathlon participants benefit from popular definitions of manliness. Even the well-known event brand name—IRONMAN—strikes a powerful cultural chord. As will be discussed later in the book, aligning themselves with this manliness empowers Iron Dads to be more visible with their athletic identity. Fathers training for a 140.6-mile event do not contend with the same social stigma as men preparing for competition in other sports, particularly those associated with femininity.

In her seminal study of gender and ice skating, Mary Louise Adams discusses the consequence of participating in a "feminine sport" (Adams 2011). By being labeled as a sport for girls, the reputation of the sport itself suffers—as do the participants. Male competitors are subjected to the devaluation of effeminacy. Their masculinity and sexuality are questioned. Compare this to the social desirability of calling oneself an iron-distance finisher. It is not hard to see how cultural perceptions of IRONMAN empower Iron Dads to be visible with their athletic identity. Full-distance racing also allows men to feel more in touch with their masculinity, both in public and private spaces.

One of the most illustrative examples of hegemonic masculinity idolization in the triathlon sportscape comes from the 2010 running of IRONMAN St. George. With approximately two miles left to go on the bike, Jeff Rhodes rolled one of his tubular tires off the rim of his wheel. His crash resulted in a broken collarbone and dislocated shoulder. After much struggle, Jeff got back on his bike, rode back into transition, and walked the marathon. He ultimately finished the race. What compelled Jeff to keep going? He could have easily quit the race during his bike-to-run transition. Whatever it was that kept him going, Jeff has been praised within the triathlon community. One blogger responded to his story by saying, "He gets man-points for sure!" Another blogger offered, "bravo," while a third suggested that he should "win the HTFU [harden the fuck up] award." This competitor is being praised for playing through what most would consider excruciating pain. Among some triathletes, he has been put up on a pedestal as a gold standard. This speaks to a subscription to hegemonic masculinity on the part of both Rhodes and the triathletes publicly commending his story.

Some iron-distance competitors train and race while injured, reflecting the idea that it is not "manly" to drop out or stop training due to pain. This reality applies to women just as much as men. In one of the most dramatic IRONMAN World Championship finishes, Sian Welch and Wendy Ingraham, two female professionals, literally crawled their way to the finish in 1997. The NBC television announcer narrating the event noted, "Their bodies were obliterated, but the spirit held firm." The fact that both competitors persevered through pain was highly celebrated and led to one of the most widely idolized finishes in the sport's history. Notably, this historic finish was for fourth and fifth place, so these two athletes were not pushing themselves for the glamour of a top podium spot. They were driven by a deeper competitive spirit that challenged the limits of their bodies, which suggests that endurance triathletes, like the surfers that Jason Laurendeau (2008) studied, follow a "gendered risk regime." That means that even in risky or extreme sporting environments—as some may view iron-distance competition to be—the production of gender is at the forefront. Specifically, the risk that these athletes are willing to take helps to solidify heterosexual masculine norms (Beal and Wilson 2004).

Encompassing more than just playing in pain, iron-distance racing is reflective of a variety of other key principles that define hegemonic masculinity. For this reason, I argue that such events can be characterized as a masculinized sportscape. This is evident when considering each segment of the race. The swim is brutal. Athletes kick, punch, and swim over other competitors. This leads to a highly combative environment in the water. Slow swimmers are viewed as weak and noncompetitive. Class and materialism also come into play, aptly visible in the cycling component of the race. People spend upward of $10,000 building up custom bikes. These bikes reflect one's personal wealth, socio-economic status, and the ability to provide for a family. The run also represents an arena to express materialism and physical dominance. People invest in equipment such as compression socks, high-end running shoes, heart rate monitors, and expensive nutrition products. As I discuss in chapter 5, flashing this gear creates symbolic capital. Men can demonstrate that they are both high-income earners and serious athletes. Further, the run demonstrates one's ability to withstand pain while overtaking other competitors. The race winner represents the strongest warrior. In a caption describing Craig Alexander's 2009 IRONMAN World Championship win, commentators noted that as he crossed the line he "appeared to roar like a lion who had slain his prey." This comparison implies a physical dominance that parallels one embraced in hegemonic standards of masculinity.

Commercialization, Symbolism, and the Iron Dad Identity

While iron-distance racing is full of unpredictability, one thing always seems to remain constant: the line for buying event finisher gear the day after the race. As one Iron Dad explains, "Early bird gets the worm at the post-event store. If they say open at 7:00 [A.M.] be in line at 6:30 [A.M.] if you want the full selection. It goes incredibly fast. We showed up one year an hour late and the pickings were next to nothing. Bring a crapload of money, too." The expansive selection of what is commonly referred to as "finisher swag" is quite notable. Beyond simple clothing items such as shirts and hats, merchandise tents also often feature large finisher flags, stickers, mugs, and custom event-centered competition outfits. Many of these items prominently display the race distances. Take for example the 2015 IRONMAN Texas finisher jacket, an item that sold for $144.99 plus tax the day after the event. The front of the jacket features an embroidered event logo on the chest. The distances are laser-etched parallel to the front zipper: "SWIM 2.4, BIKE 112, RUN 26.2." "FINISHER" is etched in capital letters down the left sleeve. The back features the IRONMAN Texas logo, date of the competition, and the finisher label.

What compels individuals who just raced 140.6 miles to get up the next day at 6:00 A.M. and patiently stand in line for hours as they wait their turn to enter the merchandise tent? The answer, in part, is the competitor's desire to display him- or herself in a particular way. The symbolism of race finisher gear is clear—it distinguishes competitors from finishers. The clothing does not simply say, "I was there." It says, "I did it. I traveled 140.6 miles." The powerful symbolism behind finisher gear helps to explain its heightened desirability. The inflated cost of these products also shows that people are willing to pay steep prices to display this symbolism in public. Competitive masculinity has become a commodity for sale. Iron-distance athletes consume this commodity by purchasing access to the activity itself (entry fees) and necessary gear (bikes, wetsuits, and other equipment). As discussed in chapter 5, not everyone can afford to purchase this commodity. Between the costly entry fees for branded events and an expansive list of required equipment, an endurance triathlon is an exclusive place. Buying finisher gear is a key way that individuals can display not only their experience, but also their success in a competitive, exclusive, masculine environment. This gear helps establish symbolic capital, a means of displaying one's affiliation with an insulated class (Bourdieu 1984). It also helps establish distinction from non-finishers and those who only compete at shorter distances (Bourdieu 1984).

At its core, the self is a socially constructed entity. Through social interaction, individuals encounter and learn the meanings of cultural symbols, such as wearing particular types of clothing, using specific language, or acting in a specific manner. Symbols play a key role in how Iron Dads express their identities as athletes, fathers, and men. To consider the social-psychological basis for how and why this presentation occurs, it is useful to draw from sociology's symbolic interactionist (SI) perspective (Cooley 1902; Mead 1934; Goffman 1959). Stemming from George Herbert Mead's *Mind, Self, and Society*, the SI framework focuses on individuals and their daily interactions with one another (Mead 1934). It further stresses that the mind has the ability to interpret symbols and that society is a product of daily social interactions. Individuals are seen as dynamic, conscious actors who use symbols to communicate different expectations, ideologies, and perceptions in their daily interactions as they progress through their life course (Mead 1934). This framework is a useful tool for understanding how Iron Dads use the power of symbolism to negotiate their multiple identities.

Further informing the symbolic interactionist framework is Erving Goffman and his classic text, *The Presentation of Self in Everyday Life* (1959). His work helps us to understand how ordinary people present themselves in a multitude of situations and how individuals attempt to control the impressions that others have of them. Goffman's dramaturgical approach illuminates how dynamic everyday social interactions are much like that of a performance (Goffman 1959). As individuals, we go through life on a variety of different stages. While acting in a specific capacity, according to Goffman, we will attempt to win over our audience members by persuading them that we are fit for that role. More specifically, Iron Dads act to persuade others that they are good workers, partners, parents, and triathletes. To do this, men may elect to emphasize or de-emphasize certain aspects of their personality, training, or family responsibilities. For example, buying a high-end triathlon bicycle may be more about convincing others of one's dedication to the sport than actually benefiting from the aerodynamic gains of the machine. As another example, Iron Dads may feel that they need to work extra hard at convincing others of their success outside of triathlon. This is particularly true if the dad perceives that others think that he is not dedicated to his non-triathlon roles. The concept of the looking-glass self suggests that the dad will adapt to how he thinks others see him (Cooley 1902). Given that Iron Dads spend so much time training, they may go out of their way to "prove" that this rigorous preparation does not get in the way of other responsibilities. If this is the case, convincing the audience of one's prowess at a particular role becomes increasingly important.

The work of British sociologist Anthony Giddens provides interesting theoretical expansion to Goffman's insights on presentation of self. Giddens (1991) suggests that one's self-identity is based on their own "reflexive biography," or understanding of their own history. In being a project of self, human identity is rooted in "the capacity to keep a particular narrative going" (Giddens 1991, 54). The sociologist goes on to explain how individual biographies must "continually integrate events which occur in the external world, and sort them into the ongoing 'story' about the self" (ibid.). These insights suggest that Iron Dads are continually working to make sense of their own histories. In doing so, they are creating an ongoing narrative about the self. The Iron Dad identity allows for a very explicit narrative consistent with specific meanings surrounding masculinity, the athletic body, and the self. As I describe in the next section, the IRONMAN narrative is one that focuses on extreme "endurance," or the ability to persevere through hours of mental and physical anguish.

Establishing Expectations

Popular conceptions of iron-distance competitors, and endurance athletes more generally, become important in understanding how Iron Dads deal with others' expectations. The concept of endurance is revered in the United States. This can be found in common discourses surrounding the topics of work, health, sex, and sport. It is also evident in popular colloquialisms such as "go the extra mile" and "tough it out," implying that one has the mental and/or physical toughness to keep going when facing adverse conditions. When it comes to IRONMAN, the brand name itself helps to establish an image of stamina. The word "iron" conjures up thoughts of a material that is nearly unbreakable. Coupling the words "iron" and "man" lead one to think of a robotic man, an image that is further perpetrated by the Marvel Comics superhero who fights crime in a suit of armor. These popular images have ramifications on the real iron people of the world—men and women who, unlike fictional superheroes, have limitations.

People think of iron-distance competitors as individuals who can be successful in all things. Again, the popular racing brand has a hand in establishing this image. IRONMAN's trademarked motto is "ANYTHING IS POSSIBLE." Perhaps anything is possible, but is *everything* possible? A number of study participants spoke about how popular images of IRONMAN led to unrealistic expectations being placed on them. Isaac describes how his IRONMAN identity is referenced in his home:

> So that identity of feeling like that's you; it's not, at least for me. I don't feel that way. It's more of a thing my wife will get to use anyway. If I'm tired and don't want to do things on my household list, she'll be like, "You're tired? You're an IRONMAN. You can do this if you want to." I'm like, "Oh yeah, that's right. I suppose I can do that." I don't know. I would like it to be, but it just isn't. I would like it to feel like it is important to my identity, but it just isn't. First, it doesn't mean anything to anybody, really, anybody else, and second, I don't feel it. You know, I don't feel like tomorrow I could run out and do it, so it's not important that way. What is important is that I feel I like the lifestyle. That's what matters most.

Greg, a computer technician and father of two, similarly talked about the pitfalls of the inflated expectations that often accompany the IRONMAN identity. He warns fellow competitors that "you can't be everything to everybody, so you have to learn to draw lines somewhere." The lines that Greg is referring to—boundaries that help one establish what is and is not possible—are informed by the larger social contexts.

The popular narrative surrounding the iron-distance context has a complicated effect on individual Iron Dads. For some, the words are a source of empowerment. The narrative of being a tough, durable machine can bring a sense of security, particularly in uncertain economic and environmental times. Aaron described how, as a multiple-time 140.6 finisher, he felt that he could "get through anything in life." This is clearly an empowering influence. At the same time, though, some use the iron-distance narrative to create unreal expectations. As Isaac mentioned, family and friends may come to see an Iron Dad as being a person without limitations. Ideas surrounding hegemonic masculinity are applied, sometimes at great detriment, to the lives of Iron Dads. These men must conquer all obstacles, regardless of the pain endured or sacrifice required. In such instances, the iron-distance narrative becomes an unobtainable self. Social paradigms surrounding these particular contexts often perpetuate unrealistic expectations. These unrealistic expectations can also be seen in the way that society views women surpassing men in athletic environments. In reality, even professional men have been beaten by their female counterparts. In the 2014 Ironman World Championship, female champion Marinda Cafrae came in thirty-third overall, earning the third-best run time of the day among all competitors (2:50:26). In the 2011 running of Challenge Roth, on her way to setting a new world record for the 140.6 distance, Chrissie Wellington overtook all but four men. She had the second-best marathon time in the entire field, setting a new world record of 2:44:35. Only the overall race winner, Andreas Raelert, had a faster showing on the run. Unfortunately, the sporting narrative suggests that women should not defeat men—particularly in a masculine domain. Getting "chicked" is a source of embarrassment for some men. Unrealistic expectations also rear their head at home and workplace life. What happens when we expect Iron Dads to be engaged parents, dedicated employees, and successful athletes? In the next section, we consider the influence of fathering and employment landscapes.

Fatherhood and the Workplace

For Iron Dads, athletic participation takes place with the ever-present backdrop of fatherhood. Fatherhood is a complex role with multiple orientations and demands. The expectations of fathers in today's society are not clear. On the one hand, fathers are subject to traditional demands of fathering, namely being the financial provider (LaRossa and LaRossa 1981). These conceptions of fatherhood stress how the man is occupied with employment-related activities, often leaving him emotionally and physically unavailable for family responsibilities. Recent conceptualizations of fatherhood have challenged this traditional model, emphasizing involved and caring fathering (Dermott 2008; Dienhart 1998; LaRossa 1997; Marsiglio and Roy 2012; Pleck 2004). One should not think of these fathering constructs as being "either/or," as the two are not necessarily mutually exclusive. Many Iron Dads construct a fathering identity that values both contributing to the financial health of the family and being an active father. This means striking a healthy balance between being successful in the employment realm and being successful in the family realm. All of my research participants experienced these complex and sometimes competing desires.

Over recent history, societal views toward fatherhood have shifted from the breadwinner role (Kay 2009); however, such evolutionary change takes time. As Tess Kay (2009) notes, "no one can quickly overturn a culture in which for so long men's identities have been inextricably bound up with their occupation" (16). It should come as no surprise, then, that work remains a central focus in the lives of most Iron Dads. Recall from chapter 1 that, in 2008, USA Triathlon commissioned a study called "Mind of the Triathlete" (TribeGroup 2009). Findings revealed that the plurality (49%) of the 15,000 triathletes surveyed hold white-collar jobs. Nineteen percent are in professional jobs, such as lawyer, doctor, or accountant. Twelve percent are students, 12 percent are blue collar, 6 percent are government or military, and 2 percent are described as "other." Since USA Triathlon's study was looking across race distances, it is reasonable to expect that we will see less occupational diversity among Iron Dads. Specifically, iron-distance athletes tend to occupy more white-collar and professional jobs.

While holding a white-collar or professional job is financially rewarding, occupants of these positions likely bear more work-related responsibility than those in a blue-collar position. Hours may be longer, weekend trips into the office may be expected, and business trips may be more frequent. This effectively lessens the amount of free time a father has away from work. If the window of opportunity to do things away from work is smaller, time allocation becomes increasingly stressful. This can lead to what is known as the work-family spillover, which occurs when work responsibilities affect the father's participation in other things, such as family activities or sport (Voydanoff 2004). Further, job stress impacts a person's marriage and parental involvement (Amato et al. 2007). National studies have repeatedly shown that the majority of parents feel that work constraints keep them from spending enough time with their children (Milkie at al. 2004). Given this, how do Iron Dads manage to add endurance sport into the mix? The upcoming chapters reveal key processes that these men use to help juggle their multiple identities.

3

To Tri or Not to Try

After competing in six iron-distance events, I finally decided to attend my very first athlete welcome dinner two days before the 2012 edition of IRONMAN Texas. My rationale for attending was to give Ryan, my undergraduate research assistant helping me handle our exposition booth, additional exposure to IRONMAN culture. This was his first time experiencing endurance sport in any capacity. As it turns out, we both got a healthy dose of exposure and personal inspiration. Upon entering the Waterway Marriott ballroom, we were stunned by the number of people packed into the room. We both stopped in the corner to take photographs of the scene. Thousands of people had their eyes glued to a large television screen. Flashes of athletes competing in the 2011 running of the Texas event occupied the current year's competition field and their families. The crowd roared as the video came to an inspirational conclusion, highlighting the very last finisher to cross the line at this exact race last year—Shana Richardson, with a time of sixteen hours, fifty-five minutes, and forty-eight seconds.

Ryan and I grabbed some food and walked around to look for two seats. They were hard to find. We finally came upon a place to sit at a large table next to a family of four. I immediately surmised that we were sitting with an Iron Dad, his wife, and two children. I anxiously waited for a lull in the action so I could engage the father in conversation. The father's name was Justin. He worked in a bank about twenty minutes from the race venue. The location of the race itself was enough to push Justin to consider competing in the event. Even more remarkably, this was his very first triathlon. "When the IRONMAN came to The Woodlands, I knew I had to do it. I couldn't have a race in my backyard and not even try," he shared with a smile.

A great quality of IRONMAN welcome banquets is that everyone shares a common bond—they are either competing or are supporting a competitor. In some ways, sharing this common bond allows people to ask seemingly invasive questions right from the beginning of a conversation. I overheard a lot of talk about personal records, race-day pacing plans, and projected finish times. Any awkwardness associated with touching upon these topics with strangers seemed to lift that evening. Everyone spoke with confidence and optimism about race day. Justin was no different. As the meal went on, I continued to engage him about his life as an Iron Dad.

Justin spoke extensively about the benefits of having a race twenty minutes from his home. I found myself becoming moved as he talked about the volume of friends and family that would be supporting him on race day—work colleagues, training partners, members of his church, and both immediate and extended family members. The list of supporters seemed to go on and on. Aside from Ryan, I had come to Texas alone. I was not even sure if Ryan was planning on spectating on race day. This was the first IRONMAN competition where my husband was unable to join me. Justin, on the other hand, was able to experience the event with a sizable support group that he playfully referred to as his Iron Posse.

I prodded a little more to get a sense of just how Justin had used the convenience of the race venue to his home. His emphasis on common space was notable. On weekends, he and his family have shopped, dined, and seen movies in the same town as the race. They have ridden The Woodlands Waterway Cruiser, a boat that takes passengers in the same body of water that competitors swim in. In essence, his family has forged intimate memories in the same physical spaces that incorporate the swim, bike, and run courses. They have played Frisbee in the park where the transition area is set up on race morning. This common frame of physical reference and positive memories associated with these spaces had created meaning for Justin and his family.

Throughout the evening, I had the pleasure of speaking with numerous Iron Dads and their families. Like Justin, some fathers registered for the event because they lived within reasonable driving distance to the race venue. For others, motivations stemmed from a variety of intrinsic and extrinsic reasons. A few fathers were competing to raise money for charity or increase awareness of specific causes. One father, a former marine, was raising money for the Semper Fi Fund, an organization that offers financial assistance to the families of injured U.S. armed forces members. Others wanted to serve as a role model for their children. While the reasons behind registering for the race varied considerably, everyone shared one common goal—to cross that elusive finish line. This chapter explores the seven most commonly cited reasons for participation that arose from my grounded theory analysis: (1) using iron-distance training as a catalyst for bodily change; (2) being a role model; (3) undertaking an iron-distance event as a way of doing the extraordinary; (4) coming to iron-distance competition through media influence; (5) joining an event because of its proximity to home; (6) taking part in something larger than the self; and (7) exploring the extremes of pleasure and pain. Drawing on the conversation I had with Justin and others I met in Texas, I situate the importance of time, space, faith, and health in the 140.6 registration process.

Motivation for Endurance Sport Participation

Previous literature has explored participation motivation in various sport contexts. As examples, a number of studies center on marathon runners (Bond and Batey 2005; Ogles and Masters 2000, 2003) and cyclists (Brown, O'Connor, and Barkatsas 2009). However, as noted by Matthew Lamont and Millicent Kennelly (2012), little attention has been focused on amateur triathletes. Of the work focusing on triathletes, sparse research has focused on ultra-distance events like IRONMAN (Grand'Maison 2004; McCarville 2007). Iron-distance racing is worthy of its own consideration because it is one of the few sporting activities that take the majority of a day to complete. This book attempts to fill that gap by understanding the motivations of active iron-distance competitors, specifically Iron Dads.

Some common themes have emerged from the endurance sport participation motivation literature. Physical benefits, such as changes in weight, body composition, and body shape, all serve as motivating factors (Bond and Batey 2005). Using self-determination and flow theories, Lamont and Kennelly (2012) identify a number of intrinsic and extrinsic motivations for triathlon participation. Intrinsic motivations include factors such as sport enjoyment and competence, while extrinsic motivations include factors such as well-being, ego involvement, and sociability. Despite identifying these common themes, scholars have yet to reach consensus on the most influential reasons for participating in endurance sport activities (Lamont and Kennelly 2012).

While this body of research helps us understand sport motivation, the studies all share one common methodological limitation. Scholars tend to lump motivations of all endurance sport athletes together. This is problematic because not all sport and leisure contexts are identical. There are unique structural and cultural properties associated with each sporting environment. Triathlon represents a unique context because it takes place in multiple landscapes, both on land and in water. It challenges competitors to gain proficiency in three separate sport disciplines—swimming, biking, and running. This is in contrast to other sports focusing on a single discipline. One limitation in Lamont and Kennelly's (2012) study is that the authors do not make distinctions among triathletes competing at different distances. By not doing so, they may be missing nuances that are specific to athletes attracted to particular distances. The financial and time commitments associated with various triathlon distances differ substantially. For example, registering for a $25 local sprint is not nearly the financial commitment of registering for a $895 IRONMAN event, as the 2012 U.S. Championship race was. Preparing for a race that lasts approximately 1.5 hours does not require the same training schedule as undertaking one that can last upwards of seventeen hours. The motivating factors for registration may not necessarily parallel one another at the various triathlon distances. By focusing exclusively on iron-distance triathletes, this chapter is able to generate a more detailed understanding about the motivating factors of Iron Dad competitors.

One unique scholarly piece helps shed some light on iron-distance participants' motivation. In his autoethnographic work, Ron McCarville (2007) set out to understand why he decided to embark on the challenging undertaking of completing IRONMAN Lake Placid. He describes IRONMAN's transcendence from a "someday" to a "why not today?" endeavor. One day, while trying on pants, his toddler son inadvertently locked himself in a neighboring dressing room. As McCarville struggled to climb over the dressing room wall to come to his son's assistance, he realized that he had become quite sedentary in his lifestyle. The author recalls, "Physically, I was bleeding and bruised, but it was my sense of self that took the greatest blow. I realized that I had become sedentary and that there was a better way. I decided to become more active" (163). It was then that McCarville turned toward a life of fitness. Due to a combination of influence from friends, media, and personal desire to be physically fit, he signed up for his first full-distance triathlon. McCarville concludes that IRONMAN allowed him to find what Johan Huizinga (1950) refers to as a "world within a world" (10). This world was a place marked by a unique blend of pleasure and pain—a place to test the limits of the human body and spirit.

Iron Distance, Motivation, and the Body

Active leisure and the human body are inextricably linked. Echoing McCarville (2007), a number of Iron Dads cited bodily changes as a motivation for registering for an iron-distance event. In further exploring this point, it is important to consider that seeking bodily changes is a gendered experience. Women have clear points of physiological change that are reflective of their place in their life course. Events such as pregnancy and menstruation serve as "bridging points" between different phases of life

(Watson 2000). People may be quick to assert that the existence of these bridging points adds to the intrigue of Iron Moms' stories. That is a reasonable assertion. How and when Iron Moms embrace sport in relation to these dramatic physiological changes adds a unique dimension to the study of gender of sport. However, at the same time, we must not neglect the implications of men's lack of these clear bridging points.

Sociologists such as Jonathan Watson (2000) have argued that through economic and social constraints, men create bodily transitions. After marriage, for example, many men "let go," linking a physical settling down with a social settling down (Watson 2000, 89–90). Iron-distance participation seems to pose a contradiction to Watson's findings. As opposed to letting go, many older men who compete in these events seek to shape their bodies into finely tuned machines. In addition to challenging workout routines, many endurance triathletes place a significant emphasis on nutrition. What is the basis for this deviation from Watson's findings? Is it that some full-distance competitors reject the idea of embracing bodily transitions, such as "letting go," between life-course stages? My findings suggest that iron-distance racing represents an ability to stay in touch with one's youth, both physically and emotionally. This is, in part, because participation allows men of all ages to feel competitive.

One of the attractions of triathlon is that it is one of the few sports that attempts to equalize age in competition. Men and women compete in age-group categories defined in five-year increments. Consequently, athletes seek to be competitive within their age group. This is in stark contrast to many team and individual sports where age is not considered in the construction of match-ups. Take, for example, a local softball league. Men might feel that competing against younger athletes would lead to embarrassment. Older men may fear being dominated on the scoreboard, getting thrown out because they are slow, and so on. Triathlon is set up in a way that attempts to mitigate these age concerns. While an older athlete might not win the race, he or she might win his or her respective age group, a prize that is highly recognized in triathlon. Most triathlons offer prizes and public recognition to age-group winners. At one point, prior to its relationship with the Challenge Family brand, the Revolution3 triathlon series had become popular because it offered financial prizes in all age groups. The IRONMAN World Championship, arguably the most high-profile event in the sport, reserves competition slots for all age groups. This allows men and women of all ages to compete in a less threatening context. Individuals can condition their bodies to excellence knowing that they will be competing against athletes in a similar age and gender category. Athletes of all ages also receive recognition in World Triathlon Corporation's media channels, including its website and print magazine. Lew Hollander, an eighty-one-year-old physician, was awarded the 2011 "performance of the year" by World Triathlon Corporation (Mackinnon 2011). Upon finishing his twenty-first IRONMAN World Championship race, he became the oldest person to cross the finish line at Kona to date. He completed the event in sixteen hours, forty-five minutes, and fifty-five seconds. Ultimately, the age group tiered system allows men and women of all ages to feel like champions, or at the very least, competitors. This undoubtedly adds to the attraction of the sport.

This sense of competitiveness allows athletes, especially men, to distance themselves from a sense of failed or threatened masculinity associated with struggling athletes (Messner 1997). Even though men hold a privileged place in society, they often feel powerless in many social situations (Kimmel 1992; Miller 1998). Success in sport is one way to regain a sense of control (Messner 1997). My findings reveal that the decision to register for an iron-distance event is a source of empowerment for Iron Dads. Men can become role models to their families and co-workers while participating in an extraordinary athletic event. As the general public learns more about others taking the 140.6 journey, interest in entering the triathlon community as a source of empowerment will increase. This could help explain why the full-iron distance has seen such a recent jump in popularity. It is with this understanding that we explore the seven reasons why Iron Dads register for such an event.

Seven Motivations for Iron Distance Registration

Iron Distance as a Catalyst for Bodily Change

Desire for weight loss and increased physical fitness were some of the most commonly cited motives for full-distance registration among Iron Dads. Athletes expressed a desire to get lean and toned, and to increase their aerobic capacity. When discussing the type of body that they were seeking, many participants drew on preconceptions about the attractiveness of the triathlete body style. In doing so, participants constructed narratives about prospective athletic identities. They drew on visions of "possible selves" as a way to frame their view on a future body physique (Markus and Nurius 1986). The use of the possible selves framework allows men and women to talk about the "kind" of self they wish to transform into (Kiecolt 1994). They then use that idealized vision of the self to help reach their goals (Markus and Ruvolo 1989). In this study, some dads embraced a type of idealized vision of the triathlete body. For example, John talked about his desire to "get the body of a triathlete." When prompted to elaborate on what this image meant to him, he talked about the "ideal balance

of strength and aerobic capacity" needed to compete in endurance triathlon. Unsatisfied with his current weight and physique, John looked to the
iron-distance as a catalyst for change. He dropped almost seventy pounds
in his training for IRONMAN Texas. Contrary to Ellen Granberg's (2006)
finding that possible selves are often not realized in weight loss efforts, a
number of participants for this study did reach their goal for the ideal self.
Some even transformed themselves well beyond what they initially imagined was possible.

Significant bodily transformations are often publicly celebrated in
IRONMAN culture. One such example is evident at the welcome dinner
events that typically take place two days before the competition. The dinner
serves as a place for athletes, friends, and families to gather in celebration
of the upcoming triathlon. It is customary for the master of ceremonies to
engage the crowd in a series of athlete recognition exercises. Mike Reilly
often leads the exercises. Mike will ask competitors who lost thirty or more
pounds while training for the race to stand up. He repeats the question,
asking for athletes who lost forty to fifty, then seventy or more pounds, to
remain standing. This continues until there are only three or four people
remaining. These people are then asked to join Mike on stage to talk about
their story. The crowd stands up in a roaring applause as the competitors
introduce themselves. Public celebrations such as this one remind us that
even though endurance triathlon is an individual sport, the athletes are
part of a larger sporting community—a community that recognizes the
middle-class sensibilities of hard work and personal achievement. In this
instance, the body becomes a vehicle for expressing those sensibilities.

For some competitors, construction of the idealized possible self was
coupled with a clear "turning point" in that individual's life (Marsiglio and
Hutchinson 2002). Turning points represent an experience that "transforms
[a person's] perspective on self" (Marsiglio and Hutchinson 2002, 3). These
moments can fundamentally shape a person's identity moving forward.
While Marsiglio and Hutchinson explore the turning point experience
as it applies to the reproductive realm, the concept can also hold significance in sport and leisure contexts. For example, think back to McCarville's
(2007) autoethnographic piece discussed earlier in the chapter. McCarville,
an Iron Dad, discusses an important experience in his journey to the
IRONMAN Lake Placid finish line. Recall that while trying on pants,
McCarville's young son inadvertently locked himself in a neighboring dressing room. The author could not fit under the door of the dressing room, so
he decided to climb up to a support beam, swing across from his room to
his son's, and unlock the door from the inside. "It shouldn't be too difficult
to swing across and drop into the dressing room," McCarville recalled (162).
Things did not quite play out that way in actuality. "My body is refusing to

do what I ask. I instruct my legs to lift to my chest. They do not. I ask my hands to grip the beam with vigor. They too are unwilling to comply" (163).

Like McCarville, a number of Iron Dads experienced a turning point when they realized they were out of shape. While describing these turning points, participants often keyed in on a single incident or moment when they had an epiphany about their bodies. "I looked in the bathroom mirror and was horrified," Bryson, a father of two, explained. He went on to detail his turning point. "I was tired of being fat. I realized that something had to change immediately, so I started to set fitness goals." Bryson's story was not uncommon. In experiencing these turning points, participants construct a new possible self that is rooted in the new athletic challenge of the iron-distance. Nick, a business owner and father of two young boys, recounted, "About five or six years ago, I decided to make a change. While looking at myself, about twenty pounds overweight and not the healthiest, I decided that it was time to change. I decided to get back into cycling and cross country running because I used to do cross country in high school as well, so let's get back to triathlon here. I decided to jump right into the IRONMAN then."

Some athletes project bodily transition, moving from unhealthy weight and habits to a more fit body. John, a lawyer and father of three, recalls, "I knew something had to change when I didn't have the energy to play with my kids. We were out in the yard playing Frisbee with the dog when I realized that this was it for me. Something had to change. [. . .] I have always felt that the athletes in Kona were something that I could aspire to be like. I decided on that day to sign up for Lou [IRONMAN Louisville]." After being in a state of depression for many months due to his 400-pound weight, Dan, a father of two, similarly decided to take action. On his website, he discusses his journey from being a morbidly obese body to an iron-distance athlete. "My wife often told me that she felt like a single mom because I had no energy to help out with the kids. I broke a colleague's brand-new guest chair in his office because of my extreme weight. [. . .] After coming to the realization that I was going to die if I didn't do something about my severe morbid obesity, I decided to have gastric bypass. Not only have I lost 201 pounds in fourteen months, I have completed dozens of triathlons including 3 full 140.6 mile IRONMAN triathlons."[1]

In Dan's case, iron-distance racing itself was not the sole catalyst for bodily change. Combined with the gastric bypass surgery, it became part of a larger life narrative about health and fitness. Dan has also gone on to expand his fitness journey well beyond triathlon, competing in ultra-distance runs and swims. "I decided to make the choice of health over food," he explains. The defining turning point for Dan occurred when he realized that he could die if he continued to neglect his health. His story has since been featured in numerous local news outlets.

Many 140.6-distance registrants consider triathlon to be the cornerstone of an overall healthy lifestyle that includes positive changes to a myriad of habits—sleeping, eating, training, time use, and friend selection, among other things. For these competitors, the commitment requires making a series of decisions throughout the day to support one's capacity as a healthy triathlete. This takes financial and emotional commitment that extends well beyond the event itself. These habits coalesce to construct something much more substantial than a hobby. Similar to findings centered on "lifestyle sports," these habits come together to form a way of life (Rinehart and Syndor 2003; Tomlinson et al. 2005; Wheaton 2004).

Of course, most Iron Dads do not simply go straight from realizing that they are out of shape to wanting to compete in a daylong athletic event. Nor do they necessarily identify triathlon as their immediate means to a healthy lifestyle. As in the case of Dan, the father who suffered from depression and overcame morbid obesity, my analysis reveals that turning points often signify the start of a lengthy process of change. This process is seen as a gradual transition to health. With Iron Dads, this health is then maintained through training and racing. So why go from one end of the health spectrum to the opposite extreme? Eventually, as participants' "possible selves" began to emerge as "real selves," the desire to explore the boundaries of their bodies and spirits become more real. As I talk about later in the chapter, iron-distance racing is viewed as a means of doing the extraordinary. Participants described their path to health as a continual quest, moving from one challenging goal to the next. They also expressed a strong desire to be role models for their children. Being an endurance triathlete allows one's kids to see, in the flesh, that transitions to a better state of health are possible.

Being a Role Model

For Dan, the journey toward the iron-distance finish line became part of a quest for better overall health. It also became part of his quest to be a better father. Weighing four hundred pounds had serious consequences for his wife and three children, Ayden, Ava, and Austin. In an interview conducted with Ben Murphy, founder of *The Father Life*, an online magazine for dads, Dan explains:

> I really don't remember every pound I gained along the way. I started after high school with a 36-inch waist, then I bought 38-inch and kept going up in size year on top of year until I reached my biggest pant size of 56 inches. The weight really crept up on me, and it was easy to ignore as I just bought baggy clothes, avoided being in pictures,

dodged every mirror that came in my path, and secluded myself from the outside world to an extent. When I hit my highest weight and became a father, I really felt the effects of my weight in every aspect. I was embarrassed to go to public functions with my family because I knew I would be the biggest dad there. I had no energy to do anything that involved physical activity including shopping, basic chores, and going to public places where I knew I would not fit in chairs, seats, or booths. (Murphy 2010)

Dan went on to explain how, after losing the weight, he became more active in his kids' lives. He became a soccer coach and went camping with his family. He wanted to be active and also to serve as an inspiration for others.

A number of Iron Dads reported registering for an iron-distance event as a means of being a role model for their kids. In doing so, they seek to demonstrate what it means to live a healthy lifestyle while embodying the Iron Dad identity. The fathers use triathlon as a vehicle for influencing other social worlds—their workplace, their family, their churches, and other communities that hold value for them. This means teaching good habits to others by demonstrating a dedication to healthy principles. While his children are too young to understand endurance triathlon, Ian blogs about his experiences. Asked to elaborate on why he thought blogging was an important activity, he said, "Honestly, it's for me a little bit of keeping history, so when my kids are old enough [pause]. I don't know if I will do this [a 140.6 race] again. I'd like to think I will, but I don't want to sacrifice anything either. It's something that they'll be able to look back and say, 'Wow.' Or hopefully they will say, 'Wow.' Or maybe they'll say, 'No big deal.' I don't know. But they'll be able to look back on and say, 'You know, this was pretty cool—look at what daddy did on this day.'"

Many fathers desire to serve as strong role models for their children. In doing so, they convey values and wisdom to their kids. This idea of passing on a particular set of values to future generations is known as "generativity" (Erikson 1950). A generative person seeks to impart wisdom to help nurture the growth of younger individuals (de St. Aubin, McAdams, and Kim 2004). In the case of Iron Dads, these men seek to instill valued skills and traditions related to health and fitness in their children. This means teaching their kids the value of sleep, healthy eating, and physical leisure activities. In essence, these men teach by doing.

The concept of generativity speaks to a larger philosophy with which fatherhood can be approached, often referred to as "generative fathering" (Dollahite and Hawkins 1998; Dollahite, Hawkins, and Brotherson 1997; Snarey 1993). Viewing fathering as a type of generative work emphasizes men's abilities to serve in a caring and nurturing capacity. It also emphasizes fathering through a larger set of ethics—one that establishes a healthy connection between parent and child. Establishing this connection does not happen automatically. It is the outcome of fostering a father-child relationship based on "daily care" and "sustained emotional engagement" (Daniels and Weingarten 1982, 161). Many Iron Dads engage in this type of relationship work through both physical and emotional means (Ahlander and Bahr 1995; Brotherson, Dollahite, and Hawkins 2005). Given the prominence of sport in an Iron Dad's life, the centrality of physical relationship work should not be unexpected.

A number of the Iron Dad participants talked about registering for an iron-distance race as a way to set a positive example for their children. In this way, men would actively engage their children in the training process. Parker, a college professor training for his first 140.6 event, talked about the importance of taking his young daughter outside. When asked if he was seeking to set a good example to his daughter, he replied, "Oh yeah, I do think that's probably true. I do think about that actually when we are out especially, when she's out in the jogging stroller and things like that. I think about how much influence an athletic family can have. You know, routinely being with her outside, already she hates coming inside. [. . .] I will always try to set an example of a Catholic healthy lifestyle and athletic lifestyle, and I think my wife and I both hope that that she will adopt that behavior on her own."

Like Parker, a number of participants spoke about the idea of transmitting the values of quality leisure time to their children. Instead of sitting in front of the television, these fathers encouraged their kids to get off the couch and be involved in athletics. By engaging their kids in a physical and emotional way, these men are able to "do" generative fathering in a sport and leisure context. Ian, a physical education teacher, discussed the importance of his daughter knowing about triathlon:

> My daughter will sit downstairs when I'm on the trainer and we will watch TV together. My daughter at five years old knows what triathlon is. She's involved. This summer she will be doing her first mini race. She knows that daddy's getting ready for something. I don't think she knows how big it is. But yeah, my wife is a triathlete as well so when one of us isn't training, the other one is, so that makes us work our schedule even better. Our kids know what an active lifestyle is. Like tomorrow we are doing a 10K race, my wife and I, and then my daughter is doing the quarter-mile race because she knows that's what we do.

Mike Reilly has called finishers home in more than one hundred IRONMAN races. His iconic voice and exciting personality entertains finish line spectators for hours. While at IRONMAN Texas, Mike stopped by my exposition booth to talk about fathers' participation in the sport. He pointed to generativity as a main reason he thinks people are getting involved in 140.6 racing:

Well, I think a lot of them [parents] are taking on the challenge. Don't get me wrong—it's for themselves, but it's also [that] so many of them feel that they need to lead by example instead of by just word. And so, when their kids see that happen, it has a tremendous benefit for the kids. I have eighteen-, nineteen-, and twenty-year-olds coming up to me now going, "Mike, you called my mom an IRONMAN in Lake Placid," they say, "and I watched her when I was ten years old and now I'm doing the IRONMAN. I want to meet you." And I'm going, "Oh my gosh! Now the kids are coming back." So it's passed on, and even with my own kids. I worked out all the time. Same with my wife. And now my daughter is doing the Boston Marathon. My son has done half IRONMAN. So it's lead by example. They really know that they're doing something that's more powerful than telling their kids what to do.

The influence of the generativity spirit is not limited to immediate family members. Mitch, a doctor and multiple-time iron-distance finisher, discusses what it is like to engage in cultural generativity with his youth group and patients. "All the kids in the group see that [me having an active lifestyle] as well. My younger patients as well. Anytime you talk to kids and you tell them how far you went swimming, biking, and running that day or that event or whatever, kids are like, 'Wow!' Yeah, it's an awesome feeling." Mitch reminds us that the influence of the Iron Dad role model can expand well beyond the confines of the family. He went on to explain how he is regarded as a role model to his fellow hospital employees:

The whole lifestyle of working out all the time and all the doctors in the hospital are like, "Wow, you're looking thin, you're looking pretty strong, you look good." They always comment on my training. And now that I'm adjusting my diet and stuff too, I try to be an example even for older physicians. You just make yourself an example and you make yourself a better person and everyone around you gets to see that. That's your personality and that character trait goes with you until the day you die. You can't take it away. It's just an incredible accomplishment to try to do this.

Be it with patients, kids they mentor, or with their own children, many Iron Dads see participating in endurance triathlon as a means to influence current and future generations.[2] These men view this as a positive outcome of their iron-distance journey, a daily contribution that they can make to society. The creative ways that men integrate their families into their training is further explored in the next chapter.

Iron Distance as a Means for Doing the Extraordinary

The very mention of IRONMAN can elicit emotions from people. As noted by professional triathlete Matt Lieto when asked about the iron-distance journey, "When they first see it and first hear about it, they think they've either misheard or think it's not possible for someone to be able to do that" (World Triathlon Corporation 2012). For this reason, participating in such an event is a gateway for doing something that many see as physically extraordinary. A number of Iron Dads used that exact terminology to describe their experience—"extraordinary." It is precisely for this reason that many competitors decide to take on the iron-distance challenge. When asked why he registered for IRONMAN, Lance, a lawyer and father of two young girls, explains, "Because it's one of the hardest things you can do and one of the biggest accomplishments in life. I wanted to do something extraordinary—and I did it. Nobody can take that away from me, ever." This vision of perceived difficulty was shared by many. One Iron Dad, a first-time triathlon competitor, described how he "loved the challenge of endurance races" and forecasted IRONMAN to be "probably the hardest thing I will ever do."

These sentiments reveal that a sense of doing something "extraordinary" in a sporting context is often couched in risk, thrill-seeking, and challenging adventure—all elements of a sporting lifestyle (Fletcher 2008; Wheaton 2004). When people register for an iron-distance event, they know they are challenging themselves to push the limits of their bodies. There is a risk that they may fail in that endeavor. The thrill of attempting something so difficult, and making it part of an overall lifestyle, is an attraction for many prospective competitors. Isaac talked about the excitement and challenge of trying to master three disciplines. "I do like the training, but it is kind of a problematic thing. The fun part is that you never really feel like you're mastering it. You've got three disciplines. Usually, if you've got two out of three going, you're feeling good. If you've got one out of three going, you're feeling bad. And there are times when you've got none of the three going all that well. So, it's difficult to have that be an identity."

Participants explained how racing and training helps them grow in both their athletic and non-athletic pursuits. As described by one Iron Dad, "I do it [prepare for 140.6] to become a better person. It allows me to have personal breakthroughs." When prompted to identify what breakthroughs he had experienced, the father cited gaining clarity and focus on issues related to family, employment, and friendship. The sentiments expressed by this individual suggest that taking on an extraordinary task in one realm of life may have a positive impact on other parts of life.

Coming to Iron Distance through Media Influence

Every year since 1991, NBC has produced a broadcast featuring the IRON-MAN World Championship race. First aired in 1980 as part of ABC's *Wide World of Sports*, the broadcast has gone on to win sixteen Emmy Awards and more than forty nominations.[3] Traditionally one hour long, NBC decided to expand its coverage to two hours in 2010. Research for this book indicates that people not only are watching this broadcast as a form of entertainment, but also are highly influenced by the program as a motivation to participate. The influence of this broadcast has even ascended to the highest ranks of the triathlon organization. In July 2011, USA Triathlon hosted a virtual forum with the head of its organization, Rob Urbach. A forum participant asked Urbach how he got his start in multi-sport competition. He replied, "Like many of our members, I was inspired by the IRONMAN broadcast. I was not a competitive swimmer or biker at the time, but the enormity of the event really resonated with me."

It is no wonder why the NBC broadcast is so influential to prospective competitors. IRONMAN lends itself well to visual motivation. Thousands of spectators line the streets on event day. A cannon shot signals the start of the race. While this approach is largely being eliminated at other sizable 140.6 events in the name of safety, a mass swim start with approximately 2,200 athletes moving in the same direction remains the icon of Kona. The spectacle of transitioning between swimming, biking, and running is stunning. After exiting the water, athletes zip out of the transition on their bikes. Finally, many courses loop over themselves multiple times. This allows for spectators to get numerous glimpses of athletes on the swim, bike, and run. For example, in IRONMAN Coeur d'Alene, a Ford vehicle signifies "the hot corner," a turn that athletes pass by four times on the bicycle route. When talking about why they registered for this specific event, a number of Iron Dads cited the spectator-friendly nature of the course.

Events like iron-distance triathlon hold a unique place in the sporting literature. Each sport operates on a continuum, falling somewhere between the extremes of "play" and "spectacle" (Coakley 2009). Play suggests that the activity is free-flowing and done for internal rewards, such as feeling good about oneself. Spectacle suggests that the activity is highly orchestrated and done for external rewards, such as getting a roar from the crowd. Iron-distance triathlon falls somewhere in the middle of this continuum, embracing elements of both spectacle and play. While people typically participate in the event for internal rewards, it is nearly impossible to ignore the fans that line the streets when competitors cross the finish line. It is precisely at this complex intersection between spectacle and play where IRONMAN-branded events become attractive. One individual described how he watched the IRONMAN on ABC's *Wide World of Sports* as a child. After being out of shape for nearly two decades, he decided to "revisit a childhood dream" and start training. Mitch, a doctor and multiple-time 140.6 finisher, recalled, "I love watching Kona. I always watched it as a kid and thought that could be me. I asked myself, 'Why not me?' and started training. Watching it [the Kona documentary] reminds me that anyone can do the race with proper training." As it turned out, Mitch was able to live his dream. After years of applying, he won one of Kona's highly coveted random lottery slots.

Both of the above competitors wrote about being influenced by the spectacle aspect of the IRONMAN World Championship. Seeing the event on television piqued their interest. At the same time, these athletes allude to the importance of personal gratification, a cornerstone of play. The NBC documentary was not the only inspiring media source cited by iron-distance registrants. Individuals also discussed being influenced by sport books written by current or former athletes. Peyton, an account manager for a telecommunications company, talked about the power of reading *Becoming an Ironman: First Encounters with the Ultimate Endurance Event* by Kara Douglass Thom (2002). "I never really thought that IRONMAN was something that I could do, and I am still amazed that I did it. But I had been curious about it for a long time and decided to pick up this book to learn a little more. I still read it before each race for motivation and repeat some of my favorite sections."

Sport receives an "enormous" amount of attention in mass media (Eitzen 2009, 69). As triathlon continues to push its way into mainstream media channels, the visibility and popularity of the sport will most certainly increase. From 2009 to 2015, Universal Sports, formerly part of the NBC network, televised full IRONMAN events from the around the world (World Triathlon Corporation 2009). These events were also streamed on the Universal Sports website. International Triathlon Union (ITU) events, as well as other high-profile distance races, are also televised. While still extremely rare, clips from triathlons can now be spotted on ESPN's *SportsCenter*, one of the strongest metrics of what typical sports viewers consider to be "good television" (Clarke and Clarke 1982). These recent media developments, alongside the expanded Kona coverage, have created more opportunities for people to encounter iron-distance triathlon in everyday life. This visual exposure to iron-distance competition is enough to push some fathers to register.

The Appeal of Proximity

Like Justin, the banker I met at the athlete welcome banquet at the beginning of the chapter, a number of competitors were drawn to iron-distance triathlon by a race venue's proximity to their hometown. This attraction stemmed from a variety of factors. Hometown races allow for family and friends to accompany the athlete to the race. Jayden, a business owner and father of two, discussed his excitement in bringing his "IRONMAN posse" to Lake Placid. This posse included friends and both immediate and extended family members. While speaking with him at IRONMAN Texas, first-time 140.6 competitor Adam told me about how his wife designed custom shirts for the entire family. The shirts featured Adam's race number and a picture of the World Triathlon Corporation logo.

Racing close to home allows different social worlds to overlap. Individuals who occupy a social world share "perspectives, unique activities and language, common channels of communication which arise out of common interest in the production of a social object" (Crosset and Beal 1997, 81). Social worlds can include families, religious organizations, or participants in sporting communities such as golf (Crosset 1995), horse racing (Rosecrance 1985), and swimming (Chambliss 1989). Registering for a race in one's hometown allows for the social world of the family to peripherally experience the social world of endurance triathlon. The connectedness of these worlds is enhanced by the sharing of mutually known physical space. Kevin talks about the allure of being near friends while at the race venue:

Well, I live in the Twin Cities and we have a lot of friends in Wisconsin, so if I'm going to do an iron-distance race, that makes the most sense. It's the only one I can feasibly drive to. There's Kentucky [IRONMAN Louisville], I guess. I could get to Kentucky, but this makes the most sense. I know people who have done it [racing near home], and there's more support that way. But we'll see. In the future, there are other races that are in other areas of the country where we have family I'd be looking at next year or the year after.

Gary, a surgeon and first-time iron-distance competitor, describes the benefits of having an event in his hometown:

I mean, I never thought I could do one [iron-distance event]. I was just gonna do the half [70.3]. I sort of looked at IRONMAN as like a different species. And then they put it in The Woodlands, where I live, and I thought, "I can't let them do this every year and rub my nose in it." So I'm just doing one, and then I'll go back to the half distance. [. . .] On race day, my wife and kids, they'll come to the swim start and then probably see me once on the bike and then go back for the run. They're familiar with the area, so they shouldn't have a big issue getting around.

Gary went on to describe how the bike course for IRONMAN Texas went right by his front porch. This highlights the importance of physical place in the fathering process (Marsiglio, Roy, and Fox 2005). This mutual use of space allows Gary's family to share a physical bond—and perhaps an emotional bond—with members of the triathlon world. These connections empower Gary as he fathers within an endurance triathlon context. Family members can enter the iron-distance social world itself by engaging in activities such as volunteering, attending the expo in the days leading up to the event, or attending the athlete banquet. While this type of entry into the iron-distance social world is somewhat peripheral in nature, it still represents a type of access. This access allows for the Iron Dad and his family to experience a deeper sharing of the event. The relationship between fathering and space is further explored in the next chapter.

Hometown races also present a more cost-effective way to enter an iron-distance competition. Traveling long distances to an event can get very costly, especially if multiple members of the family are going. Airfare, baggage fees, ground transportation, and bike shipping expenses add up quickly. Signing up for a local race allows for fathers to bring social worlds together with the endurance triathlon experience. It also allows for these men to take a more cost-effective approach to racing.

Something Larger Than "Me"

Participation in triathlon is often viewed as a selfish undertaking. Competitors spend countless hours training and thousands of dollars on a leisure activity that is typically focused on the self (Lamont, Kennelly, and Wilson 2011). Some can let the sport "virtually dominate" their lives (McCarville 2007, 160). While some degree of selfishness is unavoidable, registration motivation can often stem from reasons well beyond the individual. These reasons include raising awareness for certain causes and helping others share in religion and spirituality.

A number of interview participants discussed their affiliation with the Fellowship of Christian Athletes (FCA), an organization dedicated to spreading the word of Jesus Christ. This organization is one of the many religious-based groups present in the iron-distance community. The FCA has a wing of its organization that is dedicated to endurance sport, known as "Team FCA Endurance." Members of this community are often identifiable by their custom FCA race apparel. Part of FCA's objective is to challenge competitors to reflect on why they race. Their mantra, reflective of this challenge, is "Why do you race?" This question can be seen on the brim of team visors, stickers, and uniforms. The back of their triathlon tops features a scripture quote, ". . . those who trust in the Lord will renew their strength" (Isaiah 40:31, English Standard Version). A number of interview participants discussed the importance of mentally challenging fellow competitors while on the race course. Lance, a father of two, cited his desire to spark an "internal dialogue" with fellow iron-distance competitors. He went on to discuss how he races to, "spread the word of God and worship Him while competing." He used the FCA as vehicle to help him share his religious beliefs while training and racing.

Numerous Iron Dads spoke extensively about the relationship between their training and their faith, a theme that will be explored extensively in chapter 6. Josh, a father of two, described how he "raced to spread the word of God." He viewed himself as an uplifting spirit for struggling competitors. "Maybe someone struggling would see my jersey and be reminded of the fact that God is with them." Ian, also a father of two, talked about the connection between his training and his faith:

> I truly know that the reason I'm doing this is for a reason bigger than myself. You know, I'm racing for a team called Fellowship of Christian Athletes. I'll be spreading the Gospel while racing. I'm also raising money for a camp that works with troubled teens. So I know that the time I am spending away from my family is benefiting other people—I do. But I also know that there's a reason and a rhyme behind it, and I know that's what God sent me [to do], so that helps justify it a little bit.

Ian's comments point to the idea that in addition to religious motivations, some participants register for iron-distance races to help raise awareness about specific social or medical causes. Often these efforts to raise awareness are coupled with fundraising for that specific cause.

World Triathlon Corporation helps competitors with fundraising efforts through their "Your Journey, Your Cause" initiative. As part of the IRONMAN Foundation platform, this initiative allows event registrants to fundraise for the nonprofit cause of their choice. They can create a dedicated website that explains why they are racing. The "Your Journey, Your Cause" website reads:

> More than 22,000 athletes compete in IRONMAN events throughout North America each year, and many of these triathletes are participating in an IRONMAN event as a result of being touched

by something bigger than themselves. Whether it is a battle with cancer, the loss of a loved one or surviving a tragedy such as 9/11, many IRONMAN athletes are racing to demonstrate that ANYTHING IS POSSIBLE. In this vein, The IRONMAN Foundation provides athletes with the opportunity to transform their racing from a selfish sport to a selfless endeavor, by racing for a charity or cause of their choice through the Your Journey, Your Cause program. (World Triathlon Corporation n.d.)

From the program's inception to the time this book goes to press, more than 850 athletes competing across sixty-five different events have taken advantage of this program initiative. More than 17,000 people have donated to the program, with the average athlete raising over $5,000.[4] Other competitors fundraise in direct partnership with specific nonprofit organizations.

These findings suggest that there can often be a philanthropic motivation tied to iron-distance registration. This philanthropy may be viewed as both an intrinsic and extrinsic motivation. Competitors are helping others through their racing, and in turn, feeling good about themselves. Another prime example of this is the establishment of the IRONMAN Foundation–Newton Running Ambassador Team. Built in 2013, this team performs community service in the locations that they race. They also raise money for initiatives within WTC's race communities.

Exploring the Extremes of Pleasure and Pain

Pain is a topic that has been of sociological interest since the early 1990s. A decade later, sport scholars started investigating the subject in earnest (Roderick 2006; Young 2004). We now see a flourishing literature exploring the relationship between body, pain, and sporting pleasure.[5] Often, the topic of pain is something that is problematized in the literature. This is particularly true when competitors internalize pain as a measuring stick of success (Loland 2006). Given that one must fight to overcome pain, an individual's ability to rise above it becomes a barometer of both physical and emotional will (Loland 2006). While literature addresses the topic of pain in a variety of recreational contexts, the literature on endurance sport more specifically is comparatively sparse.

Is it possible for pleasure and pain to coexist? Iron-distance racing represents a ripe place to observe the collision of pleasure, pain, body, and health (Bridel 2010). It is a unique context in that it is not a contact sport, an area of study that has received quite a bit of scholarly attention (Gard and Meyenn 2000; Pringle 2009). Recent scholarship suggests there is an overlap between pain and pleasure for some iron-distance competitors

(Atkinson and Young 2008; Bale 2006). This literature also shows that athletes may use triathlon as a way of finding "exciting significance" in their lives (Atkinson 2008). This is to say that through pain and suffering, competitors find personal fulfillment and connection with others. Experiencing this "pain community" with other athletes is part of the triathlon culture (Atkinson 2008). Adults of age eighteen to over eighty compete in endurance triathlon, indicating that men and women of all ages are willing to enter these pain communities. Pain is something that is expected and, to varying degrees, welcomed by those who register.

My findings suggest that in the minds of Iron Dads, pain can be a place of solitude and loneliness. The emphasis was not solely on community. Many participants spoke of pushing their body through pain as a natural and expected part of the training and racing process. One study participant shared an excerpt from his IRONMAN Texas race report. In it, he describes his mental justification for pushing through discomfort in the later miles of the marathon. "I want the world to know that I conquered something that most people would never even consider. If I quit now, I am nothing. I convince myself to harden up, push on, and ignore the sensation of my body begging me to quit. Suck up the discomfort and keep pushing. This race is within my grasp. This is why I do this."

In this narrative, Dylan, an engineer and father of two young girls, places a tremendous emphasis on managing pain and discomfort. He enjoys the challenge of overcoming instances when his body wants to quit. It is also notable that Dylan's focus is squarely on the self. The rhetoric is emblematic of Jay Coakley's (2009) description of the "sport ethic"—principles that stress winning at all cost. A key aspect of adhering to the sporting ethic is negotiating and overcoming pain. Iron-distance training teeters in a precarious place, constantly walking a fine line between pleasure and pain. As my Iron Dads revealed, this is part of the allure of the distance for many competitors.

4

The Juggling Act

Now that we know why Iron Dads compete, we must start to examine how. What processes enable these men to take on such a lofty goal? Using a grounded theory approach, this chapter explores the various social and social psychological processes associated with constructing the Iron Dad identity. Specifically, I focus on the following three processes: managing sporting guilt, managing one's status on the athletic visibility continuum, and identifying and utilizing balancing mechanisms. Collectively, these processes reveal how one crafts an existence as an iron-distance competitor, father, husband, and man.

The Power of Intersectionality

Gender, class, race, and privilege all play a role in fostering athletic processes. For example, guilt is often, on some level, the acknowledgment of taking advantage of a privileged place in society. In the case of Iron Dads, some of these men use their position of relative power to impose their leisure desires on their family—as well as to manage those desires. The power of intersectionality had a strong presence throughout many of the study participant interviews.

Established by legal scholar Kimberlé Crenshaw, intersectionality is a powerful theoretical tool for understanding logics of oppression (Crenshaw 1989). The theory explains the "multidimensionality" of oppression (139). It can broadly be described as the specific context in which multiple layers of political, social, physical, and cultural differentiation intersect. Race, gender, physical features, class, and other variables all come together to capture the collective essence of identity. Avtar Brah and Ann Phoenix (2004) remind us that "this concept [intersectionality] emphasizes that different dimensions of social life cannot be separated out into discrete and pure strands" (76). Instead, these factors can come together to create powerful experiences surrounding identity, privilege, and oppression (Nash 2008). These experiences play out in both public and private places, including the home and places of sport.

One of the greatest values of intersectionality is that it moves us away from thinking in binary terms (Nash 2008). One is not simply a woman. One is, for example, a white, middle-class, able-bodied American woman. By viewing identity in a more complex fashion, we can more aptly understand cultures of oppression. This theoretical lens is valuable when considering the lives of Iron Dads. Iron Dads are athletes, fathers, and men. While this is certainly not universally true, many of them are also able-bodied, well-educated high-income earners. To put it bluntly, in the aggregate, this is not a marginalized group.

Ultimately, the vast majority of endurance sport participants compete for pleasure. This is particularly true for average age group athletes, individuals who are not making a living from triathlon. To the contrary, age-groupers pay to play. I argue that for some fathers, drawing on their position of privilege is a critical part of their daily routine. As I discuss later with the concept of intentionality, this happens in both the conscious and subconscious realms. Iron Dads use their status as men, breadwinners, and athletes to establish training and racing opportunities. Toward the end of the chapter, I identify how men rely on this same privilege to give back or offer compensation to their sacrificing families.

Managing Sporting Guilt

The first key process associated with managing the Iron Dad identity is negotiating what I refer to as sporting guilt—guilt that can be felt with the prioritization of sport or leisure over other life responsibilities. In my interviews, men used a variety of words to describe this concept—"guilt," "burden," "uneasiness," and "remorse" were all commonly mentioned. Sporting guilt does not speak to a generic guilt. Instead, it speaks to feelings that arise when a person prioritizes sport above other roles. Using grounded theory analysis, I dove into this finding more thoroughly. Through this process, the complexities of sporting guilt emerged. I identified three characteristics of sporting guilt that make it distinctive from generic guilt. Each of these characteristics is described below:

1. For non-professionals, sport is socially categorized as a hobby and/or leisure.

2. Sport can be internalized as a lifestyle, which can be at odds with society's view of the place of sport in life.
3. Sport can turn dark, meaning that it can become obsessive and destructive.

Societal versus Individual Views of Sport

Over time, societies develop dominant cultural discourses about sport. These discourses reflect what a society values, communicating standards on what is and is not preferred (Holstein and Gubrium 2000). For example, in their study of soccer, Adi Adams, Eric Anderson, and Mark McCormack (2010) found that coaches and athletes use what the authors refer to as "masculinity establishing" and "masculinity challenging" discourses. Players use such language to dominate other men, gaining masculine credibility in the process. Such findings are a sharp reminder that language serves as an important regulating force in society. At the same time, however, the values that we as individuals hold do not always mirror those reflected in dominant cultural conversation. For example, Adams, Anderson, and McCormack (2010) also found that some athletes engaged in acts of "invisible protest" with fellow teammates when masculinity challenging discourses emerged. This suggests that individual views on topics can sometimes be at odds with the more commonly held perspective.

Gauging dominant social views surrounding sport can sometimes be a deceptively daunting task. This is because society produces complicated and often conflicting views surrounding the place of sport in society. On the one hand, sport is revered. It is viewed as an institution that can teach kids good habits, be an outlet for healthy competition, and assist people in maintaining a healthy lifestyle. Sports falling under the four major professional sports leagues in the United States, particularly their athletes, are revered. At the same time, society offers a contradictory narrative to non-professional athletes. For amateurs, cultural discourse categorizes sport as a hobby or leisure activity. It is viewed as fun; something that is accomplished during one's free time. The issue is that the definition of "free time" is subjective. Society places expectations on when and where sport can be performed. In making this characterization, there is often an accompanying social pressure to de-emphasize sporting activities in favor of other life priorities. This is reflected in popular sayings such as "work before play." Consequently, when non-professionals make choices to prioritize sport in their daily lives, those choices can be called into question. For example, missing an informal social gathering of friends in order to do a trainer ride may be perceived by others as crazy or a mis-prioritization of leisure activities. Missing a child's softball game to go on a long ride is viewed as selfish. This suggests that American culture reveres sport—*to a point*.

If society tells us to take care of business before going out for fun, what happens if play is work? This question speaks to one of the themes to emerge from this research—the continual conflation of work and sport. As I listened to my participants, at times, work and training became strikingly indistinguishable. Training time took on the same properties and significance of formal work. This included a deep sense of obligation, a desire for accountability (having a coach), feelings of guilt when objectives were not achieved, and the need to make up for failure. One of the key ways that training resembled a job was evident in how Iron Dads described and executed their training programs.

Perceptions of Training Programs

The fact that negotiating sporting guilt plays such a key role in the lives of Iron Dads speaks to a unique way they view the iron-distance training schedule. "Fun" was not a commonly used word when study participants described their training regimen. More frequently used words included "routine," "execute," and "grueling." This language suggests that training is often viewed as a job, not a hobby. Training sessions are something that must be completed. Workouts become obligations. When asked to describe their training routine, many participants spoke with great detail about which workouts occurred on which day. The degree to which this "personal workout calendar" was embedded in the minds of the participants was notable. These findings raise the question: if training is about business and execution, is it really a hobby? By definition, iron-distance racing is a hobby for the participants of this study. They do not carry a professional triathlon license and thus are not eligible for prize money at World Triathlon Corporation events. They do not get paid to train and race. To the contrary, some shell out thousands of dollars, even tens of thousands in some instances, to compete. Most are not sponsored. However, the way that these men internalize their training warrants a different interpretation of their workout activities. This internalization has consequences for the way Iron Dads approach their day-to-day choices.

When training is viewed as an occupation, a sense of obligation is created. Feelings of obligation heighten the perceived importance of executing each training session. What this means is that sometimes Iron Dads decide that training must trump family time, leaving them with the guilt of being absent in the home. In addition to being physically absent from family activities, participants identified another component of sporting guilt—dealing with emotional absence. By attempting to be present physically for the family later in the day, many fathers complete their training early in the morning before their children and spouse wake up. However, after long hours of exercise, it is hard to be engaged in activities with the family. Ryan describes his dilemma:

> In my mind, I would have wished I was more perky and engaged with them [my kids], as I probably wasn't a lot of the time. I always felt a little bad that I wasn't more energetic with the kids when I would just get home, shower, eat, and lay around after long rides. Sometimes I would play games with them or just watch movies. I was never really pressured to do those things because I was tired, but I personally felt guilty for not doing those things as much because of all the training. It's not just the exercising. It's the periods after. It's how after a complete day has gone by and not feeling like I have contributed at home because I'm just too tired to do anything else, like go out and run errands or play with the kids.

As a first-time iron-distance competitor, Ryan expressed remorse for underestimating the extent to which his training would impact his family. A number of study participants echoed similar sentiments. For this reason, a number of Iron Dads suggested that they would not attempt another 140.6 race until their children were older. One such individual was Josh, a lawyer who decided that he would temporarily halt his endurance racing career after his upcoming 140.6 race. This decision was made before the training for his first full-distance event had even concluded. Josh explained, "you only get to watch them [two daughters] grow up once." The way that some men come to terms with feelings of sporting guilt is to race shorter distances until their children grow up. These fathers perceive that as their children get older, they will become more independent. This, in turn, will give them more flexibility to engage in sporting activities. The phenomenon of dropping to shorter distances as a result of sporting guilt is the focus of chapter 7, "Throwing in the Towel." That chapter also identifies the conditions under which Iron Dads may leave the sport of triathlon entirely.

A Lifestyle or Dark Leisure?

Just as conceptions of work and play may become indistinguishable, so may lifestyles and obsession. Where can we draw the line between sport being a key part of one's lifestyle and being a dark place? Perhaps one answer is when the wives of competitors feel totally abandoned. There is a term used in triathlon called "iron widows," a concept that refers to the perceived physical and/or emotional abandonment of competitors' spouses. This term applies to many other activities, including hunting widows, marathon widows, and so on. Numerous study participants spoke about the guilt that they felt from leaving their wives alone with their children for hours at a time. Textual analysis of online discussion forums revealed a number of intriguing posts about the iron widow concept. One in particular, posted by a blogger writing under the screen name of "IronWidow," received a tremendous amount of views and responses. The post reflects the essence of what spouses of iron-distance competitors may come to feel when they believe triathlon has taken an undue priority in their partner's life. The blogger writes:

> Hi, there. Remember me? I'm the one you promised oh-so-many-year[s] ago to love and cherish for all eternity. And I don't remember there being an exception made for IRONMAN years. Maybe you whispered that part. I know that crossing that finish line takes an incredible amount of hard work. And I admire that effort; you know I do. You have inspired me with your ability to come home from work and do a five-hour ride on the trainer because it's getting too dark to do it on the road. I am in awe of your discipline. I could use some of that myself.
>
> But do you really think about what your family is sacrificing to get you to that finish line? And, I mean, Really. Think. About. It. We've given up any free time with you; when you are around, you're so beat from working out that you're really not there anyway. A family trip to Europe would have been lovely this year. But that money got spent on gear and coaching and massages and physical therapy and Gatorade. (Remind me to buy their stock next year.) That's okay. I've been able to use the time we would have spent on vacation to do all the chores that need doing around here, because you're too busy to help out anymore. Working, cooking a nutritious dinner every night, keeping the house clean and in good repair, paying the bills, showing up at all the kids' activities, and hiring babysitters so I can at least go out with the girls keeps me busy. And it keeps my mind off the fact that an IRONMAN is too busy and tired for sex.
>
> I know I sound mad. Really, I try not to be. But I feel very taken for granted. Maybe you could think about showing some love for what your IRONMAN widow puts up with. Maybe your buddies here will have some suggestions. Or maybe they could use some ideas themselves. (You know, I might just be YOUR IronWidow.) Or maybe they'll just feel sorry for you and be glad I'm not their spouse. If so, I hope they can refrain from mentioning it; I'm having a bad day, and I don't think I could take it. Besides, I think I probably speak for most IRONMAN widows when I say that I AM proud of my

IRONMAN; you are a rare and special kind of person. But you know so am I. So am I.[1]

Even though the general consensus is that this posting was offered in humor, there is a strong undercurrent of truth. The words are a sharp reminder about the importance of not ignoring family. The post also shows the consequences of obsession. Some may argue that the message is suggestive of leisure turning destructive, otherwise known as "dark leisure" (Williams 2009). Among the responses this posting received were those from bloggers hoping the writer was not their spouse, wondering who it was. Exercise addiction is a legitimate concern for Iron Dads, a theme that weaves throughout the narratives of study participants.

While many Iron Dads attempt to integrate family into their training and not let exercise reach obsessive levels, numerous participants addressed the dark side of their passion. After talking about his history of drug and alcohol abuse, Mayson observed that he "traded one addiction for another." He referenced hitting significant lows if a single training session did not go well. Logan mentioned that he did not go on a honeymoon because he had a big race planned just days after his marriage ceremony. The theme of exercise addition in triathlon is supported by scholarship in the field of exercise psychology. Michelle J. Blaydon and Koenraad J. Linder (2002) found that over half (52%) of all triathletes in their sample exhibited symptoms of exercise addiction. Further, research has affirmed that the longer the race, the greater the risk for exercise addiction. Jason D. Youngman (2007) suggests that we see a habituation effect among triathletes. He argues, "The more years that triathletes participate in their sport, the more hours they would devote to training, which in turn would lead to a greater risk for exercise addiction" (27). This finding places Iron Dads, men training for a 140.6-mile event, in a particularly risky cohort.

The theoretical lens of intersectionality also raises a troubling concern. My interviews revealed how the social, economic, and physical statuses of Iron Dads foster opportunities to both feed and conceal exercise addiction. Many of my study participants had some degree of flexibility in their work schedule, with a small but noticeable cohort having complete control of their time. These men were typically well compensated, often serving as the primary breadwinner of their family. Compounding this with the internalization of masculine behavior, particularly success in the masculine environment of iron-distance racing, perpetuated a culture of obsession for some fathers. As Bryson mentioned, "I'm keeping up my end of the bargain. As long as I keep earning, I have the right to train, and I have the ability to do it. It's the only way I stay sane." Men felt compelled to train—their schedules permitted it, and their status as breadwinner justified it.

The Athletic Visibility Continuum Model

What does it mean for something to be "visible?" *Merriam-Webster* offers a definition that emphasizes being "readily noticed" and "unobstructed" from view. When we think of something having the quality of being visible, we often consider tangible items that can be touched, such as road signs, other people, or books. At the same time, intangible items can also be visible, such as projecting a specific attitude, affiliation, or identity. A more specific example would be the projection of confidence. When we comment that someone appears confident, we are observing intangible characteristics or properties in action that lead us to make this assessment.

Visibility is relative in that some things are not strictly visible or invisible. It is possible to have a partial or obstructed view. When observing tangible objects, the concept of visibility is more definitive. Imagine that a father takes his son to his first professional baseball game. The Red Sox are playing their American League East rival, the New York Yankees. The father and son take their seats in Fenway Park. To the son's dismay, one of Fenway's many "pesky poles" obstructs his view of the field. The father, sitting one seat over, suggests they switch places. They switch, and the son now has an unobstructed view of the action. This example shows us that physical placement relative to the tangible object of interest matters. I argue that the same visibility concerns can emerge when attempting to observe intangible items such as identities. However, instead of one's physical location in relation to the object, other factors become relevant. One's ability to observe and make sense of intangible aspects of another person depends on the extent to which those aspects or characteristics are visible. I argue that Iron Dads negotiate the self-perceived visibility of their athletic activities in managing their overlapping identities.

The athletic visibility continuum suggests that an athlete's sporting identity, and all activities based on that identity, can take on varying degrees of visibility in the eyes of others. Through my grounded theory analysis, four equally important dimensions emerged as components of this continuum:

1. Obtrusiveness. Iron Dads manage their perceived level of obtrusiveness to others. This is often conceptualized as their activities being visible or invisible to others.
2. Intentionality. Iron Dads can manage their placement on this continuum in both intentional and unintentional ways.
3. Integration. Iron Dads will seek various levels of family integration at different points in time.
4. Context. The extent to which individuals can control their placement on the continuum is dependent on the larger social context in which the

interaction is taking place. This includes factors such as physical place and the father's level of progress in his overall training program. Pure invisibility is very difficult—and sometimes impossible—to obtain.

Obtrusiveness

Many participants spoke about the way that they managed the visibility of their training in the eyes of others. What fathers described as visibility was actually more about obtrusiveness. Fathers used words such as "hiding" and "masking" their training from family members, indicating they measure obtrusive behavior through the proxy of perceived visibility. It is important to note that this concept speaks to the Iron Dad's perception of visibility in the eyes of others, a perception that may or may not be shared by members of his family. Many participants went to great lengths to try to hide their training as it was occurring. Some of these same men later described, however, how the lingering physiological effects of this training became apparent in family settings.

Clear patterns emerge when fathers ask other Iron Parents for advice on how to better integrate training into their lives. Using NVivo, I was able to evaluate the type of advice that was most frequently cited in these sorts of discussion threads.[2] Advice relating to visibility and obtrusiveness emerged as being the most commonly cited responses. In one such thread, an Iron Dad starts his post by saying "I need some help." He goes on to describe his personal situation. He is a father with a one-year-old son, an MBA student, and a full-time professional with a job that requires heavy travel. "Triathlon and the training/community that come with it are a vital part of who I am." The father goes on to describe a contentious home life. After going on a group ride, a rarity for him, having ridden only a few times that calendar year, his wife was "absolutely flaming." He inquires: how do other parents do it? Many answers spoke to the concept of visibility and perceived obtrusiveness:

Bike trainer—and use it when they [family] are sleeping. The running when you are away for work is a good idea, too. If you hide your training then there is no problem. You might get less sleep though. I have no time to hide my training because I do not own a bike trainer yet, and because I have no time for sleep as I work nights.

I can only suggest that you get in your longer training early in the morning before they're [family] awake. Trade off hour breaks with her [wife] during the week if possible (if she has something she likes to do, such as running, biking, whatever), so that there is a mutual exchange and she understands you're valuing her time as much as yours. And do as much training during travel as you can.

Keep training as invisible as possible. In the middle of the summer I leave on my bike at 5:30 A.M., get in four hard hours, and give the family the rest of the day . . . even if I am tired!

Iron Dads continually negotiate dimensions of the athletic visibility continuum. This is evident in the fact that as an important race gets closer, participants exhibited different attitudes towards their placement on the continuum. This was particularly true in their consideration of obtrusiveness. As their goal race approached, they allowed themselves to make training more visible. A number of Iron Dads mentioned how they identified the most rigorous training weeks to their family well in advance. This suggests that when fathers perceived that their training would become more obtrusive, they gave warning to their family.

The reality is that training can be obtrusive to family activities in a variety of ways. When the father was out exercising, the burden of shuttling the kids from activity to activity fell to their spouse. This, in turn, limited the spouse's opportunity to have personal time. A number of my study participants described how their spouse was willing to put up with this added burden. Such an action was often internalized as a signal that their wife supported the sporting activities. Paradoxically, many of these same men described how they valued egalitarian division of labor. During heavy training periods, these self reported egalitarian attitudes did not translate to equal division of labor in the household. To the contrary, heavy training periods often meant that the wife had to compromise her own leisure time.

Intentionality

When engaging in athletic invisibility, individuals can consciously attempt to shield others from their athletic identity and/or athletic activities. This speaks to the notion of intentionality of behavior, a key dimension of the athletic visibility continuum. Many participants described getting up at 4:00 A.M. on weekends, a time when their family members are typically sleeping, to complete their training sessions. This suggests that while their capacity as an athlete is very salient to them during this time, it is markedly invisible to their family. Such timing of training on weekends represents a strategic choice. The father is consciously attempting to make his training as invisible and unobtrusive as possible in hopes of maximizing family time later in the day. While this may seem to be a considerate move on the part of the Iron Dad, we must be concerned about the possibility of invisibility signaling a turn toward dark leisure. Dedicating a lot of time to invisible training may reflect an underlying exercise addiction. We must also question the extent to which invisible training actually leads to maximized family time—a point that I elaborate on later in the chapter.

At other times, Iron Dads may go out of their way to make their athletic activities highly visible. In so doing, they are often making a conscious choice to integrate family into their athletic activities. An example could be when a father wants to involve his child in a training session. Ryan, a father of two, routinely invites his children to bike alongside him while he runs. Larry, a father of a five-year-old son, lets his child swim in his lane while he works on stroke enhancement exercises. This strategic use of athletic visibility is often used as a tool to teach the value of a healthy lifestyle to children.

Intentionality is influenced by perceptions of social values and acceptability. Participation in long-course triathlon events not only has become an accepted indulgence but is socially valued. Further, being an iron-distance competitor carries a social currency. As described by Samuel, a triathlete from Colombia, "When I tell others that I have completed numerous 140.6 races, I am often applauded for my efforts. People are in awe of me." This type of response encourages Iron Dads to make their athletic presence known. It also empowers them to get their children involved in the triathlon culture.

It is important to remember that Iron Dads operate from a socially desirable standpoint in sport culture. Recall from chapter 2 the discussion about how long-course triathlon participants benefit from popular definitions of manliness. After all, the most well known competition is called IRONMAN. This cultural perception of IRONMAN allows for fathers to feel more free in being intentionally visible with their athletic identities, both in and out of the home. The narratives of Iron Dads indicated that intentionality is strongly influenced by perceptions of social desirability. For example, the desire to be seen as an active father and dedicated employee plays an important role in managing one's athletic visibility. However, fathers training for a 140.6-mile triathlon do not contend with the same social stigma as men preparing for competition in other sports, particularly those associated with femininity (Adams 2011).

Integration

Intentionality and integration go hand-in-hand. Earlier in the chapter, I described the way many Iron Dads take their training programs very seriously, a perspective that often results in the sacrifice of frivolous family-centered exercise opportunities. Study participants spoke about how family inclusion required careful planning. Sometimes this planning was quite elaborate. One father described how he rode his bike to his daughter's soccer games. Upon getting to the game, his wife would be waiting with a bike trainer. The father would spin on the sidelines and cheer on his daughter. "I even held up signs as I rode," the Iron Dad shared.

Family integration can be a powerful way to shield an underlying exercise addiction. Justin, an IRONMAN Texas participant, hinted at this while discussing his desire to become more competitive. "I had to find more hours to train. Getting over twenty [hours per week] became really hard, so I started taking my son with me to the pool in the afternoons. I couldn't do much with thirty minutes, but it was better than nothing." Justin's narrative reminds us that there is a fine line between being an exercise enthusiast and an exercise addict. In seemingly propagating health benefits for both himself and his son, Justin may justify what could potentially be seen as an addiction as being socially permissible. These dangerous waters are a real concern.

Context

The specific context in which Iron Dads make decisions impacts how they negotiate dimensions of the athletic visibility continuum. In that sense, the continuum can be examined through the lens of Erving Goffman's dramaturgical model, the view that the world is a stage on which we all perform (Goffman 1959). Goffman identifies two arenas in which impressions are managed—front stage and back stage. Iron Dads have daily experiences on both of these stages. The front stage represents situations in which a person feels most compelled to act out a specific identity. An example could be the starting line of the IRONMAN World Championship. With tens of thousands of eyes watching, an athlete may feel compelled to act the part of triathlete in a way that shows off confidence and competence. On the back stage, that same person may discuss the fear he has surrounding the event. The man may feel more freedom to relax and be himself on the back stage.

The front stage and back stage settings relate to the athletic visibility continuum in meaningful ways. I argue that the practice of athletic invisibility from family opens up the opportunity for more back stage interactions with friends. That is because, while in the company of a select few, an Iron Dad may feel free to open up and be himself. One father, Adrian, talked about the therapeutic power of running with his training partner. He described these runs as an opportunity to "be himself" and discuss "the things he would never admit to others, including family." When probed what those things were, he cited peeing on the bike (urinating while engaged in the motion of pedaling) and throwing up in the middle miles of the run. Adrian was embarrassed to admit these things to his family, but he felt free to be honest about his potentially less-than-desirable behaviors while in the company of his training partner.

Sometimes Iron Dads believe that they are being invisible or unobtrusive when, in reality, they are not. This is because true athletic invisibility is extremely hard to obtain with their athletics. In a training context, to have complete invisibility would mean that the workout session had no impact on other segments of life. While this may be obtainable in select situations, as training time demands go up, underlying consequences become more visible in other areas of life. These are areas where sporting guilt can often manifest. A father may project that a training session will be invisible only to later find out that there are real consequences for that workout. For example, even if a father is able to execute a long training session before his family gets out of bed, physical and mental fatigue become concerns for activities held later in the day. One blogger explained:

> I have two kids, 4 and 8. As the years of training have gone by, I will agree with others that making the training as "invisible" as you can is the best option for reducing the tension that your absence creates. Problem is, you will sacrifice sleep and that [may] make you irritable. You may have to ditch the group [training] thing. Get a trainer and ride very early in the morning before anyone is up. Here I am at 4:45 A.M. typing this as I get ready to jump on my trainer so I can finish my workout by 7:00 A.M.

In the circumstance described above, a seemingly invisible training session becomes visible when the man is too tired to engage with his kids later in the day. This was a common misperception among Iron Dads. Fathers tended to evaluate the obtrusiveness of activities as they were happening while downplaying the after-effects of the session. After the longer workouts, which fall on the weekends for many working fathers, dealing with fatigue is a real challenge. Sport-related tasks also tend to emerge after the workout is complete. Participants cited responsibilities such as cleaning gear, uploading and reviewing data, and giving feedback to a coach. Recovery activities, such as using a foam roller or stretching, also consumed precious moments. All of these responsibilities take time, yet often are not accounted for when a father calculates the anticipated time a workout will take.

Failed practices of athletic invisibility also appear when Iron Dads attempt to conceal their athletic identity in non-sporting contexts. Carter, a father of a three-year-old boy and three-week-old daughter, attempted to conceal his athletic identity from colleagues at a law firm. As a relatively new hire in the firm, he did not want to reveal the fact that he had a substantial interest in a non-work-related activity. He feared that colleagues would see his training as a potential time drain. He realized how hard the practice of athletic invisibility was when he attempted to swim during lunch. Carter lamented, "I thought I would be able to get in a solid thirty-minute workout at the gym. Unfortunately, I couldn't find a solution for my raccoon eyes." Raccoon eyes is a term that refers to the imprint that goggles can often leave on one's face after a long swim. This imprint can be quite obvious to others. In an attempt to avoid questioning by colleagues, Carter decided to skip the idea of swimming at lunch. He feared his invisible practice would, in actuality, be quite visible.

Balancing Mechanisms

In addition to dealing with their sporting guilt and managing their placement on the athletic visibility continuum, my analysis revealed another key process that helps Iron Dads handle their competing identities. Identifying and strategically employing balancing mechanisms is a powerful tool that my participants had at their disposal. I define a balancing mechanism as a specific tactic that an individual employs in an attempt to reach a state of self-perceived identity equilibrium. As we will explore, balancing mechanisms can be tools of either inclusion or exclusion in integrating others into a sporting identity.

As individuals go through life, they develop habits and guiding principles. These habits and principles evolve in ways to help minimize stress and make life more enjoyable. A common example is the value of leaving work at the workplace. This represents the physical, and ideally emotional, delineation of responsibilities. When you are home, your focus is on the family. When you are at work, your focus is on work. While your thoughts will naturally wander while you are at home, the hope is to minimize focus on the workplace by not bringing work through the front door of the house. Leaving paperwork at the office is one way that this physical and mental division can be achieved.

Throughout the course of my interviews, it became apparent that Iron Dads identified these juggling tactics to help negotiate the competing demands associated with their identities. Participants employed these tactics as a way to foster a sense of balance. It is important to note that this sense of balance is based on the Iron Dad's perception. In actuality, using these tactics may not foster a sense of balance at all. The word "balance" implies that identities have equal value. However, a sense of equilibrium is seldom achieved. This is because identities are not equally weighted. Sometimes fathers referenced the desire to establish balance when, in my mind, they were really evoking the concept of restitution. Still, I use the term "balancing mechanism" because *in the eyes of Iron Dads*, that was their purpose in using these tactics. The concept of balance is an NVivo code that emerged through my qualitative analysis. Although it may not accurately describe what is actually happening, it is noteworthy that the word "balance" was evoked time after time by my study participants.

When fathers develop balancing mechanisms, they do so with sensitivity to a few key variables: time, space, and the immersion of others. My analysis suggests that such mechanisms are adopted in conjunction with two main processes, compromising with family and enabling family involvement.

Compromising with Family

Compromising with family is a central way that Iron Dads balance their multiple identities as triathletes, fathers, spouses, and employees. Time and space are important considerations in the compromising process. Iron-distance training takes place in pools and lakes, on roads, in basements, and on race courses. Likewise, fathering occurs in a variety of physical and social spaces (Marsiglio, Roy, and Fox 2005). Men often struggle to create common space with their children. They want to be present for their children but are limited by physical, social, and cultural restraints. Be it prison walls or life on the road as a trucker, many dads must be creative in finding space and time to be physically close with their children. One can apply the same spatial lens to fathers in an endurance sport context. While Iron Dads may not be limited by the presence of prison walls in a literal sense, they may be in a figurative sense. Many triathletes refer to the area where their stationary bicycle trainer is located, usually in the basement of a home, as a dungeon. Even though Iron Dads participate in triathlon as a hobby, on some level, the idea of physical entrapment may apply.

Given the amount of time that men dedicate to the sport, many fathers are inclined to find ways to incorporate family into their training routine. To do this, they draw on a variety of balancing mechanisms that allow them to be physically present with their children. For example, a father may elect to ride his bicycle trainer while watching a movie with his child in lieu of riding alone on the roads. Alternatively, a father may decide to swim in a lap pool with his child instead of swimming alone in a local lake. The degree to which Iron Dads base their selection of physical training and racing spaces on family considerations points to sophisticated integration of fathering and sporting identities. It also points to recognition that the sporting and fathering roles are both important, and that these roles do not always need to be mutually exclusive. In short, a balancing mechanism can be used as a tool of inclusion. This means that space and time can be used strategically to include both training and fathering opportunities.

In conceptualizing space, there is no location more intimate than the home. Important aspects of this territory include how rooms are furnished, the proximity of the rooms to one another, and the meaning that each room may take on to individual family members. Many Iron Dads attempt to improve training efficiency by having workout equipment readily available in the house. This often includes installation of items such as bike trainers, treadmills, and lifting equipment. Some make further investments in tools such as an Endless Pool or Vasa Ergometer swim trainer. Iron Dads refer to their indoor training spaces using a variety of colorful expressions—training cave, man cave, sweat sanctuary, amusement park, or as professional triathlete and father Andy Potts puts it, a pain cave. In a promotional video released by Asics, Potts describes his home training space. "It's where the hard work gets put in, and when I come out of it, hopefully I'm a better man because of it."[3] Even though the references elicit visions of a personal dungeon, these spaces represent areas where fathering and training opportunities can and often do overlap. How space is set up in the home can be seen as a balancing mechanism in itself. For example, in addition to the training equipment, entertainment systems are often prominent features in a workout room. Televisions or computers with streaming media capabilities are common staples for many Iron Dads. Netflix was a particular favorite. Some invest in big televisions with elaborate sound systems. These entertainment systems can be enjoyed by both father and children alike.

The home can also serve as a powerful means of dealing with one's geographical climate. Bill, a thirty-seven-year-old lawyer from New England, commented about his desire to ride outside after spending much of the winter indoors on his trainer. "The trainer is a critical element for me. I don't have a treadmill at my house but I do have a trainer. My bike, actually, it's just now getting to where I want to be outside because most of my winter workouts are on the bike at home. I don't go to the Y [YMCA] to work on the bike much." Greg, a father of two, mentioned how he had to consider the Arizona heat during his training. "When I was doing that heavy IRONMAN training, especially here in Phoenix, you have to do a lot of your training in the morning. Training for a November IRONMAN means you're training through summer. Peak temperatures here are above 110 degrees; it's not uncommon. So you have to do morning training. Pretty much during my morning training, I did as much of my load as I could. Otherwise, I would be indoors for everything else." While some fathers expressed disappointment over having to contend with climate limitations, a clear benefit from these situations often emerged. Dealing with climate limitations often forced Iron Dads to exercise indoors. This created more opportunities for the men to interact with their children and, in so doing, lessened the need for balancing mechanisms.

Greg's insights bring up another important consideration: time. The concept of time dominates the life of an Iron Dad. Its centrality on the race course is clear. Clocks are everywhere—at the starting line, at the swim exit, as one comes in and out of transition, and, of course, at the finish line. Racing performance is judged against the clock. For people at the front of the pack, time can be an ally. It dictates age group awards and coveted IRONMAN World Championship slots. For those who fail to make published cutoff times, time can also be an enemy, ending a race prematurely. Just as the concept of time plays a pivotal role on the race course, it has a prominent place in the day-to-day maintenance of the Iron Dad identity. Employing balancing mechanisms often involves strategic consideration of time barriers.

Time management is at the forefront of the Iron Dad juggling act. Iron-distance training is all about following a schedule. Most athletes either hire a coach or follow a plan downloaded from the Internet or taken from a book. Participants described training as a continual buildup, starting with a base and with workouts becoming increasingly difficult as their target race became closer. As the race neared, hours spent training became more critical. One Iron Dad likened this buildup to having an "IRONMAN baby," indicating that training increases considerably as time goes on. This parallel also applies because many individuals spend upward of nine months preparing for the event. Athletes often refer to this build as "putting the time in," meaning doing the training necessary to prepare for the event. During the peak training window, beginning approximately two months before the race, study participants reported an average weekly training volume of 17.5 hours, with an overall range of 14 to 22 hours. Iron Dads identified the key workouts in the training week as the long ride and long run, sessions that can last upward of six hours. These long sessions are what really separate iron-distance competitors from athletes focusing on shorter distances. While someone training for a 70.3 or Olympic-distance triathlon may possibly train for twenty hours a week, the necessity for super-long rides and runs is not the same as when training for the iron-distance.

The Long Ride The need for employing balancing mechanisms is perhaps most evident when considering the cornerstone of iron-distance training—the long ride. These key sessions are where athletes build the endurance required to complete the bike portion of the race. Virtually all of the Iron Dads interviewed for this project specifically addressed the challenge of fitting long rides into their schedules. Focus is typically placed on maintaining a desired race pace, refining a nutrition strategy, and testing out clothing and equipment. The difficulty with a long ride session is that an athlete must identify an uninterrupted five- or six-hour block of time. This is challenging to do in light of work and family constraints. Most participants identified weekends as the best opportunity to fit the session in. The issue then becomes how to minimize the training session's impact on family time. Church and youth sports were frequently cited as habitual weekend outings. Greg, a father of two and finisher of IRONMAN Arizona, reflected on the difficulties presented with fitting in long sessions:

> The Sunday long ride was the hardest because there's just no way to keep that from having an impact on the family. Fundamentally, you're gone for a good portion of the day. There's no way around it. My wife recognized it was part of the goal. But that was probably the hardest part of the training schedule. There are more difficult sessions, but just the training schedule itself, that was probably the hardest. And then occasionally, because I actually had a coach, occasionally we would have clinics that were fundamentally full-day events, and that would just fill up a day or a weekend.

Like Greg, many Iron Dads struggle to fit in the long workouts. To carve out this training opportunity, numerous participants negotiated time barriers with their spouse. Engaging in this negotiation is a balancing mechanism in and of itself. One popular strategy was to agree on a time when the training would conclude. As discussed by Cooper, ten o'clock was a common delineation. "I told my wife I would be unavailable anytime before 10:00 A.M. on the weekends, and for the most part this worked out. But occasionally I would have to go on really long rides and runs where I asked her to give me until 2:00."

Many fathers attempted to practice athletic invisibility in conjunction with the longer sessions. Ryan, an IT department manager and father of two, discussed how he would get up very early to start his endurance workouts:

> There were times when I would get up so early, when the sun wasn't even up, and start my training on the training bike indoors, and when it was light out, finish up outside. This allowed me to finish my training without biting too much into my schedule. There were other times where I would have to rearrange the schedule a bit and have to take half-days. On Friday, for example, where my long bike ride would be done and out of the way before the start of the weekend while the kids were still in school.

Bill, a lawyer and father of two young children, also took the strategy of starting long workouts early on Saturday mornings:

It's my commitment to my wife that family is first, period. And I will do this [training] around it. So, every day is different, and that has worked for us because I have honored that commitment pretty much all the time, other than Saturday mornings normally. The only consistent piece is I will get up early on Saturday mornings and be gone before everybody gets up and we'll do my long training day on that day. Everything else works around their schedule.

Jeremy, a physical education teacher and father of two, echoed the sentiment:

The majority of my winter workouts, I get up at 5:30, like last week for example. I had a three-hour thirty-minute ride. I got up at 5:30 in the morning and I was done by nine o'clock so I could be with my kids. Tuesday nights I do a run, but my kids are at daycare when that's going on, so I don't have to worry about that. Thursday I ride my bike after getting back from working with a church youth group at ten o'clock at night. I'll usually get on the bike and get that done. Then I do my long runs on Sundays at seven o'clock in the morning before my kids get up and we all go to church together.

Both Bill and Jeremy attempt to finish their long weekend training before the rest of the family gets out of bed. They use this time delineation as a balancing mechanism. When they are done exercising, they can then focus on being engaged with their families for the remainder of the day. In Jeremy's case, this includes the weekend ritual of going to church. What makes these stories of time management even more remarkable is the additional time spent preparing for and concluding the training session. This time includes tasks such as preparing equipment and training-specific nutrition, cleaning and putting away gear after use, and showering. These are added demands that are built into every training session but very often not reported when someone talks about the time they spend working out. These hours add additional responsibility to an already packed calendar.

Employing balancing mechanisms can become even more challenging for families where both spouses compete. Frank and his wife are both active iron-distance competitors. As parents of a ten-year-old-boy and two-and-half-year-old girl, they find that scheduling can get complicated. Frank explained how he and his wife manage scheduling:

Well, we do running during the week and sometimes we do our sprints on the weekends, but it's [training] every day. We only take one day off. The white board on our fridge, we take it down every Saturday or Sunday night and plan the week out. It has got every-thing from, you know, it's every day. Anything from morning to dinner. Then at night, it'll be for the kids. You know, if they have practice or play time with the other kids down to doctor appoint-ments and things like that. But then, we also get our training done there [nighttime].

The long ride is where role conflict became the most pronounced. With many of the men in this study electing to do their long session on the weekends, training often interfered with the events of both children and spouses. Further impeding this juggling act was the fact that feelings of obligation were at their highest when the men faced a long ride. Ian describes his preparation for IRONMAN Texas: "I missed soccer games on Saturdays. There was just so much pressure to be successful, so I felt like I had to get on the bike." While many fathers described having some flex-ibility in their daily routine, long rides were a clear exception. This some-times meant that Iron Dads put their needs before those of their family members, missing their child's game or not allowing their spouse to take much-needed personal time.

Enabling Family Involvement

One key way that Iron Dads balance their multiple roles is by recogniz-ing and embracing their overlapping identities. Being a father and being an athlete do not have to be mutually exclusive. While their kids and spouse may not be active triathlon competitors, there are many ways that they can be involved in the training process. Iron Dads use a variety of very creative balancing mechanisms to enable family involvement.

Involvement in the Racing Environment Companies that put on long-distance triathlon races are becoming increasingly cognizant of the importance of family inclusion in endurance sport. This is evidenced by, for example, the growth of youth activities in pre-race festivities. In 2009, World Triathlon Corporation announced its expansion of offer-ings to include youth-oriented races.[4] Dubbed the "IRONKIDS," this global series is aimed at increasing interest and participation in triathlon among America's youth. Children from ages six to fifteen compete in age-appropriate triathlon distances. For example, kids aged six to eight compete in a mini-sprint consisting of a 50-yard swim, 2-mile bike, and 500-yard run. Those aged twelve to fifteen compete in a 300-yard swim, 8-mile bike, and 2-mile run. The event features an IRONKIDS expo, a smaller version of the IRONMAN expo, where children can browse products. IRONKIDS has expanded its offering around the globe. The series currently features races in locations such as the Philippines, France, Japan, and New Zealand.

The World Triathlon Corporation (WTC) recognizes that interest in sport can begin at a very young age. To market to children under the age of six, WTC also has a series of kid "fun runs" during their pre-race festivities. For example, at IRONMAN Lake Placid—one of the most popular races in the 140.6 circuit—WTC hosts a youth fun run on Mirror Lake Drive the day before the race. This type of activity allows for fathers and children to occupy the same place not only with one another but also with other families, creating the perception of a family-oriented environment.

Some Iron Dads may elect to go to a specific race venue because of the attraction of these pre-race events. A number of participants talked about how their kids were very excited to participate in these festivities. Mike Reilly elaborated on the importance of these youth-oriented events:

> They [World Triathlon Corporation organizers] realize IRONMAN is all about family. They're in the process of looking at ways you can incorporate family more into the whole experience of the weekend. And by its natural progress of IRONMAN, it is family. If you're going to go 140.6 miles, you want to be able to do it in front of loved ones. And so, they've realized that family members are here whether they've asked them to come or not. But when they're here, you want to make sure they're part of the process and part of the race.

When asked how he thought the World Triathlon Corporation has tried to reach out and make family part of the racing experience, Mike replied:

> I think by doing the kids' races, the IRONKIDS events, even the IRONGIRL events where young girls can do events throughout the country now. But I think the biggest experience for a family is being able to see what their loved one is going through. Because, yeah, race day is tough, but the preparation of setting up, getting the bike in the transition, doing the practice route, checking in, you know what that's like. All that is just a bunch of stuff, and it's part of the race. But when family come in and see it and go, "God, this is harder than I thought!" Then they appreciate it more. So, we love the families.

The concept of involving kids in races is also starting to become more prominent in shorter-distance events, within both the running and the triathlon communities. For example, the Hartford Marathon Foundation, a not-for-profit organization founded in 1994, includes youth opportunities in many of their events. A number of their road races include kids' races. The foundation's marathon includes a program called Jeff's Running Partners, a children's relay team where each child runs one or more miles with an adult.[5] By getting young kids involved in racing together with their parents, the children may take more of an interest in the adults' training activities and races. This interest can open up opportunities for parents to take their kids along on training sessions. When considering various race venues, the opportunity for youth-oriented festivities is a consideration for some Iron Dads.

Careful planning of race venue selection is a key balancing mechanism for Iron Dads. There are iron-distance races all over the world and at varying times of year. Some of the fathers sought out destination races that had more family-friendly environments. Others sought out races that were close to home in hopes of minimizing the travel burden on the family. Seeking a family-friendly venue was especially popular with fathers of young children. A number of study participants talked about targeting IRONMAN Florida 70.3 as a tune-up race for their main full-distance event. They selected this race specifically because of its proximity to Disney World, allowing for a family vacation after the race. This also shows how intersectionality plays a powerful role in household negotiations. Eli drew on his status as both a competitive athlete and lone household-income provider while describing a past race selection: "I get to race hard, they [kids and wife] get to go to Disney." The use of the word "they" is particularly interesting. Eli is effectively separating his experience from that of his family. Someone speaking from a family-centered mindset might use the word "we," suggesting that everyone gets to go to Disney. The language used by Eli suggests that he is providing the Disney experience in exchange for an opportunity to race, like a quid pro quo transaction.

Consideration of physical and social space plays a key role when an Iron Dad decides which races to compete in. Some iron-distance courses are known as being more spectator-friendly than others. IRONMAN Arizona, for example, features a three-loop bicycle course. By comparison, IRONMAN Florida offers a one-loop bike course. Fathers are sometimes inclined to pick races that maximize their family's ability to see them in action, allowing the family to feel included in the sporting environment. Additionally, some fathers are inclined to pick courses that are near a vacation destination. Throughout my interviews and my textual analysis, there is much discussion of race vacations, or "race-cations." These occur when the race is situated in the context of a long family-oriented trip. Races near theme parks or beaches are especially popular.

Given that competitors can be on the course anywhere from eight to seventeen hours, family members are left watching on the sidelines for long periods of time. Participants discussed how family comfort was a key element of race selection. Availability of things to do and the proximity of hotels to the race venue are often key factors in the race location decision. Mike Reilly talked about the ease of spectating on multiple-loop courses. "Families can get around the course and see them on a bike, see them on a hot corner, see them on the run, and things like that. The loop courses are easier, like in Arizona. There's three laps on the bike and three laps on the run, so you see your family member more. Most of them [bike courses] are two laps, so you still get to see your family members during the day." In addition to World Triathlon Corporation's event in Arizona, its Wisconsin (IMWI) venue was also a popular destination among the study participants. This was due to the perceived volume of things that the family could do while the event was taking place. Also, with numerous hotels being close to the race location, families could go back inside and relax while their Iron Dad was on the course. A number of the study participants selected Wisconsin for this exact reason.

Involvement in Training Environments While a race occupies a full day, this time represents just a small fraction of the effort put into the larger iron-distance journey. The bulk of the time dedicated to this effort is spent training. This period represents the best opportunity for Iron Dads to involve their families in the 140.6 experience. To varying degrees, many fathers are able to have some level of family involvement in their training. This does not mean that a family member is always by their side. To the contrary, training can sometimes be quite lonely and isolating. It often calls for early mornings or late nights. However, with careful planning, many fathers are able to identify opportunities for their children to be involved in some aspect of their training routine. With that said, Iron Dads often walk a difficult tightrope when it comes to involving family in their race preparation. On the one hand, many of these men desire to get their families involved in some way. This makes sense, given the level of commitment that they are putting into the activity. At the same time, however, they are also attempting to minimize the impact of training on the lives of these same family members. This leads to an interesting dialogue about when, where, and in what capacity children and spouses can and should join training sessions.

One of the primary concerns is disparity in athletic capabilities between father and child. This study included men with children of diverse ages. The call for participation was rather broad in that sense, seeking participation from men who had children from one day old to twelve years old. Naturally, there is a substantial difference in athletic capabilities within that window. Further, grown men are capable of producing sizable power and endurance output. While riding around the neighborhood at a few miles per hour with his child is great for building an intimate father-child relationship, it does not necessarily allow the dad to challenge his capabilities as an endurance athlete. Generally, Iron Dads value the importance of unhindered exercise. How does one address these two seemingly conflicting desires? Study participants were very creative in finding ways to balance the tension between wanting an intense training session and finding a physical space to allow children to be present. Some dads embraced identifying these balancing mechanisms as a personal challenge. As one blogger notes, the track can serve as a mutual location:

> Yes, it [iron-distance training] is selfish, but on the balance it works for our family. I was out racing all morning then came home, whipped up [an omelet] and rye toast, grabbed a coffee, then my son and I were out on XC skis all afternoon as I am coaching his team. Good fun. And how many families get to do a father and son sprint around a 500m XC ski track in 76 and 50 seconds? We had a blast this afternoon. Closed things off with [a] game of touch football on skis. So yes, it is selfish. But because of my athletic abilities, I can give opportunities to my family and community that other parents cannot. So I think it balances out. My wife and son only come to two races per year. The rest I do with my friends or solo. I don't think them hanging around in the sun all day waiting to watch me whip by for 3 x 10 [3 repetitions of 10] seconds is a fair request. On that front I totally agree.

This father clearly enjoys the challenge of juggling family and sport. He feels his athletic prowess enables him to offset the fact that he is absent during training. He works hard to enhance the lives of his family members through sport.

Sometimes the age of one's children can be a difficult challenge to overcome. Frank, an IT specialist, is the father of three girls, ages seven, five, and two. He explained how the young ages of his children serve as a barrier to training participation: "I do try to get them involved some. Unfortunately, because you're trying to minimize the impact on them, I'm not getting my kids up at five in the morning to go to the swimming pool with me. It's not an appropriate environment there, especially at their age. I do try to get them out and go run. I have brought them to other races and they really enjoy it. But, in general, my kids are so young I can't really take them out for a lot of my training stuff."

When it comes to age and athletic disparities, the issue of safety can often cause tension. Frank mentioned how the swimming pool was "not an appropriate environment" at his kids' ages. Other participants expressed similar concerns. Early swim times tend to attract adults looking to get in a high-intensity workout before going to work. The safety concern is not limited to the pool environment. As another example, while a child may be old enough to bike alongside his or her father while he runs, it may not be a practical means for furthering the father-child bond. This is because the father now must give additional consideration to factors such as traffic, the presence of sidewalks, dealing with major intersections, and other variables. My study participants repeatedly talked about how they were able to focus more on their own performance when training alone.

As an alternative means of involving children and spouses, some Iron Dads participate in local running events with their family. Jeremy talked about involving both his wife and daughter in a hometown race. He and his wife competed in the 10K while his two daughters attempted the quarter-mile youth challenge. Jeremy used the race as part of his iron-distance preparation. Leo, a doctor and first-time 140.6 competitor, routinely brought his kids to the track: "Well, both my kids run at school, so when I started doing track workouts, I started [to] bring my daughter. Well, she actually asked if she could come do track workouts with me, which is pretty nice. And that lasted a while. And then my son, he runs twice a day, so he had no interest in coming for a third run with me. But they're kind of excited. My daughter said, 'Please finish [the IRONMAN]. Otherwise I'll be really embarrassed to tell my friends.'"

Other dads found creative ways to get their families involved in more detailed aspects of the race preparation process. Alex, a personal trainer from California, talked about how he allowed his three kids to help out during longer workouts. He reflected on his preparation for his sixth iron-distance race: "During my long run, my daughter would bring her bike out for support. She would give me food, nutrition, and stuff like that." Managing and decorating equipment served as another balancing mechanism to help engage family in the training process. One can look at equipment and think of it as a tool of the sport, but some Iron Dads look at it as a canvas for creativity with their children. On one triathlon blog, a father posted images of his very expensive Cervelo P3C triathlon bike, a $4,500 machine. He let his two children create a design for the down tube prior to his event. The bike served as a blank canvas for the family to become involved in the iron-distance experience. We can regard the images depicted on the down tube as reflections of the father's commitment to involving his two children into the training process, integrating the roles of father and athlete. In the course of his blog posting, this dad went on to discuss how his children came up with the design, which he immediately painted on the bike. The tone is clearly one of a proud father. This posting alerts readers to the concept that space can represent not only the physical place where one stands, but also the physical space on artifacts that we come in contact with through the course of our day.

Competitive Aspirations

If you speak with athletes at the start line of an endurance race, competitors will cite a wide variety of goals for the day. In iron-distance racing, these goals range from wanting to finish to wanting to win their age group. Those seeking a finish are often registering for the experience of the event. In WTC events, those in contention for an age group podium are likely seeking a highly elusive IRONMAN World Championship qualification. The vast majority of competitors fall between these two ends of the spectrum, seeking a personal best time or personal course record. These differing goals manifest themselves in the ways that Iron Dads approach family integration.

Generally, seasoned, highly competitive athletes engaged in more invisible training. These athletes often had rigid training schedules that centered around hard solo efforts. These individuals also gravitated toward starting their training further out from the race date. By contrast, those interested solely in the race experience tended to include family members in their event preparation more often. They also tended to be more flexible when family conflicts emerged. These athletes identified themselves by using language such as "I just do this for fun" or "I am just looking to finish." Dan, an iron-distance participant for more than ten years, transitioned from a hard-nosed competitor to one who participates for fun. In expressing his newly discovered less-competitive sentiment, he explained, "The finish clock doesn't matter. I do this for fun. If I get upset because the clock reads 12:05 and not 11:59, my priorities are out of whack. Ultimately, the race could take me two additional hours and I wouldn't care. If my family is happy with me, it's worth it, and I am still a finisher."

5

Why Class Matters

※

"You need some income to be able to support the
lifestyle of racing in IRONMAN." (Mike)

In December 2012, *Bloomberg Businessweek* columnist Elizabeth Weil
ignited the triathlon world with the publication of her article "The IRON-
MAN: Triathlete Executives' Ultimate Status Feat." There, she profiled the
emergence of World Triathlon Corporation's "Executive Challenge" (XC),
a program aimed at providing VIP race experiences to top-level business
executives. Admission to the program is granted through a competitive
application process, with packages ranging from $4,900 for 70.3-distances
races (California 70.3 and Mont-Tremblant 70.3) to upward of $10,000 for
the IRONMAN World Championship. Weil called IRONMAN the "ultimate status bauble for a certain set of high-earning, high-achieving, high
VO2-max [maximal oxygen uptake] CEOs" (Weil 2012). It was not just
these words that sparked controversy among triathletes—it was her depiction of the typical Executive Challenge competitor. Emblematic of contemporary political discussions about the handling of the national economy
and the fiscal cliff, the article ignited a heated discussion about class war-
fare on rich triathletes. It is worth asking: was there any truth to this depiction? Are Iron Dads nothing but a bunch of wealthy, classist men?

In her article, Weil paints the picture of a wealthy male executive check-
ing an iron-distance triathlon off his "bucket list"—the list of activities that
he wants to do before he dies. The executive athlete will do so, she argues,
while paying "about 10 times the regular registration cost" to receive

VIP race status (Weil 2012). This price, Weil contends, affords competitors super-elite status, including privileges such as not having to wait in line for a bike mechanic and mingling with professional athletes over lunch. The only thing that Executive Challenge athletes don't have access to, according to the piece, is dedicated port-a-potties on race day. This, the VIP coordinator for IRONMAN suggests, "would start a riot." Weil describes, "XC provides its 25 athletes with what it refers to as 'high-touch' service: breakfast with the pros, a seat up front at the welcome banquet, [Troy] Ford [director of the IRONMAN Executive Challenge Program] at your disposal. He books your travel. He'll find out your favorite snack is Oreos and have a pack waiting in your suite. When your kids get bored in the hotel restaurant, he'll improvise with an entire box of Coffeemate creamers that they can use as building blocks" (Weil 2012).

So what, exactly, made the triathlon blogosphere go ablaze the day after this article was released? Was it the data-centric, spend-at-all-cost depiction of the typical Executive Challenge athlete? Was it the suggestion that these individuals are spending tens of thousands of dollars on a "status"? Was it alluding to the fact that Executive Challenge athletes are throwing money away "needlessly" by spending ten times the regular registration cost? Is this the epitome of what it means to be an IRONMAN? These questions, and the answers to them, capture the significance and sensitivity of the larger class debate that is occurring in American society today. The *Bloomberg Businessweek* article serves as a stark reminder that, contrary to popular colloquialism, all is not fair on the athletic playing field.

Class and Sport: An Overview

One of the attractions to sport is the belief that athletics can be a uniting force. With sport serving as a common ground, people who may not otherwise meet each other cross paths. People of different ages, races, and religious backgrounds can come together to enjoy a pick-up game of basketball, a trail run, or an Ultimate Frisbee tournament. In addition to viewing sport as a uniting entity, many see it as an equalizing force. This belief is further reinforced by popular language. People commonly use sport-related references such as "leveling the playing field" or "playing on the same team." Unfortunately, these terms can often represent nothing more than hollow rhetoric. This is because, in both subtle and overt ways, class defines athletic opportunities.

People often make the mistake of looking at challenges presented by sporting events in absolute terms. A common example is the distance between the start and the finish of a race. To finish a marathon, everyone must cover 26.2 miles. The sentiment among competitors is that we are all tackling the same course under the same conditions, thus we are all competing on an equal playing field. While it is true that every marathon participant must complete 26.2 miles to get to the finish line, personal experiences with training, nutrition, running technology, athletic apparel, and general marathon knowledge can vary considerably. In the context of iron-distance triathlon, an event that incorporates three sports and a highly demanding training schedule, the differences in personal experiences leading up to the event can become even more discernible.

This chapter discusses the relationship between class and the construction of the Iron Dad identity. I argue that within the iron-distance culture, class manifests itself in both subtle and overt ways. In overt terms, endurance triathlon is engulfed in an ever-present culture of consumption. Competitive masculinity is a commodity for sale. The desire, as well as pressure, to continually upgrade to the latest equipment is real for many Iron Dads. However, thinking in more subtle terms, we can look beyond simply talking about paying a race entry fee or purchasing material goods. Class concerns expand well beyond that. My interviews demonstrate that there are intangible things that class helps establish. Specifically, class resources are used to (1) solidify the authenticity of a man's Iron Dad identity; (2) help maximize workplace flexibility; and (3) facilitate conflict negotiation. In the sections that follow, I detail how these tools help some fathers to juggle multiple identities more easily.

The Manifestation of Class in Sport

Before discussing the various ways in which fathers activate class resources, it is useful to step back and consider the place of class in sport more broadly. Class and sport are inextricably linked. While society likes to think of sport as an egalitarian institution, it is anything but that in reality. Starting in the late nineteenth and early twentieth centuries, sport became a mechanism to create and reaffirm class consciousness (Bourdieu 1985; Coakley 2009). Sport has remained a highly stratified institution, continually working to affirm and reaffirm the larger social inequalities in society (Eitzen and Sage 2009). For example, numerous sports, such as golf, sailing, and horse racing, are prohibitively expensive for many segments of society. Max Weber's (1978) concept of social closure can readily be seen in these environments. Class cohorts use sport as a mechanism of exclusionary behavior, effectively creating a dominant and subordinate social grouping within an athletic space (Karen and Washington 2015). This trend applies to triathlon, particularly iron-distance competition, where the $600-plus event entry fees for many popular races serve as an economic gatekeeper to widespread participation.

Sociologists recognize how varied, and at times contested, the term "class" can actually be. Does it refer to income? Level of educational obtainment? Occupational status? Within the sociology of sport literature, the concept of class has been operationalized in numerous ways. The dominant way is to conceptualize class as a combination of income, education, and occupation (Eitzen and Sage 2009). Collectively, these attributes create societal hierarchies that produce different life chances. These chances create opportunities for entry into specific sporting contexts. Studies have shown how this definition of class stratifies people into certain sporting opportunities. One example is the game of golf, a sport largely played by high-income, highly educated individuals (Varner and Knottnerus 2002). As a result, the golf course has come to be regarded as an elite space. The same can be said of equine facilities, expensive tennis clubs, or even IRONMAN courses. This stratification of space has real social consequences. As Pierre Bourdieu observes, certain spaces hold symbolic power in society. It is in these spaces where the social elite can "keep their distance" and "maintain their rank" from common people (Bourdieu 1989, 17). Elite spaces reaffirm not just physical distance but also social distance between members of varying social classes. This is, in part, why these elite spaces are popular locations for business meetings. These meetings can be completed in the comfort of casual yet exclusive leisure contexts. As noted by Luis Alvarez, an IRONMAN Executive Challenge participant and CEO of a Mexican fuel tank company, "I do business with these people [iron-distance triathletes]. They're my family. IRONMAN is the new golf! If you know someone through IRONMAN, you know they have commitment, you know they are for real. They are not just talking, not a hot-air balloon" (Weil 2012).[1]

Some studies have focused on more peripheral concepts of class. For example, a recent stream of literature has examined the building of social capital in voluntary organizations, specifically looking at sporting contexts (Seippel 2006, 2008). Diversity in conceptualization of class was evident in my study as well. Specifically, I found that participants referenced class, and the resources associated with class, in different ways. This was admittedly a very difficult part of the grounded theory process. Participants would not say, "Heads up, professor, I am talking about class now." Instead, they would use words that are indicators of class itself. It was my job to uncover and further understand those indicators.

Many participants made reference to class resources, or more specifically benefits acquired because of their socio-economic status positioning. For example, a number of Iron Dads talked about the flexibility of their job, something that I categorized as a reflection of occupational status. Recognizing that flexibility can also be associated with lower-paying jobs, I took care to listen for other characteristics of the man's workplace. Some fathers talked about the ability to pay for a housekeeper, something that I categorized as a reflection of income. This was a commonly used class resource. Finally, other men described benefiting from elite social capital networks, something that I categorized as a reflection of one's overall social location. Scholarship suggests that these personal networks may be more powerful than "income" itself (Erickson 1996; Lesser 2000; Putnam 2000). The ways in which individual Iron Dads drew on class resources varied considerably. It should come as no surprise, then, that class has a profound impact on many spheres of life—especially sport.

Further Exploring the Iron-Distance Demographic

Previous chapters have offered a general overview of the iron-distance participant demographic. Certain elements of that demographic profile are easily observed. For example, we can visually observe that competition fields tend to be dominated by middle-aged white men. Naturally, there are other dimensions to this profile that may be more difficult to ascertain from simple observation. This could include things like occupation, class, and level of educational attainment. Figures published by both World Triathlon Corporation and USA Triathlon, the sport's governing body, reveal some additional information in this regard. Participants tend to be well educated, white collar, and middle to upper class. These patterns of participation do not emerge by accident. Instead, they speak to a systemic bias about who can afford to make it to the starting line.

Given that this work looks exclusively at iron-distance competitors, we must recognize that the research focuses on a more elite social class. I discussed this reality in chapters 1 and 2, citing a USA Triathlon-commissioned study called "The Mind of the Triathlete." The results reveal that the average income of a multi-sport athlete was $126,000.[2] The study also shows that 8.4 percent of triathletes have incomes between $200,000 and $299,999, and 5 percent with incomes over $300,000. In an interview with the New York Times, the vice president for K-Swiss, an athletic shoe and apparel company that formerly partnered with WTC, suggested that "triathletes are a discerning group of alpha consumers, with $175,000 average salaries" (Gardner 2010).

The 2010 IRONMAN World Championship featured a male-dominated field (72.4% men, 27.5% women). A press release issued by WTC prior to the race outlined the demographics of the entrants. The largest age groups, percentage-wise, were men 35–39 (12.7%), men 40–44 (13.8%), and men 45–49 (10.2%). Work is a central focus in the lives of many of these athletes. Recall from chapter 1 that TribeGroup's 2009 study findings reveal that the majority of triathletes (49%) hold white-collar jobs. Nineteen percent hold professional jobs, such as lawyer, doctor, or accountant. The economic and employment exclusivity of iron-distance racing is not without its consequences. One key consequence is the reflection of consumption-centered culture. While some study participants rejected the idea that they subscribed to this culture of consumption, the reality is that it is within these cultural boundaries that men establish their identities as Iron Dads.

Consumption in Iron-Distance Racing

One thing is for certain when it comes to the world of triathlon. Irrespective of the distance that one competes at, it is an expensive sport. Individuals must equip themselves with gear for three separate athletic segments—swimming, biking, and running. While many triathletes get by with less-fancy equipment, the temptation to spend is internalized by numerous Iron Dads. This is because iron-distance racing is engulfed in a culture of consumption. Athletes are bombarded with messages to spend money—big money—and many do. USA Triathlon's 2009 study reports that over a twelve-month period, the average triathlete spent $2,274 on bikes, $564 on race fees, $524 on bike equipment, $370 on athletic footwear, and $277 on training/racing nutrition. That comes out to $4,009 spent on triathlon each year. In contrast, the vice president of marketing at K-Swiss felt that "the average Ironman spends $22,000 a year on the sport" (Gardner 2010).[3] The costs of triathlon were recently profiled in *Bloomberg Businessweek*'s "Real Cost of" series. The series is intended to educate readers on the actual costs of participating in some activity or accomplishing some task. Previous series topics have included the real costs of the lottery, home improvement, a designer-decorated holiday, a saltwater aquarium, and weight loss.[4] The *Bloomberg* piece looks at what it refers to as the real cost of competing in two local sprint triathlons and one Olympic-distance race. It estimates the expense to be $4,782. These expenses are broken down in the "Real Cost Expense" column in table 1. The "140.6 Expense" column represents what a high-budget athlete might pay for these items while racing at the full-iron distance.

Selecting triathlon as part of the cost estimation series was a creative idea. Thanks to the increase in media attention that the sport has received, such as broadcasts of International Triathlon Union (ITU) races and some of the Xterra off-road series, more people will be aware of triathlon. Many, however, would likely experience some sticker shock if they decided to participate, particularly at the iron distance. The *Bloomberg* article likely opened up the eyes of many readers who were unfamiliar with the real cost of triathlon competition. As noted by table 1, these expenses can get exponentially higher for an iron-distance athlete—particularly someone with a big budget.

TABLE 1. The Cost of Iron-Distance Racing

Item	Real Cost Expense	140.6 Expense
Coaching (4 months)	$1,250	$1,200
Training books	30	50
Gear	1,663	8,200
Race day clothing	663	900
Training clothes	249	500
Pool membership (1 year)	300	435
Swimming extras	31	100
Biking accessories	88	300
Running accessories	18	200
Maintenance	23	400
Transition	85	100
Body care (1 season)	61	150
Nutrition (1 race)	5	25
Race registration (3 races)	316	2,025
Hotel (per event)	not documented	1,100
Airfare (per person)	not documented	550
Training nutrition (per event)	not documented	250
Bike transportation (per event)	not documented	325

SOURCES: For real cost expense data: Bloomberg Rankings and Nikhil Hutheesing, "The Real Cost of Completing a Triathlon," http://www.bloomberg.com/consumer-spending/2012-11-05/the-real-cost-of-completing-a-triathlon.html. The 140.6 expense figures are estimates based on the author's personal experience at a single iron-distance event.

NOTE: Unless otherwise noted, all prices are for training for and competing in a single race. This table does not reflect the expenses *required* to participate in triathlon. One can compete on a much smaller budget. Instead, the table reflects an example of what one could spend if purchasing new gear and, in the case of 140.6 expenses, flying to a race location.

Virtually all of my Iron Dads were quick to point out the cost of participation in iron-distance racing. Greg talked about how, after race fees, he was into the sport for thousands of dollars. "Bikes, especially, are a sticker shock. Honestly, in our family, I'm the more fiscally conservative saver type. I tend to think about them [prices] a lot and probably have more reluctance to buy very expensive things than my wife does. She just knows that that's the way I am. That being said, the equipment is expensive—there's no doubt about it. I think I've looked at it and last year I was probably in, after race fees and everything, I think I was in several thousand dollars."

To non-triathletes, the price of gear is extremely unreasonable. Arnold recalled a last-minute trip to the IRONMAN Florida expo:

While at IRONMAN Florida, I decided to make a last-minute clothing purchase for race day at the expo. You know, I wasn't sure what I was going to wear coming out of the water given that it might be cold, and I wanted to give myself the option of a few things, so I purchased a pair of thermal arm warmers. Sugoi [a brand name] or something like that. So I quickly ran into the expo while my family was looking around and purchased them, secretly hoping my family wouldn't realize how much I just spent on such a small item. I ended up not needing them and decided to return them after the race. I commented [to my wife] that they were really expensive, and when she asked how much, I was embarrassed to admit that I spent $42. She looked at me totally shocked, like, "What the fuck? You spent $42 on a pair of arm warmers?" I mean, I know the cost was ridiculous, but you do what you have to do when it comes to options, particularly in the heat of the moment.

This story reminds us that discretionary spending is a relative concept. For most people, the idea of spending $42 on arm warmers would be perceived as beyond reason. Under less stressful conditions, this expense may even be unreasonable for Arnold. However, for an iron-distance competitor thinking in the heat of the moment, this may be seen as an essential purchase. Similarly, views on the price tag of triathlon bikes can vary in a person's mind. There is an element of sticker shock that many triathletes initially experience. As one becomes more immersed in the sport's consumption culture, this shock goes away. Bikes that cost $5,000 come to be seen as a good value for the money. This is interesting, given that the same person may have viewed the price tag differently at a previous time. Immersion in a consumption culture clearly has transformative powers. It is within this culture of consumption, class, and gendered paradox that Iron Dads operate. With that in mind, a key theme from my analysis was that Iron Dads activate class for strategic processes. The first is to solidify the authenticity of their Iron Dad identity.

Solidifying Authenticity

In chapter 2, I discussed the importance of presentation of self. Goffman (1959) suggests that we are like actors on a stage, continually configuring, refining, and displaying our identities to others. A key part of that acting job is establishing an aura of "authenticity." That is, we seek to craft in others a belief that we are good in the roles that we play. Part of establishing authenticity is based on the idea of consistency. We want to project a consistent presentation of self, be it as a dedicated athlete or a loving and engaged father. Iron Dads use the power of physical and cultural symbols to help solidify their identities as triathletes, fathers, and men.

Symbolism plays a significant role in the construction and maintenance of the Iron Dad identity. More specifically, symbols are a crucial mechanism for individuals to display identity affiliation (Burke and Gusfield 1989; Goffman 1959). Class enables men to engage in this symbolism to varying degrees. The acquisition of symbols can be expensive, both financially and emotionally. However, this acquisition can pay off, as symbols serve as a visual proxy to commitment. In this regard, there is perhaps no other piece of equipment in triathlon that is more iconic as the bike. By buying an expensive bike, men are purchasing cultural and symbolic capital (Bourdieu 1984). They are also purchasing marks of distinction within the triathlon world (Bourdieu 1984). This distinction, and accompanying capital, draws attention to a man's financial and athletic accomplishments. As described below, it also bestows feelings of authenticity on his athletic identity.

The Triathlon Bike as a Symbol of Authenticity

The bicycle is a pivotal part of any triathlon. The bike is the longest portion of the race, both in distance and (under typical circumstances) time. For iron-distance competitors, athletes must ride for 112 miles, a journey that can take anywhere from four to eight-plus hours. To the average passer-by, making distinctions between types of bicycles may be a difficult task. To cycling enthusiasts, however, the variety of bicycles is seemingly endless. Road, triathlon, mountain, cruiser, fat, and cyclocross are just a handful of the many styles available. Triathlon bikes are a type of bicycle specific to time-trial cyclists and triathletes.[5] These bikes are evinced by aerobar extensions and aggressive geometry. Together, these features are meant to assist in cutting down drag by positioning the rider as low as possible.

The type of bicycle that one rides is indicative of that individual's "location" in the cycling community. Cycling communities can be protective of their territory, to the point of excluding other breeds of cyclists. For example, triathlon bikes are typically not allowed on cycling group rides. Road riding enthusiasts, otherwise referred to as roadies, insist this guideline is about safety. Among cohorts of competitive athletes, I suggest the social construction of such guidelines is also a way of protecting an identity. Generally, roadies would argue it is the former, while triathletes would contend the latter. While it is undoubtedly true that some triathletes lack sufficient bike-handling skills to ride in a group, it is unfair to suggest that such a statement applies to all. For this and other reasons, many triathletes feel that banning triathlon bikes on group rides is a way to engage in the politics of exclusion. It is a way to mark territory and cast triathletes as outsiders who do not excel at the craft of handling their bikes, a topic that has been discussed extensively on triathlon blogs.

Beyond announcing one's location within the cycling community, the bike is symbolic of personal wealth. People within the cycling and triathlon worlds are well aware of the price tags of bikes, wheels, and mechanical components such as derailleurs and cranks. For example, many athletes in the cycling world know that SRAM Red is a much more expensive group-set than SRAM Apex. Likewise, these athletes lust over electronic gear-shifting systems such as Shimano's Di2. Having one of these groupsets on a bike signals dollar signs. This is important in a society that equates money with sincerity. *To have a Di2 system, that athlete must be a pretty serious competitor!* Beyond component groups, visual inspection of a bicycle can also produce other valuable clues about a person's identity. One such clue is bike stickers, items that hold tremendous significance in the world of iron-distance racing.

Bike Stickers

When competing in a triathlon, all athletes must pick up a race packet containing a bib, stickers for their bike and helmet, and a timing chip. In IRONMAN-branded races, athletes' bike stickers and bib feature the event logo and respective race number. Displaying these items post-race can be seen as a symbol not only of status but also of accomplishment. These race artifacts say, "I was there." It is a common practice for competitors of IRONMAN-branded events to leave previous race stickers on their bike. This may include stickers on both the stem and top tube. IRONMAN World Championship stickers, representing participation in the ultimate 140.6 venue, often find a permanent home on a competitor's bike. Other stickers may stay on until participation in the next event or beyond. In a plea to competitors on a blog, one IRONMAN Arizona volunteer asked participants in the upcoming race to please "remove your old stickers. I look at them and get confused!" This volunteer went on to discuss how, by referencing the race number from a vintage sticker, he accidently racked a competitor's bike in the wrong place. This caused a major disruption in transition. Despite these pleas from volunteers, many competitors con-tinue to leave old stickers on bikes as a way to display their affiliation with IRONMAN. As an active competitor, I am not immune to this trend. I cur-rently have stickers from two different iron-distance events on my racing bike. One sticker is located on the seat post while the other is situated on the stem.

The symbolism of bike stickers becomes even more significant when you contrast them to helmet stickers. Helmet stickers do not typically con-tain event logos, even when issued at an IRONMAN-branded race. They are a generic black number in bold type. Leaving this sticker on simply displays, "I raced somewhere at some distance," not "I raced IRONMAN St. George or IRONMAN Mont-Tremblant." You don't see many athletes leave vintage stickers on their helmets. The lack of identifying event logo is the likely explanation. In other words, the actual event being referenced matters. A great example can be seen in a photograph that circulated around the Internet. In December 2012, professional triathlete and Iron Dad Jordan Rapp shared a photograph of his bike on Instagram. He also shared this photo on Facebook. Jordan's caption reads, "Motivation. Simple but effective. And less dorky than a race bracelet." The picture is a close-up of his triathlon bike, with only select components being visible.

A person with an untrained eye might not be able to tell what is being displayed in the photograph. The left crank arm, water bottle, and wheel in the background may be enough for someone to say that this picture is of a bicycle. Then again, maybe not. To those familiar with rides of the two-wheel variety—and with iron-distance racing more specifically—a lot more can be taken away from this image. The picture reveals important clues about Jordan's identity. The top tube, down tube, and "S-Works" logo are all visible. The black with red-and-gray piping and white logo paint scheme identifies the bike as a 2013 Specialized S-Works Shiv. The module (frame, aerobars, and partial component set-up) has a retail price of $5,800. To bring this module to a condition in which it can be ridden, one must purchase additional components such as wheels, a chain, shifters, derailleurs, and other items. Put bluntly, this is not a cheap bike. To the contrary, it falls under what many in the industry refer to as the "superbike" category. *Boy, this competitor must be serious to own a new S-Works Shiv!* Looking more closely, there is an additional clue that this bike may be owned by a serious competitor. When Jordan speaks of the motivation in the photograph caption, he is referring to the shiny sticker visible on the top tube. To those who compete in iron-distance events, this sticker is unmistakable. It is the mark of an IRONMAN World Championship competitor. When Jordan says "less dorky than a race bracelet," he is making reference to the blue race bracelet that athletes receive at event check-in. This bracelet identifies the athlete as a competitor in the race. It gives them access to privileged spaces such as transitions and post-race food tents. Some wear this bracelet for weeks after an event has concluded. However, as the event logos fade with each shower, many come to terms with clipping it off. The bike stickers are a different story, as they could potentially stay on a bike for years.

Authenticity, Body, and Self

Extending beyond the bike, it is possible to plaster every inch of your body, home, and workplace with IRONMAN symbolism. Stickers on cars, in the office, or at the home all serve as important reaffirmations of one's status. Many competitors also hang up their race bibs (numbers worn during the race itself), medals, and event posters. Symbols can serve as important marks of distinction within the endurance triathlon community itself. These symbols can distinguish between two types of iron-distance athletes—finishers and non-finishers. In the iron-distance world, finishing is a highly valued accomplishment. Completing a WTC-branded race is a particularly coveted status. Competitors want, without hesitation, to call themselves an IRONMAN. That registered trademark cannot legally appear on the merchandise of other race management companies. For this reason, after an event is over, the merchandise store at WTC's full-distance races always has a huge line. People crave finisher gear, with the most popular item being the finisher jacket. People spend $144.99 plus tax for this item. While the exact design varies from event to event, you can guarantee that the word "finisher" is present on each version. Typically, the back of the jacket prominently displays this word. The front displays the event logo and date. Why is this jacket so significant? The item is a way of saying, "I was there, and I did it. I am part of the 140.6 club." Ryan, a father of two and manager of an IT department, discussed how he was not immune to the IRONMAN event swag bug: "I have a bunch of IM items from my previous events all around my house. It's really ridiculous. Should I sit down and take a tally of everything? [. . .] I have a large garden flag, ten water bottles, car stickers, luggage, probably twenty shirts, twenty hats, posters, mugs. You get the point. These things are everywhere."

Some of the items that Ryan mentions are transportable to a variety of social settings. Things like hats and luggage serve as traveling props, helping Ryan to display his sporting identity wherever he goes. Spending money on these props is a way to reaffirm and further legitimize one's status as an IRONMAN finisher. They are traveling vehicles of athletic and economic distinction. The ability to spend this type of discretionary income brings class to the center of attention. This becomes clear when we compare the price of an event-branded item to the price of a comparable piece of merchandise sold at a big-box store (see table 2).

Shopping at event stores is certainly not for the budget-minded. Why would an Iron Dad such as Ryan feel compelled to spend more than four times as much on a soft-shell athletic jacket? The answer, in part, is to reaffirm his identity as an IRONMAN athlete and finisher. Those who are financially strapped for cash may feel confined in what they can purchase at an event expo. As one father reported, due to his personal finances, he decided to limit himself to one small souvenir. This decision bothered him. He conveyed a feeling of entitlement in purchasing multiple items at the post-race finisher store. This may be partially due to the man's wish to be the object of envy and desire. These feelings, coupled with our consumer society, create a powerful motivation to spend.

TABLE 2. Event-Store vs. Box-Store Merchandise Pricing (2015)

Item	Event-Store Price	Big-Box-Store Price
Soft-shell athletic jacket	$144.95	$35.49
Polo shirt	49.99	12.97
Athletic hat	24.95	10.00
Beach towel	39.99	6.60
Grey cotton t-shirt	24.95	5.97
Technical wind jacket	141.95	14.88
Technical long sleeve t-shirt	34.95	6.88

SOURCES: For event-store data, prices reflect those given on the online IRONMAN merchandise page. For big-box store data, prices reflect those given on Walmart's website.

Symbolism in a Consumption Culture

Much of the Western world is centered around activities of consumption, with sport being no exception (Horne 2005; Norris 2006). Consumption is a focal point of obsession, desire, and celebration. After the World Trade Center towers fell on September 11, 2001, President George Bush proclaimed, "We can't let the terrorists stop us from shopping."[6] This quote reflects the sentiment that the act of spending, in and of itself, is viewed as a powerful sign of cultural freedom. On both macro and micro levels, consumerism is an important means of social distinction (Bourdieu 1984).

Consumerism has opened up pathways for new social dialogues to emerge. The work of French social theorist Jean Baudrillard offers valuable insight on how the process of dialogue formation works. Speech, Baudrillard argues, comes in the form of symbols—signs that are established and transmitted through commercialization (Baudrillard 2001). He notes, "In order to become an object of consumption, the object must become a sign [. . .]. It is in this way that it becomes 'personalized,' and enters into a series [. . .]. It is never consumed in its materiality, but in its difference" (Baudrillard 2001, 25). Eventually these symbols can come to dominate all other forms of "discourse and signification" (Norris 2006, 466). The construction and reproduction of these signs hold great political and social significance, often drawing attention away from original social meaning. As an example, we can look at how the concept of feminism has changed in the consumer culture.

In their influential work, Robert Goldman, Deborah Heath, and Sharon L. Smith illuminate how feminism is packaged and repackaged as a commodity for sale—a process that they refer to as "commodity feminism" (Goldman, Heath, and Smith 1991). The authors sharply point out how select aspects of feminism have been turned into commodities that directly contradict feminism's origins. These commodities, powerful social markers, are then attached to brand names. This enables the creation of distinction from competitors. Goldman and his colleagues observe, "Feminism has been cooked to distill out a residue—an object, a look, a style. Women's discourses are relocated and respoken by these named objects (e.g., Hanes hose, Nike shoes, Esprit jeans)" (336). This observation directly applies to the men in this study.

Iron-distance racing is a means of commodifying masculinity, albeit a particular type. Drawing on select social markers of hegemonic masculinity, including concepts such as endurance and power, manliness becomes something that can be purchased. Consider World Triathlon Corporation's positioning in the marketplace. We see a clear subscription to the "binary semiotic opposition" evident in commodity culture (Brown 1987). In this instance, the binary is "male" or "not male." We need look no further than the brand name to know where IRON*MAN* falls on this particular binary. In attaching themselves to this particular brand name, men, as well as women, can be a part of a socially desirable commodity. Paying the price tag premium at the event store allows for this attachment to be visible just about anywhere. Car magnets, jackets, computer bags, and beach towels all serve as moving symbols of attachment to a revered masculine identity.

While much of the focus of this chapter has been centered on income, class speaks to more than what people bring home in their weekly paycheck. It also speaks to occupational status. The higher one's occupational status, the more opportunity one has for flexibility in the workplace. While not universally true, many higher-paying occupations may allow for time flexibility. In this vein, another key theme to emerge from my analysis was how Iron Dads maximized job flexibility as a way of juggling their multiple identities—a proxy for class.

Maximizing Job Flexibility

Occupational status dictates a lot more than the money that one brings home. Other variables can fluctuate substantially between jobs. This includes the scheduling flexibility of the position, the ability to delegate tasks to others, and the social networks that one engages in while at work. Work is a central component in the lives of many Iron Dads. For the purposes of the research conducted for this book, recruitment parameters required participants to have full-time jobs at the time of their iron-distance training. Employing this recruitment parameter allowed me to investigate both the subtle and overt ways that work influences, and is influenced by, endurance sport identities.

An individual on a blog asked other triathletes what they do for a living. There were all kind of responses. Participants responding to the question were college professors, CPAs, firefighters, and attorneys. While the individuals participating in this online discussion represent a specific subset of the triathlon population, the professions listed are emblematic of the general demographic recruited for my study. Six men recruited for this research owned their own business, including one man who owned multiple franchises of a well-known restaurant. While recruiting on location at IRONMAN Texas, I spoke to a number of men involved in the medical community. This was due to the event's proximity to Memorial Hermann Hospital, the title sponsor of the event for that year. When asked his approximate household income, one cardiologist chuckled and said, "a lot." This was a stark reminder that I was dealing with a particularly unique and privileged demographic. Armed with sensitivity toward this privilege, I developed a commitment to understanding how Iron Dads used their occupational status in establishing their athletic identity. Analysis of blogs were also useful in this regard. One college professor, a 70.3 athlete, wrote about the numerous advantages of his job:

> [I] can't think of a better job. This year I have May 15 to September 8 off, and when at work my schedule is flexible enough to find enough time during the day to train. What money I don't make I save in the fact that parking is $10 year. I have a free gym with every piece of equipment I could ever want/need, a free personal trainer, and a free pool. Plus, having spring break the rest of my life is a pretty good thing, too. Only five more days until that happens.[7]

Being higher up on the managerial totem pole can enable Iron Dads to actively shape their workplace culture. This speaks to the ability to present an increased athletic visibility in the workplace. One father brought his Vasa Ergometer, a land-based swim trainer, into the office. Another put his personal spin bike in his corporate workout room. Some of the participants with management jobs felt empowered to actively shape the culture of the workplace. While a managerial position is a strong gateway to influencing workplace culture, it is not the sole determining factor of holding such sway. In other words, this is not to suggest that workplace empowerment is the normal experience for all managerial Iron Dads. To the contrary, some relayed a desire to hide their endurance sport identity at work. Sean, a father working as a retail store manager, was actually asked to "stop working out at lunch" when his boss came to learn that he went running during his lunch hour.

Having a workplace that embraces a culture of health and fitness was very important to numerous Iron Dads. One of the biggest factors in determining if a workplace has this type of culture is the presence of multiple employees who participate in athletic activities. Thirty percent of the fathers interviewed for this project specifically cited the advantages of having a fellow triathlete, runner, or cyclist in the workplace. A similar number of participants mentioned the importance of having a boss that understood the importance of their athletic endeavors. Access to a workout facility on-site was another measure that participants offered as a way to determine if a workplace embraced a culture of fitness.

An interesting quagmire that arose for some fathers was whether or not they were going to tell their boss that they were training for an iron-distance race. Don Fink, a highly accomplished iron-distance athlete-turned-coach, touches on this subject in his 2004 book, *Be Iron Fit*. Fink suggests that triathletes should not only tell their bosses, but also sit down and have a meeting with the boss and any close colleagues. This is a noteworthy idea if an athlete's employment culture is welcoming of such a notion. As some of my Iron Dads revealed, however, this advice may be unrealistic in some working environments. As one case in point, an online discussion debated the merits of listing "IRONMAN finisher" on a résumé. A number of bloggers, both men and women, expressed hesitation with such a move. One triathlete specifically cited seeing 140.6 as a "selfish endeavor." This individual offers that "to see someone who has a 20+ hour, physically exhausting side hobby [. . .] is a red flag." Others floated the possibility of simply mentioning "triathlete" instead of "IRONMAN."[8] In this economic climate, those with jobs feel pressure to keep them. This may mean concealing one's identity as an endurance athlete. Another blogging athlete addressed how often he talks about triathlon in the workplace: "As little as absolutely possible. I work in an environment where the strong survive, the weak are eliminated. Strong has nothing whatsoever to do with endurance/fitness, and all to do with alcohol and politics."[9]

The relationship that this equity trader has with his work environment is a challenging one. To not let on about his training likely means limiting strategies that others in more tolerant environments may utilize, such as taking extended lunches. This, in turn, probably means that this man reserves training for either before or after work, time that he might otherwise spend with his family. By contrast, if feasible, informing the boss of one's athletic endeavors can be of great benefit. One Iron Dad mentioned that his boss allowed him to adjust his work schedule to assist with training. The father explains, "I started coming into work earlier and taking a longer lunch so that I could get in a decent swim."

Iron Dads utilize technology as a means of juggling multiple identities. Instead of having to be present at the workplace, some telecommuted. One study participant, an employee for a major defense contractor, worked two days a week from home. He dedicated midday to training. Smartphones were also pivotal in balancing work and athletic identities. Numerous Iron Dads described responding to e-mails while riding the trainer. One dad noted, "I can ride in the aero position and text back and forth as needed." As technology continues to advance, this is one potential avenue for some parents to lessen the stress involved with trying to juggle work, family, and sporting interests. Not needing to be physically present at a specific time opens up opportunities to be other places while still addressing the needs of work. Still, even with the rapid expansion of technology, access to this workplace flexibility is largely driven by class.

Class Resources as Conflict Negotiation Tools

A final theme to emerge from my analysis is how class resources can be activated to help resolve conflict within the family. As an example, while money does not buy happiness, it can buy luxuries to help juggle multiple demands and quell disputes. Earlier in the book, I discussed the concept of sporting guilt. One of the ways that some men manage this guilt is by buying their family members goods and services. Mitch had to deal with the guilt of getting into the IRONMAN World Championship via the lottery system:

> I did my first IRONMAN in 2010. Afterward, I promised my wife I wouldn't do one in 2011 because I've got young kids, seven and four at the time. Despite my efforts to workout while everyone else was sleeping, it was still an imposition on the family. So I didn't tell her that I entered the Kona lottery. You can guess what happened next. I used the "good news, bad news" routine. The good news is we're going to Hawaii in October. The bad news is you won't see me on weekend mornings for twelve weeks. It all worked out and we had a great time in Kona. I didn't do an IM in 2012.

Mitch managed his sporting guilt by couching his athletic participation in the context of a trip to Hawaii. As he put it, he used the "good news/bad news" approach to managing the potential conflict of announcing his winning lottery application. A number of Iron Dads used the allure of a trip, or race-cation, as a means of minimizing anticipated conflict surrounding event registration.

Interestingly, a number of fathers described how it was a mistake to view traveling to the race as a vacation. This is because the event takes up more than just race day. Competitors have to pick up materials, set up a transition zone, and consider how much time is to be spent on foot in the days leading up to the event. After the race, dads are exhausted and are faced with families eager to go out and enjoy vacation. As Jeff noted, "All I wanted to do was sleep, all they wanted to do was party." With thoughtful planning, some fathers had more positive experiences. Frank talked about how his family prepared for a race vacation:

> The big thing is my wife is part of it, too. So this is just something that we decided that was our goal for this year. So, we haven't really taken any vacations this year. We have not bought many non-triathlon related purchases, so this was our big vacation. We had saved some money to go to Europe, or go on a cruise, or something like that. And this year was "let's just focus on the race and the vacation attached to the race." I can see that if my wife was not on board, and we were spending our money like that, it could be difficult.

Even though Frank's family tried to vacation once a year, he found it financially unsustainable to travel on separate occasions for racing and family leisure. With careful planning of a post-race vacation in Lake Placid, Frank and his family were able to enjoy some leisure time after the event.

Managing the Expense of Iron-Distance Racing

While some may imagine that every iron-distance triathlete occupies a place in the upper class, this is not true. Some of my participants discussed how they competed on a shoestring budget. Kevin, the sole financial provider for his family, talked about competing on a smaller budget:

> We do everything we can to do it [IRONMAN] on a shoestring. I've never purchased a new bike. My first IRONMAN was done on a Trek 1500 with a flip-around seatpost and some aerobars slapped on. My next one will be done on a used bike I got last year. It fits really well and I love it, but it's kind of like "well, do you want to do an IRONMAN this year or do you want a new bike?" If you want both you'd better save it up. My wife and I essentially give each other allowances, so it's like every week we each get forty bucks and it's no-questions-asked money. If I want to save it for a year and buy a bike, fine. But if I want to spend it all that day on candy and comic books, I can do that too. But, you know, I saved up for the race entry fee, I saved up for the bike. We are not extravagant by any means.

Setting a budget was a very important consideration for a number of study participants. Aaron talked about the financial burden of having two kids. He described the burden as "significant," adding that "just race fees or the expense of equipment can be a big consideration." Ryan discussed his strategies for dealing with these expenses with his wife:

> We are very open about these things. We are both very practical and pragmatic about those purchases. Not jump right into buying, but research the availability and pricing of the items before buying. There are things like race wheels, which come up occasionally, and you would see friends that have them or they would come up in a discussion. Travel oftentimes leads into further expenses, and that was a key part of the discussion before committing to an IRONMAN event. Some people spend a lot of money on a daily basis, whether it's for nutritional food, supplements, and so on. I didn't feel it's necessary to acquire every single item which will lead to an advantage while competing. Coaching was one, and definitely at a cost, and that came up in a discussion. It's something where my wife and I would be going through the bills and ask ourselves if it was worth paying the extra price for something that may not be all that necessary and cost-effective.

Bill also touched on having discussions with his wife.

> When we travel to IRONMAN, you know, with the entry fees, and traveling to a venue and staying there for about a week, that's why it's our vacation for a year. You know, it's just like going to the beach. So for a lot of people that are racing and are not just trying to finish, they look at it differently and eat perfectly. But for me, it's all about us because we are on vacation, and we'll be smart. When it comes to the money that we have to spend, you know, on bike maintenance, equipment, nutrition. We've tried to be smart with that and not spend too much. But that's just something that we have considered to be the best thing to do in keeping me healthy and happy.

It is notable that Bill uses the word "we" in his discussion on finances. After probing, he went on to explain how he and a wife set a budget. They regard race expenses as something that keeps Bill healthy and active.

In speaking of expenses, Ian encourages fellow Iron Dads to be upfront in talking about the financial burden of the sport.

> I guess just be upfront with your training and be upfront with the expense. Not just the registration fees, but also on what equipment

that you have and what you do not because it can be a very, very expensive sport and that can take a toll on your family as well. Especially if you're starting from scratch. You know, if you're in [the sport] and you have the equipment already it's not bad. But if you're starting from scratch, the $675 registration fee is nothing compared to what you're going to need.

Wives at the IRONMAN Texas expo gave a candid opinion of endurance sport expenses. The following is an excerpt from an interview with Chase. Chase approached the booth with his wife and children. His wife hovered over him as he answered my questions, finally jumping into the interview:

> INTERVIEWER: It's an expensive sport. How do you combat the finances of the sport?
> WIFE (INTERRUPTS): MasterCard, Visa, and Discover!
> CHASE: Yeah, and work overtime.
> (WIFE LAUGHS)
> CHASE: We really try to balance it out, the spending of the money with what you really and truly need. That's always another thing I keep coming back to, but that's also another setting-expectations type of thing. And having someone who's willing to support you, but rein you in when you see the next big thing.
> WIFE (INTERRUPTS): The $7,000 bike.
> CHASE: Yeah.

In this exchange, Chase commented on how his wife serves as an important reality check on fantasy purchases. One might interpret this as the wife serving as the financial monitor of her husband's hobby-related expenditures. Language used by other study participants supports the idea that wives frequently played the role of financial monitor. In these circumstances, spouses would enable purchases by giving their approval. As Chase's wife interjected during the interview, "Getting the support of the family is key. If the wife isn't on board with the expenses and the time [commitment], it's gonna be bad."

Is Iron-Distance Racing Only for the Upper Class?

Many of the Iron Dads interviewed for this project enjoy financially comfortable lifestyles. However, I had the ability to talk with a few men who did not fit the long-course triathlete demographic profile. Mike, a professional truck driver from the Midwest, did not have the financial resources or flexible hours that many of his fellow competitors did. Yet, he was determined to become an iron-distance finisher. He saved for six months to afford the $650 race entry fee for his goal event, stashing away bits and pieces of each paycheck. In preparing for IRONMAN Texas, he turned the sleeping quarters of his truck into a training space. He used swim cords and a bike trainer, and ran loops around industrial parks and big-box store parking lots at night. Perhaps most importantly, he shared his story wherever he could, hoping that he would influence people in the trucking industry to become more health-conscious. More scholarly research should seek to give exposure to people like Mike—individuals who do extraordinary athletic feats with sparse financial resources and little job flexibility. Further, reading such stories in popular presses may give hope or inspiration to those in similar socio-economic positions. While competing in sport is often an expensive proposition, some extraordinary individuals show us the incredible things that can be done with very little. This includes reaching the elusive iron-distance finish line.

While this chapter has focused on the benefits of class privilege, endurance triathlon is not completely inaccessible to low-income individuals. Just as competitors can take a family-centered approach to training, others can take a budget-oriented approach to acquiring gear and race registration. Like Mike, a few of the men interviewed for this project did not have sizable disposal incomes. While none of the participants in this project were students, the sport has seen a growth in its younger competitor base, especially those in school. When asked if he saw any notable demographic trends regarding IRONMAN participation, Mike Reilly replied: "I'm starting to see more younger people come and do it, which is great. That average age group is still 35–39 and 40–44 because you need some income to be able to support the lifestyle of racing in IRONMAN. If you're a little bit older, you've got a little more money and you can do that. But I like seeing a lot of the young ones come in. We're having more in the 20–29 age range, you know, and the 20-year-old age group than we ever have before, so that's fantastic to see."

While Mike Reilly reminds us that the lifestyle of the sport is costly, his comments point to an important positive trend: greater inclusivity. I argue that part of this trend is attributed to the increased recognition that the sport of triathlon is currently enjoying. This increased recognition has ramifications at the institutional level, especially in the world of higher education. A growing number of colleges and universities are funding triathlon clubs. Collegiate conferences are being established around the country. Both USA Triathlon and World Triathlon Corporation have targeted the collegiate community as an area of growth. To encourage students to race, USA Triathlon features a yearly Collegiate National Championship race. WTC also designates a Collegiate National Championship race at the 70.3 distance.[10] Full-time college students participating in IRONMAN 70.3 Austin have the option of competing in the Collegiate Division. Four IRONMAN 70.3 World Championship spots are awarded exclusively to individuals in this division. In a 2012 press release, the National Collegiate Athletic Association identified triathlon as the "next big sport in the varsity queue" (Brown 2012). The groundswell of support for triathlon to become an official NCAA-sanctioned sport is very strong. The popularity of the USAT Collegiate National Championship—a race that has sold out the past few years—shows that a healthy interest exists. Many colleges and universities have infrastructures to support training (pools, stationary bikes, tracks). In January 2014, women's triathlon was labeled as an "NCAA Emerging Sport" for Divisions I, II, and III (USA Triathlon 2014a). In December of that same year, USA Triathlon announced the commitment of a $2.6 million Emerging Sport grant. Awarded to eight U.S.-based institutions in April 2015, these grants were aimed at helping to sustain varsity women's triathlon programs.[11]

Obtaining recognition from the NCAA will go a long way toward enhancing the visibility of triathlon. As the number of participants in the sport rises, more opportunities to compete will emerge. This would lead to a greater range of 70.3 and 140.6 races, offering athletes more choice in event selection. The ability to find grassroots events with more affordable entry fees will increase, and triathlon networks, such as coaches and teams, will expand. If more young men and women grow up with an exposure to triathlon, their desire to compete may continue into future years. These individuals will then become the next generation of active endurance triathletes and Iron Parents.

6

Faith Meets 140.6

"Make sure you put Christ first in everything you do, and make sure you know why you're doing it." (Alex)

It is a beautiful day in Panama City Beach, Florida. The annual running of IRONMAN Florida is tomorrow. The weather has improved each day during the week leading up to what is anticipated to be a picture-perfect race day. The expo is buzzing with competitors and their families. It is 11:00 A.M., a time that holds significance for multiple reasons. It is the height of bike and gear bag check-in. All 3,100 competitors toeing the line tomorrow must drop off their gear in specified locations by 4:00 P.M. For a smaller group of people, 11:00 A.M. has a different significance. It is the start of the annual Fellowship of Christian Athletes (FCA) "Iron Prayer," a non-denominational worship service. FCA advertises this event as a "gathering of athletes, family, and friends for a time of worship, testimonies, and prayer prior to IRONMAN and other triathlon events around the world" (FCA website). Attending athletes and their families ask for God's blessing while out on the race course. The prayer is conducted at a variety of events, including IRONMAN, IRONMAN 70.3, major sprint triathlon, and marathon events. Today, the annual prayer for IRONMAN Florida is about to begin.

A large tent surrounds the side of the pool at the Boardwalk Resort, the host hotel for the 140.6 event. The pool area is overflowing with competitors. The audience extends outside the confines of the tent and into the warm Florida sunshine. I look around to take mental note of the audience as a man takes the podium and begins to sing. Many around me are wearing an event-issued blue athlete bracelet, a sign that they are competing tomorrow. "Sing with me, church," the man at the podium calls. The audience responds to his request in a single harmonic tone. The atmosphere is emotional as tears come to the eyes of the singer. His voice begins to crack as he looks upward. Athletes raise their hands to the sky as the singer cries. I cannot help but feel moved by the moment.

The main speaker of the day is introduced. It is Dr. Mark McNees, pastor of Element3 Church in nearby Tallahassee. Dr. McNees's presence is striking. He is an athletic competitor, father, speaker, pastor, and author. His ability to relate to the crowd of athletes is moving. The essence of his message is clear: by competing in IRONMAN Florida, athletes are living out the parable of Christ's commitment to us. The service begins with a prayer. "Heavenly Father, we just give you all the praise and glory for this day. We just ask that you be with all the athletes, families, volunteers, and workers as they go about what you called them to do this weekend. Heavenly Father, we just give you thanks for your abilities, we thank you for your strength, and most of all, we give you praise for giving us this creation that we get to enjoy. And it is in the holy and powerful name of Jesus we pray. Amen."

McNees has a healthy amount of athletic experience to draw from in connecting with the competitors sitting before him. He has competed in numerous 70.3 events as well as the very challenging Escape from Alcatraz triathlon. As the event name implies, athletes attempt to swim from a ferry located adjacent to Alcatraz Island to the shores of San Francisco Bay. In his book *Immersion: Live the Life God Envisioned for You*, McNees likens his experience of jumping off this ferry into the frigid and turbulent waters of San Francisco Bay to developing a relationship with God (McNees 2011). This experience primes him to talk to the group of excited and nervous athletes. In today's sermon, he will explore the parallel between endurance racing and a relationship with God. McNees begins:

People don't fear commitment. People fear outcome. That's why people don't sign up for the IRONMAN. That's why I haven't signed up for the IRONMAN. Fear of outcome prevents people from being IRONMAN and prevents them from becoming ministers of the Gospel. You are living out the parable of Christ's commitment to you. I find it very interesting that Christ understood the commitment that he was making when he went to the Cross. [. . .] Tomorrow when you're hurting and you want to throw in the towel, I want you to connect with the fact that you are not only competing in a race, but you are being taught something of great spiritual significance. That you are being, having a window open into Heaven to have an understanding of what true commitment means. You guys will run the race well. You will complete the race. You will hear your name and hear that you are an IRONMAN. And I have every bit of confidence that, someday, when you stand in front of your creator, you will hear, "Well done, my good and faithful IRONMAN."

McNees closes his sermon with a prayer: "I pray for the athletes [. . .]".

This Iron Prayer gathering represents the nexus of important contributors to the Iron Dad identity. In this chapter, I explore the powerful connection between faith, religion, and the construction of the athletic self. In exploring this interconnectedness, I investigate case studies that depict the place of the Fellowship of Christian Athletes and Iron Prayer Ministries in endurance sport. I argue that the link between sporting identity and faith rests on inspiring the self and inspiring others. Both of these concepts are central to the overarching theme of deepening one's relationship with God. Finally, I discuss how faith informs one's placement on the athletic visibility continuum. My central finding is that faith serves as a powerful catalyst to make one's athletic identity more visible.

Religion and Sport: What Do We Know?

When I first started conducting research for this project, I did not anticipate the significance that faith and religion would play in the lives of my participants. This link struck me when my fourth study participant, Bill, started to talk about his training routine. A thirty-seven-year-old father of two, he affiliates himself with the Church of Christ. He painted a vivid picture of a training session where he and his friends were out riding their bikes. The sun was shining, the temperature was warm, and puffy clouds lined the sky. He recalls a powerful moment he had while training with fellow triathletes:

> I pray before, during, and after training. It's probably one of the coolest things about IRONMAN. I'll tell you this one story about when we were training for a race in 2005. One of the longest rides that we did, it was particularly special because we broke barriers of mileage that we never got to before. One of the first days that we were out there training for IRONMAN, we get on our bikes and we are about three miles in. We had already prayed before, but I looked at my training buddy and my other friend. This is a beautiful morning, we've got to just pray. And they all agreed. And here we are on the straights, praying for a couple of minutes. And it was just so cool. It was, you know, adding that faith to what we were doing that made it much more meaningful.

Even well after completing all of the interviews for this book, Bill's comments still stand out as some of the most memorable. Reflecting on my research audit trail of decisions regarding this project, these comments also represented a pivotal moment in the development of this book. Upon hearing Bill's story, I immediately introduced a series of new questions into my interview guide, the most fruitful of which read: "Does faith play a role in your life? If so, do you see a connection between your faith and your iron-distance training?" The answer, as I would come to learn, is that faith plays a critical role in the lives of many Iron Dads.

While sport and religion may seem like two disparate institutions, in reality they share a strong interconnectedness. Both embrace common values of commitment, discipline, and hard work. Both are founded on rituals in both the public and private realms. And, as noted by a sizable literature, each utilizes the other to promote its respective causes (Baker 2007; Eitzen and Sage 2003; Parry et al. 2007). This reciprocal relationship creates a prime physical and emotional location for sporting and spiritual identities to coexist peacefully. One example of this coexistence that has received a lot of attention in both the scholarly and non-scholarly worlds is Tim Tebow. Scholars have examined various aspects of the athlete, including marketing (Moore, Keller, and Zemanek 2011), media communication (Butterworth 2013), and the link between sport and Christianity (Novak 2013). While playing in both college and the National Football League, Tebow was known for his frequent signs of religious devotion during games, including pointing to the sky and getting down on one knee to pray. The iconic image of Tebow lowering down to one knee in prayer, clenched hand pressed against his forehead, became globally known as the act of "Tebowing."

While the popularity of Tim Tebow shows that sport and religion do coexist, his story also shows how this merging can be a place of contested terrain. In 2012, Dan Barry wrote an article in the *New York Times* craftily titled "He's a Quarterback, He's a Winner, He's a TV Draw, He's a Verb" (Barry 2012). In this piece, Barry surmised that the widespread popularity of Tebowing may be just as much about mockery as it is respect for the act. Barry noted, "When a wedding party Tebows in Las Vegas, or a couple Tebows on Abbey Road in London, or two scuba divers Tebow underwater in Belize, it can be hard to tell whether they are celebrating or mocking him for his virtuous ways" (Barry 2012). Even in Tebow's own words, his act of Tebowing is something that needs to be controlled. In an interview on ESPNNewYork.com, the University of Florida alumnus was quoted as saying, "[Tebowing] is something I do that's prayer for me, and then it got hyped up as Tebowing. So I think [it's] just to control how it's used, as well. Make sure it's used in the right way" (ESPN 2012). It is telling that the popular Tebowing act needs to be controlled by the very man who started the phenomenon. It shows the importance of claiming socially relevant symbols and spaces.

The relationship between masculinity and religion stems from a similar desire to reclaim physical and emotional territory. For example, scholars have identified the emergence of a "Muscular Christianity" (Ladd and Mathisen 1999; Putney 2001), a concept defined as "a Christian commitment to health and manliness" (Putney 2001, 11). While it was popularized in the Victorian age (Hall 1994), the values of Muscular Christianity are alive and well today. The combination of the energy and spirit of religion with historical masculine values, particularly strength and a healthy vibrancy, is a powerful combination. The Muscular Christianity framework is useful in this work for numerous reasons. Most centrally, it gives us pause to consider the connection between religion, popular conceptions of health and strength, and masculinity. Religion and sport do not coexist in a vacuum. The interconnectedness of these institutions takes place in a larger culture that idealizes specific visions of health and masculinity. Clifford Putney (2001) classifies the Fellowship of Christian Athletes, the not-for-profit religious organization discussed earlier in the chapter, as a "neo-muscular Christian" group (10). He argues that the FCA is an important vehicle for observing the merging of these respective phenomena at play, a point that I echo throughout this chapter.

The Fellowship of Christian Athletes

The linking of participation in sport with public proclamations of religious affiliations and beliefs has been well documented (Dzikus, Hardin, and Waller 2012; Watson and Parker 2013). In particular, the influential reach of the Fellowship of Christian Athletes has been of particular interest to scholars. The power of this organization extends well beyond the endurance sport context. The FCA has a presence in intercollegiate sports, most notably with collegiate sport chaplains (Dzikus, Hardin, and Waller 2012). Scholars have argued that we have seen ebbs and flows with the injection of evangelicalism into sport, with a re-emergence of this phenomenon spiking in the 1950s (Ladd and Mathisen 1999). Evangelicalism is in a constant state of play with society. In the context of endurance sport, I suggest that evangelicalism is alive and well today.

The FCA refers to itself as the largest Christian sports organization in the world. Formed in 1954, its mission is "to present to coaches and athletes, and all whom they influence, the challenge and adventure of receiving Jesus Christ as Savior and Lord, serving Him in their relationships and in the fellowship of the church."[1] It operates with four key values: integrity, service, teamwork, and excellence. The organization has many dimensions, including a deep presence within college campus and endurance sport communities. The endurance sport portion of FCA is known as Team FCA Endurance. Members can be spotted at IRONMAN events worldwide wearing their signature maroon-and-gold apparel. Team FCA Endurance embraces many of the philosophies and characteristics of its larger counterpart, known more generally as Team FCA. FCA Endurance, more specifically, features a national offering of huddles, or small local groups that come together under a common mission. As of summer 2015, FCA featured seventy-one certified endurance huddles. This included groups in thirty-seven states, the District of Columbia, and Puerto Rico.[2] International huddles were also established in Penticton, Canada, and San Pedro Sula, Honduras. Certification for huddles lasts for one year, so this number is subject to change.

The FCA is not the only organization of its kind. We also see organizations such as Multisport Ministries, a men's athletic ministry with more than 1,500 members. The organization's mission is to "train our bodies for the sport of triathlon while dedicating our lives to pleasing God through worship, discipleship, fellowship, ministry, and missions."[3] Founded in 2007, the group's motto is "By Endurance We Conquer." Commonalities between groups such as the FCA and Multisport Ministries include features such as a statement of faith, chapters, and group clothing. The emergence and growth of such groups suggests a strong interconnectedness between endurance sport and faith. In probing this connection, I found that this link is quite strong for some Iron Dads. These men use this interconnectedness as a way to bring meaning to their lives. As noted on the FCA Endurance website, "FCA Endurance gives adult Christian runners, triathletes, and cyclists, as well as all who engage in and support endurance athletics, the chance to tell the world why they do the things they do and why they are the people they are." As a number of my study participants attested to, iron-distance racing becomes a powerful vehicle for both finding and sharing spiritual meaning.

Faith and the Athletic Visibility Continuum

In chapter 4, I discussed how Iron Dads are engaged in a continual dialogue with the athletic visibility continuum. I argued that an athlete's sporting identity, and all related activities, can take on varying degrees of visibility in the eyes of others. In speaking with Iron Dads and reading their blog postings, it became apparent that for men of faith, religion helps define their place on this continuum. More specifically, men of faith intertwine sporting and religious identities. In doing so, these individuals often seek to make these identities more visible in the eyes of others. There is a process that emerged that was unique to Iron Dads who expressed religious affiliation. This process included two steps. First, athletes internalized a connection between faith and sport. Second, they shared this connection. Collectively, this entire process served as a powerful mechanism for determining placement on the athletic visibility continuum.

Internalizing a Connection

While not all of this study's participants described themselves as religious, many did. These men perceive and internalize a connection between faith and endurance sport. This connection emerges in a variety of physical and emotional places. Some of these places are more public in nature, including racing or group training environments. Other places are more personal in nature, such as reading the Bible in the privacy of their own home. Observing men on an iron-distance course reminds us that there is no single way that an "Iron Dad identity" is constructed. For some, faith plays no role in informing this identity. For others, it serves as a very strong informing influence. While faith takes on varying degrees of significance to men, what is more universal in nature is the fact that endurance sport landscapes can serve as prime grounds for engaging and displaying a religious sporting identity.

The fact that triathlon takes place outdoors serves as a powerful connecting agent between faith and the sport. Participants used a variety of words to describe this connection, with "beautiful" and "majestic" being the most common in my NVivo analysis. Being in nature, as one Iron Dad noted, gives athletes "an opportunity to be in God's kingdom." Even those who did not describe themselves as men of faith reported experiencing spiritual feelings when training outdoors. Bryson, a small-business owner from California, talked about this point: "In training you're out in the woods, in nature for hours and hours at a time and that's definitely spiritual. There's certainly an aspect of that in IRONMAN training even though it's a lot more urban-based, but it's that being outside for long periods of time." Chase, an Iron Dad who called himself "spiritual but nondenominational" explained: "I think that there are people who experience God in different ways, and I am more the type of person who experiences Him through nature. So, being out in the elements and being out there helps me understand this world. It's just amazing, this world that God has created. And being in it is really cool."

Interestingly, none of the men who described feeling a connection between faith or spirituality and the outdoors lived in an urban setting. Iron Dads residing in more urban settings described the outdoor training environment more in terms of danger. This was most apparent when interviewing men at the IRONMAN Texas expo. One father, a resident of the nearby city of Houston, stressed the "volume of cars" and "asshole drivers." While these words certainly do not invoke a sense of serenity, this father still internalized a strong connection between outdoor training and faith. He looked to God for safety more than in reverence for nature while navigating the traffic-filled streets of Houston.

Looking to a higher power for safety was a very prominent theme among Iron Dads of faith. The seemingly ever-present thought of God watching over training and racing environments suggests that internalizing a connection between faith and the iron-distance is a key part of safety. Faith in God came alive when the men talked about exposure to the dangers of outdoor training. Samuel, a Catholic Iron Dad, discussed how he turns to God to help with the dangers of training: "It's dangerous, 'cause you have to think about safety in every ride, in every swim, in every run. I think, I say, 'God, take care of me and my family.'"

In internalizing a connection between faith and training, a number of study participants reported that they read the Bible regularly. Interestingly, these men perceived a strong connection between the Bible and 140.6, specifically. Jayden, a father I met at the IRONMAN Texas expo, painted a detailed picture of this relationship. When asked if the Bible talked about endurance sport, he replied: "Yes, it sure does. Oddly enough, just carrying you on His wings, right? He tells us that we have to finish the race. So, oddly enough, it is like putting on the suit of armor. So like, before a race, I'll pray over my bike. I'll pray for my shoes. I'll pray for all of the people, all of the volunteers. It makes it that much easier. And what better time [is there] to talk to the Man in the ten, twelve hours, or however long you spend on the course?"

When probed where in the Bible the "suit of armor" is addressed, Jayden cited Paul's Letter to the Ephesians. In this letter, we are reminded that the suit of armor serves as an important tool in fighting evil. Apostle Paul writes: "We have a fight, not against blood and flesh, but [. . .] against the world rulers of this darkness, against the wicked spirit forces in the heavenly places." This means that every Christian must "take up the complete suit of armor from God, that [he] may be able to resist in the wicked day" (Ephesians 6:11–13). Jayden continued to describe the "suit of armor" concept:

Yeah, the suit of armor, with the brass plate. I'm going to get a sticker made on my speed helmet of a tattoo of a suit of armor from one of my very good friends from car design [shop]. And, depending on the goal for Saturday's race, I'm going to get a tattoo of it. And before I race, whoever is in front will tattoo my arms. Which is almost a saying, it's a spiritual thing back to the person. Maybe talk about faith to somebody else and spreading His Love.

Jayden's reference to "whoever is in front" tattooing his arms is speaking to the concept of body-marking volunteers placing an image on his body. On race morning, competitors must get their bib numbers inscribed on their arms. Dozens of volunteers typically stand waiting with markers, ready to assist competitors as they enter transition on race day. It is common to see athletes ask for an additional "artistic touch" during the body-marking process. Some ask to have sayings written on the back of hands or down their arms. Others, like Jayden, ask for temporary tattoos or symbols to be applied. For Jayden, having the symbol of the suit of armor is a powerful way of sharing his spiritual connection with others.

Sharing the Connection

Faith can be a major factor influencing how one engages the athletic visibility continuum. Often, faith leads Iron Dads to make their athletic identity more visible to others. This is because they want to use their faith as a vehicle for inspiring others. Some competitors wear clothing with scripture from the Bible, or in the case of Jayden, have symbols tattooed on race morning. Alex, a personal trainer and father of three, discussed the importance of clothing as a means of sharing his faith with others. When asked how he made his faith visible, he explained, "Well, through various events. Sometimes we set up at the different events. Otherwise, maybe during the race you can come up to somebody and talk to them. I wear the FCA shirts and sometimes you get some questions as far as 'What is that?' And hopefully you can try to reach out to them, maybe teach them a little about Christ and what He can do for you, and hopefully plant a little seed with some people as far as what it's about."

Alex is a dedicated member of the Fellowship of Christian Athletes. He competes as a vehicle for sharing his faith and connecting with others. He talked about his experience starting a new FCA chapter:

They [FCA] branched out a few years ago and just founded an adult chapter. Normally it used to be high school and stuff like that. And we put out these things as far as "Why do you race?" So you can think about why you do it every day and making sure that it's first and foremost in your life. You can go to whydoyourace.com, and then at the FCA website you can click on some of the things. Make sure you put Christ first in everything you do and make sure you know why you're doing it.

The ever-present experiencing of a higher being is powerful to Iron Dads. Frank, a father of two, explains:

I was brought up as a religious person. I've had some things go on in my life where you could question some of my beliefs, but I think on most days my faith is very strong. But still, before the race, I say a little prayer to help me perform to the best of my abilities and to keep everybody else at the race safe. You know, make sure that everybody gets through this without any injuries. This is not part of my day-to-day rational religion, but, I do think about it on long runs. I kind of ask for a little extra strength every now and then. We can all use some strength at times.

Bill, the father mentioned early in the chapter who got off his bike three miles into a training ride with friends to worship, shared another emotional story about the power of prayer. Like the story he offered earlier, sharing this moment with family and friends was an important dimension of the experience:

We were on the beach getting ready to start IRONMAN and our training buddy, he's a pediatric doctor, had flown down after his shift from work just to be there at four o'clock in the morning, just to be there with us. We were on the beach and the three of us and my wife and child prayed together. And then he walked off with another twenty yards to get to the swim corral and he said, "I just want to pray over you guys real quick." And he prayed with us and what a peace that was. It was just God. Faith has played a huge role when it comes to praying and prayers in what I've done.

Ian, a member of the Fellowship of Christian Athletes, talked about creating meaning by racing for something larger than the self:

The first time I did the IRONMAN, I did it all myself. I wasn't a Christian and I didn't have any faith. I just did it and I had a very successful race. This time, I wanted to do it and know that I was doing it for much bigger reasons than myself. This time, I am ten years, eleven years older, and I have to rely on God to know that my strength is coming from Him. And the Bible says that all things are possible through Christ who strengthens me. So when I'm out there, for instance, tomorrow I have a four-hour ride. It looks like it's going to be twenty-five-mile-an-hour winds and it's going to be nasty. I just know that I can get through it because there's something powering me that's much greater than me.

Ian went on to explain how he would be spreading the Gospel while racing. He described what will happen surrounding his upcoming IRONMAN race: "Yeah, I'll be wearing the team FCA jersey. It says 'Fellowship of Christian Athletes Endurance Team.' It has a picture on the back that says we are 'Powered by God.' There's a big event up there at the race venue where they do a breakfast and an Iron Prayer."

Faith as a Balancing Mechanism

At various points in this project, I found myself coming back to the same question: can faith itself serve as a balancing mechanism? Recall that a balancing mechanism is a specific tactic that an individual employs in an attempt to reach a state of self-perceived identity equilibrium. Numerous participants indicated that they found a self-perceived sense of balance through their faith. In this sense, being a person of faith can not only take on a master identity (Charmaz 1994) but can also become a tool for nego-tiating other capacities. Brandon, a restaurant owner and father of two daughters, talked about finding balance through faith. When asked if faith plays a role in his life, he replied:

> Yes, but not as big as my wife's. She's very religious, and I now go to a men's group meeting every Tuesday morning at 6:30 A.M. that is faith-based. I also meet with a mentor from the church every week and we just talk about things. Of course, I go to church every Sunday with my family. That's something else that's come up as part of the balance kind of issue. My wife, that was always one of the things that she wanted—to get more involved with faith. That was important to her, and it was not important to me on the same level that it was for her. So that's something I'm doing more of. I did start doing primar-ily to make her happy. The more that I'm doing with the men's group and everything, the more my faith grows, in my personal life as well. So, before, not so much, and since that time, ever increasing.

Faith plays an important role in an Iron Dad's perception of "life bal-ance." Part of this comes in one's religious identity taking precedent over other competing identities. When conflicts arise between training sched-ules and religious events, religious events take priority. This sense of defini-tiveness in priorities led some participants to feel a sense of balance in their lives. Ian recounted:

> Sunday is Easter and you know Easter is a very big holiday for us. I switched my day off to be Easter so we could spend it together as

a family, and I sort of rearranged my training so that it's not a big conflict. My daughter starts soccer here pretty soon and I don't want to miss a game, so I sort of have to modify my schedule a little bit. It might be as crazy as getting out on the bike at six o'clock in the morning and riding until nine in the morning. Actually, riding to where her game is at and taking out the rollers [a style of trainer] from the back of the van and setting them up on the field so I can be rolling during the game, and then getting back out on the road when she's done. It's just planning, I think, what it really comes down to.

Bryson echoed the same sentiment of prioritizing religious events over other activities. He described how he worked hard to "not miss church." This definitiveness made fathers like Bryson feel confident in their ability to prioritize daily responsibilities.

Even though church attendance was viewed as a marker of balance, the sense of self-perceived balance that some Iron Dads were experiencing was not reflective of reality. One such example is Josh, a Catholic Iron Dad. He described his life as "pretty well balanced" and "manageable." Yet, at the same time, he described instances where his wife demanded that he stop competing in long-course triathlon for good. His life did not appear "manageable" at these times. In the next chapter, I identify the reasons why Iron Dads decide to leave iron-distance racing. I describe how the process of quitting racing at that distance, or putting training on hold for an extended period of time, has influenced study participants as athletes, fathers, spouses, and men.

7

Throwing in the Towel

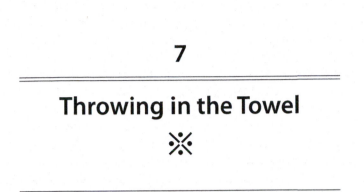

"My marriage was on the brink," Tristan recounted. "My wife, basically, in her opinion, felt that I got out of balance. When you talk about the balance of being a husband and getting things done around the house and seeing relatives, that sort of thing, she didn't feel like I did a good enough job of balancing it all together." Tristan's words shook me. After conducting sixteen interviews with Iron Dads who seemingly had their lives under control, this story was markedly different. I knew that this would be a memorable interview. Tristan is a busy professional and father of two. He owns a series of restaurant franchises in the mid-Atlantic states. I could tell right away that he was the type of person who strives for perfection. He spoke about his hands-on managerial style, traveling great distances to and from various franchise locations in a single day just to take care of small details. After seeing the IRONMAN World Championship broadcast on television, he felt inspired to try endurance racing. He signed up for a charity slot to IRONMAN Arizona that same evening.

Initially, Tristan's story did not reveal itself as one that would be well outside of the typical Iron Dad narrative. Like many other study participants, he presented himself as being dedicated to involving his children in his training. However, his story had a unique twist. He gave his children a lot of attention but inadvertently neglected his wife in the process. Tristan recounts his training for IRONMAN Arizona:

> Well, my two girls were certainly a big priority. I was involving them in every way that I could. Really, this thing started way back when, looking at my daughters when they were young, and thinking that I

had never seen my own father running a step in my whole entire life. I would see their eating habits and think, "Wow, I really have to show them a healthier lifestyle." So, everything I've been doing has been with them in mind. My wife, on the other hand, again, I made a number of assumptions that turned out to be faulty. Being married is hard that way. You know? When you have kids, there are shifts from giving each other attention to the kids being the first priority. Everything becomes about them and less about your spouse. It's not intentional that way, it's just something that develops. So I wasn't thinking that hard about my wife being a priority, exactly. I mean, of course she is one, but now, with the ability to look back on it with some hindsight, I didn't have my wife high enough on the priority list as she needs to be. She actually needs to be ahead of the kids. I learned that during IRONMAN but didn't realize it. IRONMAN, honestly and truthfully, almost created a divorce situation. However, we're actually on a better path now than we were before any of this began. It's been rough, but beneficial.

Tristan decided that in order to save his marriage he would have to put his training on hold. He was not the only study participant to come to this difficult conclusion. Simply put, iron-distance training is not for everyone. Many people realize this immediately, reacting to the thought of 140.6 miles with something like, "you call that fun?" or "you couldn't pay me enough to do that." Other people give iron-distance training a try, ultimately finding out that they cannot achieve their goals—be it personal or athletic. Even though endurance triathlon is a hobby, it is internalized as serious business by many Iron Dads. My study participants repeatedly shared stories of the strong sense of commitment required for success. Still, even with this high level of commitment, managing competing responsibilities can be hard to reconcile. As with Tristan, establishing a healthy balance between sport and family can be extremely difficult, if not impossible, given certain circumstances.

Walking away from iron-distance racing can come in multiple forms. Some competitors register for an event and end up quitting in the middle of their training cycle. These athletes never make it to the start line. Others call their 140.6 racing career quits immediately after an event. One study participant decided to pull the plug on future iron-distance events *while* he was competing. In the midst of a bad race full of pain and suffering, he decided not to compete again in the future. A more popular philosophy among competitors, particularly those with children, is to step aside from racing full-distance triathlon and return when their kids are older. My analysis revealed that Iron Dads who took the latter approach tended to drop to shorter distances, often 70.3 races. This chapter explores the ramifications of quitting iron-distance racing on the Iron Dad identity. Using the concept of the "turning point," I discuss characteristics of the moments when fathers came to realize that it was time to pull the plug on 140.6-mile events. Central to this decision-making process is the presence of multiple and sometimes conflicting discourses surrounding masculinity. In that vein, I explore the complicated array of discourses that surround the concept of sporting failure.

Discourses about Sporting Failure

When registering for an iron-distance race, people do a variety of creative things to help them envision success. We see the power of discourse when these tactics are deconstructed. One Iron Dad described writing "You are an IRONMAN" on every bathroom mirror in his house. Another put a picture of his training partner crossing a 140.6 finish line on his desk at work. "If he could do it in under thirteen [hours], so could I," Jeff recounted. While the mechanisms that Iron Dads employ in helping them envision success vary considerably from person to person, one constant remains true: competitors obsess over the finish line. As William Bridel (2010) argues, the finish line is where the "IRONMAN identity" is bestowed. While I believe that this identity can be realized before competitors hit the line, particularly in those who view starting a 140.6 event as a victory, there is no denying the privileged place that the finish chute holds. Competitors dream about it, talk about it, and visualize running through it. "They will have to drag me off the course before I quit," Jeff pronounced at the IRONMAN Texas expo, expressing his determination to make it to the finish line. The concept of success in an endurance sport context often includes some discussion of the finish line.

While nobody registers for an endurance triathlon with the intention of quitting, the reality is that it happens. The world keeps turning after an athlete shells out the registration fee. People get sick, laid off from work, have children, experience relationship issues, and the list goes on. Race management companies bank on a certain percentage of competitors not making it to the start line. While some races provide a combination of insurance, transfer, or partial refund options for athletes, as will be described in the next chapter, access to these benefits often have limitations. Upon making it to the venue and starting the race, competitors once again face a host of potential challenges. Race day conditions are a significant contributing factor to a competitor's success. Athletes sign up for many WTC-branded full-distance events a year in advance, and in so doing, spend the next 365 days hoping for good weather. Some races present athletes with brutally difficult conditions. This makes an arduous task—traversing 140.6 miles under one's own locomotion—even more challenging. In the 2012 running of IRONMAN St. George, swimmers were caught off-guard by four-foot waves that started a mere fifteen minutes after the race began. The dangerous swim conditions, combined with the notoriously difficult bike course, led to a 29 percent did-not-finish [DNF] rate. Due to low registration numbers, driven in part by the overall difficulty of the course, this race was subsequently turned into a 70.3 in 2013. The 2005 running of IRONMAN Wisconsin presented athletes with extremely warm conditions that contributed to a high DNF rate. The same can be said of the 2009 running of IRONMAN China, where temperatures topping 100 degrees pushed the DNF rate to a WTC record-high 50 percent.[1] This represented the final year that the race in China was offered.[2]

While weather conditions may account for a certain percentage of any given DNF rate, other factors play a role in an athlete's decision to throw in the towel. Sometimes competitors are severely undertrained, leading to physical exhaustion. Other times, athletes struggle to take in critical nutrition while out on the course. This frequently results in "bonking"—hitting a physiological wall due to low blood sugar levels. Finally, one may call it quits because of pain. Iron-distance competition is uncomfortable. Either due to an injury or soreness, some people see no alternative but to call it quits. How does that choice affect the construction of the Iron Dad identity? Can this identity peacefully exist in the wake of a failed competition effort?

Deciding to quit the pursuit of the 140.6 finish line can be a devastating decision for some—a choice that affects every dimension of the self. It impacts how people see themselves as athletes and gendered beings. Due to the significance that sport often takes in an iron-distance athlete's life, withdrawing from an event is unquestionably hard for both men and women. However, looking through the lens of gendered societal expectations, the Iron Dads in my study demonstrated the ways in which throwing in the towel is uniquely challenging for men. Hegemonic masculinity encourages men to keep competing at all costs. This means that there is a lot of significance wrapped up in sporting outcomes. Language is used to support this idea. The following popular colloquialisms used in the endurance triathlon community illustrate this emphasis of hegemonic ideals:

"Death before DNF" = Death before a "did not finish" (result when a competitor starts the race but fails to reach the finish line)
"HTFU" = Harden the fuck up
"Drag my dead body off the course"

All of these phrases speak to athletes' willingness to "give it their all" on the race course—including sustaining a permanent injury or even death. While such popular language reaffirms subscription to hegemonic gender norms, are these colloquialisms really reflective of what competitors are willing to endure? For example, would a man *really* feel compelled to "harden the fuck up" if lack of nutrition intake landed him in the medical tent? Are these types of discourse really internalized by Iron Dads—men whose kids depend on them?

Masculine Discourse as Pre-race Ritual

In talking with Iron Dads, it is clear that this type of hyper-masculine discourse is commonly used for motivation in pre-race ritual. I suggest that the value given to such language reflects the emotional investment that these men have in racing. This hyper-masculine discourse emerged when men talked about physically entering the course, a time that is also full of great anticipation and, at points, uncertainty. Body marking was the most commonly cited time for using such language in pre-race ritual. In the previous chapter, I described how Jayden asked a body-marking volunteer to place a temporary tattoo of the "suit of armor" on his skin just before a race. A number of fathers elaborated on how they used the same body-marking process to reaffirm their subscription to hegemonic gender norms. Proxies for subscribing to these ideas were numerous. A few Iron Dads talked about writing "HTFU" on their knuckles or back of the hand. These spaces on the body are not obscured by wetsuit sleeves. These spaces also face competitors when they have their hands resting on their aerobars. With the bike being the longest segment of the race, looking down at writing on their hands offers a constant reminder of the competitor's race philosophy.

Men Advising Men

My analysis suggests that particularly in instances of family turmoil, these hyper-masculine discourses emerge a lot less frequently. This is especially notable when an Iron Dad turns to the blogosphere to seek advice from fellow Iron Dads about quitting training. The discourse that emerges is one of empathy, support, and reaffirmation of the value of family.

In one blog post, an Iron Dad discusses the emotional turmoil that he is experiencing as a result of not having time to train. He recently had a child and now only has thirteen weeks until his goal race. Feeling horribly undertrained, he seeks advice from other parents:

> For you guys that have been through it and just decided that it's not doable, what was your final straw, or coming to Jesus moment, when you just gave up the fight of trying to train to complete another IRONMAN? I really enjoyed the first two I did and would really like

to do another one (or multiple ones), but just looking at life's priorities, a 5–6 hour training ride just seems like a challenge to get clipped in for at this point. But I'm still having a hard time throwing in the towel on the idea of limiting myself to 70.3s or less.

Fellow Iron Dads (as well as Iron Moms) applauded his consideration of his family. Other men offered support, saying that they decided to prioritize family over training. They offered recognition of the fact that they could not be the father that they wanted to be while in the midst of heavy preparation periods. One father replied, "The reality is that when I am training for an IM, not only are there the long days away from the house, but I'm also obsessed with anything tri-related. [. . .] I will go back to IMs, but not until the kids are a little older and not as needy." One father described a heart-to-heart discussion, started by his son, that prompted him to drop down to races of shorter distance. The father blogged:

> Last year I was asking the family [wife, twelve-year-old daughter, and ten-year-old son] about their thoughts on my training for another IM. My son sat me down and said "Dad, let me ask you a question." Uh-oh. He then asked me if I would rather spend the season working out very long and hard to accomplish something personally rewarding, or do what I had just done—a season of sprints, Olympic-distance tris, and one half iron, and having more fun. Hmm. I asked him if I wasn't much fun when training for an IM. He said, "Well, you're not around much on weekends and when you are, you're pretty tired and taking a lot of naps." I got it. It seems to be a good balance for my family and I for me to train to do sprints, Olympics, and the occasional half. I don't want to turn around in a few years and wonder what happened to my kids.

Another father, a Kona qualifier, sympathizes with the Iron Dad who started the thread:

> Prior to our first son being born, I had done two Konas and really had the IM bug. After he was born, IM didn't seem as significant anymore—although giving up my [Kona] slot a couple of times in subsequent years was one of the hardest things to do. Now with the birth of our second son, even scheduling for a 70.3 race is rough. But I've found a happy medium with sprint and Olympics. I don't want to miss any part of their growing up, but I still want to compete. It's a really tough balance.

The original question posted by the Iron Dad received almost 10,000 views. He received 131 responses over the course of a one-week period, making it one of the more popular discussions of the year. It is noteworthy that there were no responses emblematic of the pre-race ritual. Nobody suggested that the father "harden the fuck up" or "die trying" to reach the finish line. Instead, thoughtful, pragmatic advice emerged.

While this thread represents a small fraction of discourse surrounding the culture of iron-distance racing, I believe it offers valuable insight toward a question posed earlier in the chapter: are colloquialisms referring to hegemonic values really reflective of what competitors are willing to endure? I argue that the blog exchange presented above demonstrates that a more progressive masculinity can and does exist in endurance triathlon—a sporting culture that, quite literally, encourages people to think of an *IRONMAN* (Anderson 2005; Anderson and McGuire 2010). So why is this more progressive masculinity not observed more readily in 140.6 culture? This question is informed, in part, by a Goffmanian analysis of digital interactions. As actors on a stage, we aim to present ourselves to the audience in a particular way. This is known as the "front stage" presentation of self. In more quiet moments away from the audience, we may let our guard down and reveal more elements of our true selves. These "back stage" moments are places where we do not seek to conceal truths. The ability to hide behind a pseudonym, combined with the familiarity and comfort of a friendly forum, may create a more welcoming environment for more authentic identities and beliefs to emerge. This may explain why we see the more caring and compassionate sides of men revealing themselves in this particular social sphere.

Turning Points

In attempting to untangle the underlying and more inclusive masculinity that exists in this sporting context, it is worth exploring what happens when an Iron Dad fails to finish a race. Why does he make this choice, and how is this decision regarded by other fathers as well as by competitors without kids? The concept of the "turning point" plays a key role in an Iron Dad's decision to throw in the towel on training. William Marsiglio and Sally Hutchinson (2002) offer that, "a situation or event can be thought of as a turning point if it prompts an individual to become someone other than he or she was before" (25). This moment is typically embedded in the process of reevaluating the self (Strauss 1969). My research revealed that common turning points in endurance sport training include (1) having a negative race experience, (2) realizing the selfishness of the distance, or (3) receiving direct threats from a spouse. These turning points signal to Iron Dads that priorities are out of order and more attention needs to be focused on family life.

Negative Racing Experiences

Max, an Iron Dad who decided to drop down from full-distance races to shorter ones, had a turning point that resulted from a negative racing experience. He refers to this turning point as a "Jesus moment." "My 'come to Jesus' moment was during the last part of the run at the 2009 Silverman [140.6]. It was dark and there is a point on Sunridge Heights Parkway where you have a pretty good view of the lights of Las Vegas. For whatever reason, I knew then that I was going to finish the race but that I'd never do another IM." This father makes reference to racing in the dark, alluding to the fact that he was out on the course for a long period of time.

As expressed by a number of study participants, subpar racing experiences can serve as stark wake-up calls for Iron Dads. Keith, a father who decided to stop competing in future long-course events while participating in IRONMAN Canada, decided that "the time wasn't worth it without a PR [personal record], and I didn't get one. I knew I was done." What he means by this is that, given the amount of time he spent training, he expected to set a new personal best at the distance. While walking the majority of the IRONMAN Canada marathon, Keith experienced a turning point. He realized that his training efforts did not pay off. Consequently, he decided to drop down to the 70.3 distance and focus more on his children.

Realizing Selfishness in the Iron Distance

Some Iron Dads came to an abrupt realization that iron-distance racing is a selfish activity. After coming home from a training session, Frank realized that his wife Maggie was constantly working while he exercised. "Maggie works full time but has very flexible hours. Despite working a full-time job, she still does most of the household chores, which really includes helping me get ready for the next day's training. She does all of the laundry and cleans out my water bottles. She was doing way too much and I was just training." Frank was pointing to what sociologists refer to as the "second shift," or unpaid labor that is typically done after work (Hochschild and Machung 2012). Maggie was serving in an enabling capacity, propelling Frank's athletic participation by helping with domestic chores. The Iron Dad came to realize that the division of labor in the home was not equal. He noted, "It finally hit me that the amount of domestic chores increased as a result of my training. These responsibilities were falling to my wife." After experiencing this turning point, Frank decided to take a year off from full-distance racing.

Ryan talks about coming to the realization that long-course racing means more time spent training. He described himself as having an "obsessive" personality. Be it in the workplace or on the bike trainer, he fully invests himself at the task at hand. He realized that this obsession blinded him from being sensitive toward his family:

> I'm a little more sensitive now to how easy it is for me to fall into doing activities that are [of] benefit to me. It's selfish, definitely self-ish, to go out and ride a bike for four hours. But I have to remember it's not just me, but it's the kids, because I'm not there doing things when I should be there with them. But I'm more attuned to the fact that the decisions I make are not only a benefit to me, but what is best for my family as well. Before when I used to just do things like that, it seemed like there were smaller amounts of time, so I didn't consider the impacts. But now I think of the impacts a lot more. Now that I have done a number of longer distance events, I don't focus as much on my training now for my smaller sets coming up than I used to. I'll be fine. Whatever fitness shape I'm in at the time will be good enough.

Ryan came to see the amount of work that he was putting into his training. Once this obsession became visible to him, he went through what he described as a "learning process" for how to train more efficiently on fewer hours of investment.

Direct Threats from a Spouse

A recent online thread called "IRONMAN and divorce—the real truth" reveals that Iron Dads appear, at least on the surface, to recognize that their spouses have a breaking point when it comes to the selfishness of the distance. The language being offered by fathers in this thread suggests a valuation of egalitarian ideals. Further, numerous men suggested that marriage is something worth fighting for, indicating that they value marriage as an institution. While egalitarian ideals may not actually be practiced in the home, it is interesting to see men advocating for that in a public forum. Generally, we instead might anticipate seeing a more masculine discourse. However, as mentioned, the comfort of a familiar and anonymous online environment may make men more apt to leave a "backstage" impression (Goffman 1959). Here are some of the more provocative quotes:

> Racing doesn't kill marriages. Leaving your wife home with four kids that are being absolute hellions does! Doesn't matter what you are doing if the end result is a pissed off wife left at home. And this is why I drink beer and sit around a campfire with my wife and kids instead of getting those long rides and runs in.

I know there are a lot of accomplished triathletes here. A whole lot of real hard-asses who would not quit an IRONMAN if you chopped one of their legs off halfway through the run. They will train for a year to target one eight- to fifteen-hour event (depending on how good you really are). It means you are tough and driven, generally speaking. As I read this thread, this is the part I can't understand. If you're such a fighter, why don't you fight for your marriage like you fight for a Kona spot? Why don't you expend that same energy to make your marriage awesome, not just okay, but awesome? Do you value your half-assed age-group third place more than you value the person that promised, swore an oath, before God and your best friends, to love and cherish until death do you part? Did you not take that commitment any more seriously than your 6:00 A.M. group ride? After all, aren't you the person that told yourself you can do anything, and then proved it?

Love is not a happy feeling, or great sex, or mutual adoration (although it can encompass all those things). First and foremost, it's a commitment. The commitment you made when you got married, for richer or poorer, in sickness and in health. If you think you're so fucking tough how about proving it by working to make your marriage better every day, just like you do your power numbers and your swim stroke. That's a memory you can cherish in twenty years, and it's a lot warmer at night than a $5 plaque and a worn-out race number.

Dropping Down in Distance

Numerous Iron Dads suggested that they would be temporarily "throwing in the towel" on long-distance racing. Until their kids grew older, they would stick to sprint, Olympic, and 70.3 races. Justin describes how, despite the decision to stop long-course competition, exercise still has an important place in maintaining a healthy lifestyle:

I may take off a year or so, but yeah, I'll probably do some more 140.6 races in the future. Absolutely, it's fun. It's a pretty cool accomplishment. I don't think I'll do more than one a year or so. It's a lot of time commitment. Especially near the end when you're getting really hard training and stuff. But definitely 70.3s and definitely a lifestyle that you can manage. But just keeping active and keeping fit and becoming an athlete, it's really helped me out. All the exercise, it's a drug. It's a natural drug that God gives you in your brain. These natural drugs are just incredible and I'm addicted for sure. But, if I don't end up racing one year, or if I take off some training days, it's okay, because it is a balance once again. Things will inevitably work out.

Greg relates a similar sentiment about taking time off from iron-distance racing. When asked if he tried to give his wife some free time during his heavy training periods, he recalls:

> Yeah, I tried to do it as much as I could. I would give her opportunities to go do stuff. I would try to get her a movie or to go shopping without the kids, but that was difficult. I spent more time away from them than she did. I made that decision probably June or July, when my long training really started ramping up. I made the decision I would do this one [140.6] and be done for a while until my kids got older. Then, when they wanted me around less, I could resume the training. The impact on the family was too great to continue for a few years.

In my interviews, numerous Iron Dads were forthcoming in their decision to drop down to shorter competition distances. As we saw earlier in the chapter, this was also true of some men participating on blog forums. Looking through the lens of R. W. Connell's (1987) original hegemonic masculinity framework, we might interpret this as a sign of weakness. This framework suggests that men should be successful in all ventures—especially athletic ones. Sport is an arena where men can claim their masculine selves. To drop down in distance from 140.6 to 70.3 miles is to compromise this self. So what does it say about the state of masculinities if Iron Dads openly consider, and are publicly applauded for, throwing in the towel on long-course events? What are sociologists to make of men who are commended for vocalizing the minimization of sport in favor of family responsibilities? I argue that this shift in acceptance towards a nurturing approach to fathering is indicative of evolving notions of both masculinity and fatherhood (Marsiglio and Roy 2012). The narrative surrounding Dick and Rick Hoyt, two special endurance triathletes, is emblematic of these changing discourses.

Toward More Inclusive Masculinities

A Case Study: Dick and Rick Hoyt

Team Hoyt is a father-and-son team that many believe exemplifies what it means to be an Iron Dad. Dick and Rick compete in iron-distance races together. Dick tows his disabled son Rick on a raft for the swim portion, pedals a bicycle for two during the cycling portion, and pushes a wheelchair for the run segment of the race. The duo has competed in numerous endurance events such as marathons and IRONMAN triathlons.[3] Some may say that Dick exemplifies Connell's (1987) original formulation of hegemonic masculinity because he is physically strong and is the breadwinner for his family. Rick's participation in sport as a disabled man would be fundamentally at odds with Connell's original interpretation of the concept. Looking through the lens of Connell, Rick's efforts on a 140.6 course would be devalued. Dick would not be applauded for his engaged fathering practices but, rather, for the sheer physical strength that he exhibits on race day. Today, with more inclusive masculinities emerging in society—including sport (Anderson 2011)—a very different narrative surrounds the pair. Both Dick and Rick are revered in the endurance triathlon world. Rick, someone who is unable to pedal a bike or swim a stroke on his own, is celebrated. The resounding sentiment expressed on social media that Rick is regarded as an athlete is quite telling. Similarly, the fact that fathers who drop down in distance are applauded for their efforts to prioritize family over sport is also revealing. In my opinion, both of these examples point to the fact that new, more-inclusive views of masculinity are slowly emerging in sport. While they may not necessarily be the dominant social paradigm, a trend toward more progressive values in sport is slowly emerging.

One of the more interesting developments in Dick and Rick's story is the fact that Dick is widely regarded as a model Iron Dad. Dick is a nurturing father who, quite literally, gives his all for his son. He has been enabling his son's participation in sport since 1977. Dick's recognition as an engaged father is quite vast. If one types the words "Iron Dad" into the search box on YouTube, as this book goes to press, the first video that appears is of Team Hoyt in action. Another highly recognized part of Team Hoyt's story is its successful fight for the inclusion of a physically challenged division in IRONMAN-branded competition. In my interview with him, Dick relayed how hard he had to press World Triathlon Corporation to establish this division. He was initially barred from towing his son around the course. Using the power of his social networks, especially Boston Marathon race director Dave McGillivray, physically disabled athletes were finally welcomed into IRONMAN events. Now men and women with a variety of disabilities can be celebrated as endurance athletes.

Images of masculinity are ever-changing. Dick and Rick, a team that may not have fit in with Connell's original definition of hegemonic masculinity, are now celebrated as endurance athletes. The same is true of men who drop down in distance or quit iron-distance training. What this tells us is that gender ideologies depicting what men can and should be doing are shifting (Marsiglio and Roy 2012). As more progressive notions of masculinity emerge, commitment to children is gaining an increasingly valued place in society. Over time, this more expansive conceptualization of masculinity will present more avenues for Iron Dads to express their identities as engaged fathers. It will also offer more opportunities for the efforts of disabled competitors to be celebrated.

8

The Road Ahead

❖

This book offers the first look at the lives of Iron Dads—men who juggle work, family, and endurance triathlon training. Using a qualitative approach, I uncover how Iron Dads negotiate their multiple identities. I introduce new concepts such as the athletic visibility continuum, sporting guilt, and balancing mechanisms. In this chapter, I discuss some of the theoretical and methodological ramifications of this research. I also offer some parting thoughts for both athletes and race directors. For athletes, I suggest that competitors—especially those with children—expand the scope of their selection criteria when considering upcoming races. These criteria should include an evaluation of family-centered attractions surrounding the event. I also offer race directors suggestions for creating more family-friendly triathlon events, and I applaud some of the recent efforts of various race-directing organizations.

Athletes Studying Athletes

The process of interviewing can be seen in a number of lights—as a dance, a conversation, an act, or a speech event, among other things. It can include one person, two people, or a whole host of individuals. Each interview has its own dynamics. These dynamics have consequences for the data collection process. This research provided an opportunity for the researcher, an active iron-distance competitor, to interview other active iron-distance athletes. This presented a unique situation, as both the interviewer and the interviewees possessed detailed knowledge of a common sport culture. In this regard, one could conceptualize this research dynamic as an insider interviewing other insiders. This project does not represent the first time an athlete has interviewed fellow competitors. Academic conferences such as the North American Society for the Sociology of Sport are full of athletic-minded scholars presenting qualitative research on athletes. However, despite the existence of this insider dynamic in the study of sport and leisure, sparse scholarly attention has been given to this interviewer-interviewee interplay. This dynamic is worthy of attention. My project has generated fresh insights that can advance the scholarly dialogue on this topic.

Scholars studying sport and leisure contexts should begin a healthy dialogue about the ramifications of athletes studying athletes. Hearing the experiences of others in the field would help us advance our own methodological practices. Kathy Charmaz reminds researchers that we influence our own studies in both overt and subtle ways. As she noted, "We are *part* of our constructed theory and this theory reflects the vantage points inherent in our varied experiences, whether or not we are aware of them" (Charmaz 2006, 149). Advancing this dialogue would help us all in our practice of reflexivity. There is enough content here for the development of an edited volume. Scholars (who are also athletes) studying competitors in a variety of sports could discuss their respective experiences, standpoints, and methodological challenges.

Study Limitations: Methodology

Besides my limited opportunity to interact with spouses and children at the IRONMAN Texas expo, this research portrays one side of the endurance sport/parenting story that was presented by Iron Dads. The interviews and textual analysis conducted for this project provided access to a population previously untapped by researchers. Hearing how Iron Dads construct meaning in their lives and juggle responsibilities was a much needed step in developing our understanding of fathering through sport and leisure. However, much more needs to be done. As I explain in the next section, this is a ripe area of scholarship to expand on. For now, I begin by discussing some of the methodological limitations of the study at hand. Reflecting on these limitations will help future scholars advance this line of research.

Interview Approach

Interviews were conducted both over the telephone and on location at the IRONMAN Texas exposition. Neither of these interview approaches was ideal.[1] While the interviews conducted over the phone were quite in-depth, I missed the opportunity to collect important information. As John Amis

(2005) warned, one of the drawbacks to conducting phone interviews is the loss of non-verbal cues. He describes face-to-face interviewing practices as "preferred" because they "ease the building of rapport and collection of non-verbal data" (2005, 106). Meeting with participants in Texas allowed me to catch these non-verbal cues. However, as was true of the telephone conversations, there were some drawbacks here as well. The temperature on expo days crept over ninety degrees. Weather.com had forecast brilliant sunshine during these days, which was exactly what expo-goers were treated to. Unfortunately, standing in these conditions for long periods of time is less than ideal for people looking to rest before a big competition. For this reason, the in-person interviews were much shorter than those conducted over the phone. On top of the heat, the expo held numerous other distractions. Being sensitive to this situation, I shortened interviews on an as-needed basis. The ideal situation would have been to conduct in-person interviews at a period when competitors had more time and slightly more forgiving climate conditions.

The Web as a Data Source

One of the difficulties in utilizing blog postings for research is the issue of identity. With in-depth interviews, one is able to capture important demographic information about the participant by asking questions. With blogs, posters only write what they want others to know. This made it more challenging for me to identify standpoints that bloggers were invoking. For example, there were instances where I was able to identify that the blogger was speaking as a parent. However, at times, lack of demographic information precluded me from knowing if the person was speaking as a mother or a father. Depending on the type of information being disclosed, it may be difficult to determine if the poster is a man or a woman, young or old, if the person is employed full-time, or how many hours the person spends training per week. To determine gender, profiles of the screen names were sometimes helpful. Often individuals reveal their actual first name on their blogging profile. Many of the bloggers also had links to personal websites, a space where I could get further demographic information. In instances where it was hard to decipher the gender of the blogger, I searched prior online postings made by that individual. Some of these posts offered more detailed information about the person. For example, a prior post may make reference to a spouse, specifically discussing a husband or wife. Searching prior posts also assisted in determining a blogger's gender. For example, while not completely sure, I had a strong hunch that one particular post was made by a man. A search of the user's history showed that he chimed in on conversations about his favorite pair of male swim jammers.

Deciding to use blog postings for analytic purposes is a compromise. On the one hand, it opens up the scope and depth of discussion on the topic. On the other hand, researchers have only limited knowledge of who these individuals are. One must be careful not to make assumptions about the unknown. Some people may see anonymity as an opportunity for exaggeration or deception. One must also be careful not to claim that bloggers constitute a representative sample, unless the research itself is about habits of people in the blogosphere or, more specifically, a particular website. It is hard to ascertain how individuals in the blogosphere may be different from individuals not present on such digital forums. This is clearly an issue in recruiting interview participants on the Web. While this study does not claim to have a representative sample, readers should be sensitive to potential systematic differences between bloggers and non-bloggers. Fathers who are exceptionally strapped for time will not be blogging. Also, as we know from the "digital divide" research, people who have access to the Internet are disproportionately white, male, and of higher socio-economic status (Norris 2001). Consequently, it is important to note that the data collected via the blogosphere cannot be generalized. To mitigate these concerns as they applied to recruiting for the in-depth interviews, I did not rely on digital outlets as my only means of soliciting participants. Men were also recruited on location at an event expo. Still, even with this multi-pronged recruitment approach, limitations were still apparent.

Recruitment Limitations

This project involved participants who were already deeply embedded in the iron-distance community. Participants were either just about to compete in a full-distance race (such as those I met in Texas in the days leading up to the event) or were actively blogging about triathlon. In that sense, these men may be viewed as being more enthusiastic about triathlon than others. These recruitment strategies may have missed people who are less invested in their athletic identities. Further, men self-selected into the study. Again, this raises concerns about an oversampling of those holding enthusiastic and/or positive feelings about iron-distance triathlon. If someone recently competed in such an event and had a bad experience, and was consequently thinking of quitting the sport, he may have been less willing to respond to my call for participation.

My analysis also fails to offer insights about fathers who aspired to do their first iron-distance event but backed down in the training process. The study recruitment parameters required that men either be currently training for a race or had completed one within the past year. This excludes men who may have started the process of training for their first race but quit.

While my research was able to draw conclusions about men who decided to quit racing the 140.6 after completing a race of that distance, there is an obvious gap in understanding left to be addressed. To date, no scholarly research has addressed first-time full-distance athletes who registered for a 140.6 event but failed to make it to the starting line. Locating these individuals presents obvious methodological challenges. Recruitment via triathlon blogs may offer researchers a start toward reaching this population. However, if a sizable number of these individuals abandoned the sport of triathlon altogether, even the most popular of forums would be limited in their reach.

A Consequence of the Times

Finally, one must put this study in the context of its time. The cost of entering many popular iron-distance triathlon events continues to increase. As these prices increase, the financial barrier for entry into the sport goes up. This is particularly true in the context of the economic times in which this research was conducted. Recruitment for this research spanned from 2009 through 2012, a period of economic recession in the United States. This larger economic picture had ramifications for individuals. With the value of investments declining, people had less disposable income for hobbies such as triathlon. This suggests that the people who were able to compete during this time may be unique in certain ways. One could argue that those who have the disposable income to race in a time of economic recession are particularly privileged. As this work has asserted, triathlon is an expensive sport. Having the economic resources to race at the 140.6 distance during a recession is an enviable position for many families. The population of competitors may change as the times—and accompanying economic climate—evolve.

While the financial barrier to iron-distance participation is still sizable, as economic conditions improve, more people may be in a position to compete. Further, as long-course racing grows in popularity, more affordable race options will eventually emerge. Popularity breeds competition in the race management field. We have already seen the expansion of competing race outlets. Both HITS Endurance and the TOUGHMAN series races continue to expand its offerings. These and other race management teams offer half- and full-distance alternatives. This is to suggest that while it is certainly the most popular outlet, World Triathlon Corporation is not the only gateway to racing long-course triathlon. The continual expansion of race venues also means that more people will be able to find competitions near home. Eliminating travel costs makes triathlon much more feasible. Replicating this study ten years from now may reveal that the socioeconomic profile for clientele of 140.6 race competitors has shifted.

Directions for Future Research

Expansion of Scope

A natural progression of this work is to explore the unique complexities of Iron Moms. As we have seen in this research, many Iron Dads want an emotional and physical proximity with their children. This desire, compounded with the societal expectations of being the breadwinner, poses distinct challenges for the prospect of competing in longer events. Many mothers also share this wish to be emotionally and physically close with their children; however, contemporary narratives of parenting seemingly necessitate this intimacy. Mothers may be viewed negatively when they prioritize their personal aspirations over the needs of their family, especially when it comes to engaging in leisure. In their study of amateur triathletes competing across a variety of distances, all of whom enjoy traveling for sport, Matthew Lamont, Millicent Kennelly, and Erica Wilson (2011) conclude that athletes must contend with competing priorities. One prominent sphere that emerged was domestic responsibilities, including a wide range of parenting activities. How does gender influence how these competing responsibilities are negotiated? Expanding our understanding of how moms contend with these highly demanding social expectations—particularly while looking through the lens of endurance sport—is a valuable line of research.

While interviewing Iron Moms and Iron Dads is a useful endeavor, an equally provocative line of research is to interview Iron Couples—parents who both are active endurance sport competitors. While at the IRONMAN Texas expo, I was located next to a booth managed by an endurance sport couple. The man and woman were dating and both had children from previous marriages. Neither individual had competed in an iron-distance race. However, they were both heavily devoted to the sport of ultrarunning, participating in events of fifty and one hundred miles. The woman was sponsored by numerous companies. While the man did not qualify for this study, I did have a chance to talk informally to both him and his partner about ultra-distance running and life as a single parent. To advance this line of research, it would be informative to sit down and conduct interviews with couples, both separately and together. Interviewing couples individually would provide researchers an opportunity to hear two sides of the story in isolation from each other. If a father indicates that he is helping out around the house, does the mother agree? Or, perhaps, is the father being too modest in his assessments? Interviewing both spouses together would provide an additional opportunity to see how the couple interacts in regard to sporting identities. Interviewing single parents, such as the individuals at my neighboring expo booth, would also be a rich extension of this research. How do single parents fit endurance sport training into their lives? Lacking the advantages of having an enabling spouse, does this population offer any unique identity-juggling practices?

Expanding on the idea of interviewing family members, future research could extend this work by capturing the voices of the children of Iron Parents. Such research would represent a valuable response to Michael Messner and Michela Musto's (2014) question: "Where are the kids?" As noted by the authors, there is a dearth of sociological literature on child participation in sport. This same vacancy in understanding, I argue, extends to children with sporting parents. As I observed the children of Iron Dads milling about at the IRONMAN Texas expo, I was reminded that these individuals are far from "hopeless spectators" (Hardman 1973). Incorporating these voices more prominently into our understanding of sport and family leisure time would be a powerful asset. Projects exploring the lives of Iron Kids could include capturing the perspectives of both younger and older children. Such research could also help us understand pathways to youth participation in triathlon. What factors help explain why some children of Iron Parents participate in triathlon while other kids elect to sit on the sideline? How do children of different ages conceptualize the impact of training on the family? When and where do they experience family bonding through training? Does observing a parent train for and compete in endurance athletics inspire them to embrace their sporting identities more? How do they conceptualize an iron-distance competition? What do they see as their role on race day? Answering these and other related questions would allow the sociology of sport field to move beyond the adult-based paradigms that currently dominate the academic journals. As Messner and Musto (2014) suggest, such research would also foster intradisciplinary connections with other subfields such as the sociology of children and youth. Interdisciplinary connections with fields such as family studies and communication arts could also be enhanced.

With an eye towards expanding our understanding of fathering in sport and leisure contexts, another interesting extension of this research could look at Tri Dads, or fathers of kids who participate in triathlon. My research details the myriad of ways that Iron Dads influence their children. Through generative practices, these fathers seek to teach their kids about the values of living a healthy lifestyle. Looking more holistically, the direction of influence in a father-child relationship is two-way. To gain a more complete painting of this picture would mean better understanding how sporting children influence their parents. A few possible permutations of future research emerge here. Naturally, some Iron Dads are also Tri Dads; however, not all Tri Dads are Iron Dads (or even triathletes/athletes). How does the sporting background of a Tri Dad shape the experiences that he has with his athletic child? To what extent are non-athletic Tri Dads influenced by their athletic children to live a healthier lifestyle? How do athletic children perceive the role that their fathers should have in their triathlon careers? What do those perceptions mean for the ways that Tri Dads internalize their roles as fathers? Future studies could also embrace a longitudinal approach to understanding the dynamic nature of sporting identities. My research entailed talking to athletes at a single point in time. It would be interesting to follow up with these individuals over the course of many years. For example, some Iron Dads anticipated shelving the idea of competing until their children got older. Does this delay in participation actually occur? If so, how does the athlete's identity change over that time span? Ultimately, is the athlete's life as balanced as he imagined it to be upon moving from the 140.6 to 70.3 distance—or in abandoning rigorous triathlon training completely?

Finally, the study of professional triathletes presents a particularly ripe area for future research. Professional athletes face unique issues when it comes to juggling family and sporting identities. This is because, fundamentally, their sporting identities are their professional identities. The pressure to win could compel athletes to push their bodies to unhealthy levels. Studying elite athletes may also reveal some unique approaches not only to training, but also to issues of generativity, safety, nutrition, and finances. Very few triathlons offer lucrative professional payouts.[2] Given that triathlon is still regarded by some as a fringe sport, the opportunities for athlete sponsorship are not that vast. How do professional triathletes with children deal with this lack of financial payout? How do they manage economic risk?

Ultra-Distance Triathlon Competitors

When talking about endurance sport, it is important to acknowledge the growing popularity of ultra-distance races. In triathlon, there are opportunities to compete in events longer than 140.6 miles in distance. The Ultraman is an event consisting of a 6.2-mile swim, 261.4-mile bike, and 52.4-mile run. This 320-mile race spans across three days as participants move from stage to stage. The race organizers describe the event as the "odyssey of personal rediscovery." Acceptance is very competitive, with only forty participants being selected per race venue. Each application is thoroughly screened by the race directors before an event invitation is extended. The Ultraman has some striking similarities to IRONMAN. These similarities include a qualification-centered World Championship event in Hawaii, strictly enforced cut-offs for each event segment, and an increasingly visible following. Like IRONMAN, Ultraman continues to expand in both scope and popularity. A new Ultraman race made its debut in Florida in February 2014.

Ultraman presents sociologists with a ripe area for investigating questions related to pleasure, pain, sport and family life, and class. These men and women are training for an event that is more than double the distance of a standard iron-distance event. With entry costing $1,800, the financial commitment is approximately three times that of an IRONMAN-branded race. While no scholarly research to date has examined the lives of Ultraman competitors, we can reasonably speculate that the emotional and physical commitment is substantial. How much more do these competitors have to train, compared with athletes preparing for a 140.6 event? What does this training mean for life at home and in the workplace? The answers may not be that intuitive. Ultraman is an interesting area of study because it is extremely self-selecting. In order to be considered for admission to an event, Ultra applicants must have completed at least one iron-distance in the previous eighteen months. It is possible that in getting to that level of competition, athletes have already figured out mechanisms for successfully juggling their responsibilities. Unlike this project, there will be no first-time iron-distance competitors in the field. My study even had some instances where a participant's upcoming 140.6 was going to be his first triathlon. Ultra-distance competitors have already experienced the growing pains of making it through an iron-distance event. In that sense, they represent a more seasoned crew of athletes. What does that mean for their lives as parents, spouses, workers, and athletes? To what extent can these findings be applied to other super-long-distance sport contexts, such as brevet cycling rides (typically 200 km or more) or ultrarunning events (50 km or more)?

For family sociologists, Ultraman has another unique dimension that begs to be studied—the participants' crews. Each athlete is required to have at least two adults serving as crew members. The maximum number is four. An unscientific browsing of online discussions suggests that many athletes ask family members to crew. This could be an interesting source of reverse generativity—examples where sons and daughters attempt to expose their parents to a particular lifestyle. As mentioned earlier in the chapter, this Iron Dad research is dedicated to looking at more traditional views of generativity, instances where a father attempts to instill certain values in his children. Is it possible for sport to foster practices of reverse generativity? Sociologists could explore, for example, whether the ultra-distance crewing experience serves as a medium for such practices.

Theoretical Expansion

This research introduces the new concepts of sporting guilt, the athletic visibility continuum, and balancing mechanisms. In describing these concepts, I aimed to make them as transportable as possible to other social contexts. It is my hope that other scholars in fields pertaining to sport and society, as well as other areas of sociological inquiry, can advance these ideas.

The athletic visibility continuum is a concept that can be applied to virtually any sport or leisure context. An interesting take on this would be to explore how dual-athlete couples mutually manage their space on this continuum. How do dual-athlete couples deal with the issue of training obtruding on other areas of life? Under what conditions do sporting couples make their athletics visible at the same time? Do particular sport and leisure contexts make it easier to have a more visible athletic identity? Future research could also consider the role of training partners in co-constructing one's placement on the continuum. Athletes likely interact with other athletic-minded people as part of their identity construction. In this vein, to what extent do athletes with training partners perceive accountability with others? How does this perception influence one's self-placement on the athletic visibility continuum? Finally, a fascinating line of research would be to explore the ways in which the athletic visibility continuum intersects with identities and standpoints not discussed in this book. This research was informed by Iron Dads, fathers juggling work and sport. Do different patterns emerge among mothers? How about among individuals of various faith groups? A similar call for theoretical expansion applies to the concept of sporting guilt. How do social demographics such as race and class influence how sporting guilt is internalized and managed? What novel dimensions of sporting guilt emerge in different leisure contexts? How does this guilt relate to risk in sport? Over the past few decades, extreme sports such as rope-free climbing and BASE jumping have gained substantial followings (Brymer 2010; Pain and Pain 2005). How does participating in such activities shape the way that athletes internalize sporting guilt?

There is also ample room for expanding our understanding of balancing mechanisms. Future research should expand the conception of time and space in the construction of balancing mechanisms. Generally, I found that balancing mechanisms tend to fall under two themes— compromising with family and enabling family involvement. What other relevant themes can be uncovered? How do the characteristics of specific sociological contexts or unique sportscapes influence the ways we balance multiple identities? Are the processes through which balancing mechanisms are identified and utilized different for members of under-privileged groups? If so, how?

Policy Advice for Race Directors

This study was conducted within the confines of a particular time window. Where will long-course triathlon go from here? Fortunately for partici-pants and fans of the sport, the long-term health of endurance racing looks positive. Mike Reilly forecasts:

> I think it's going to be very strong a few years down the line. We're still now getting—in this race alone in Texas—we've got almost 800 first-time IRONMAN athletes. Every IRONMAN race now, espe-cially in the U.S., we're carrying between 800 and 1,000 first-timers. That's not going to go away. And the ones that are doing the race, sure you have some that check off IRONMAN on a bucket-list deal, but most don't. Most, once they become a triathlete, they stay a triathlete. They always have the swim, bike, run between their ears. If they don't do an IRONMAN, what they do is maybe every three years they do one. So I see the sport being very healthy for a lot of years to come.

In order for the sport to sustain and be a positive experience for com-petitors, race directors need to do more to accommodate families. We already see some market challengers stepping up to the plate in this regard. In the section that follows, I offer some race policy and event-management advice for race directors.

Refund and Transfer Policies

Race directors need to be sensitive to their clientele. At the time that inter-views for this project were conducted, World Triathlon Corporation had a very limited refund policy for its events. Competitors could request what was referred to as a "standard refund." If registration withdrawal was requested two months or more in advance of the event date, the athlete was entitled to a $150 refund. That means that athletes stood to lose around $550 on regular registration rates. Numerous Iron Dads reported that this policy was not thoughtful. Competitors and their families experience train-ing disruptions such as the birth of a child, losing a job, or getting injured. Others come to grips with the idea that training for the distance requires too much attention. Of further concern is that WTC's standard refund policy may result in athletes competing when they may have preferred not to start the race. A few study participants commented that they had injuries but felt compelled to give the race a go because of the financial commitment already made. Instead of seeing the situation as getting $150 back, these athletes were focused on the financial loss. This suggests that a $150 refund is not compelling enough to pull the plug, given everything else that competitors have invested. Smaller-market challengers have room to shine in this regard.

In 2014, World Triathlon Corporation showed the initiative to advance a more progressive withdrawal policy. It introduced a North American Transfer Program, a concept that was fully launched in 2015. In addition to the standard refund policy of $150, athletes now have the option to transfer their entries to alternative North American 140.6 or 70.3 events in that same calendar year. A transfer fee of $50 is required. There are some notable caveats with this program. First, an event must be open for general registration for at least ten days prior to accepting transfers. This renders many popular events ineligible because they fill in less than ten days. Second, athletes can only transfer to events offered in the same calendar year. This means that individuals seeking to transfer out of late-season races have limited or no alternative options to turn to. Individuals registered for these races would likely have to compete in an event scheduled earlier in the calendar year. If the reason for the transfer request is an injury or a life-changing event, competing earlier may not be possible. It does not help that some of the last races in the calendar year, such as IRONMAN Cozumel and IRONMAN 70.3 Miami, are currently ineligible for the transfer program.

The introduction of this transfer program has been applauded by many in the triathlon circle. One blogger commented that the program "shows that they [WTC] are starting to care for their customers." Another stated that "as long as athletes get some more flexibility, then it is a good trend."[3] Providing additional registration options, however limited, is an enhancement. Currently, the transfer policy only applies to athletes registered for full-distance races. These competitors have a choice of transferring to either a full-distance or half-distance event.

Offering athletes the opportunity to move to a shorter distance is a big positive of the policy. Individuals who find the demands of iron-distance training to be overwhelming can now salvage an alternative racing opportunity with their original entry fee. Further, recall that event popularity necessitates individuals to sign up for many races one year in advance. Competitors who are suddenly faced with an unanticipated date conflict, such as friend's wedding or school reunion party, can shift the timing of their event. Further, athletes who experience heavy demands at work could elect to push back their event date. This policy allows for some maneuverability, giving individuals critical flexibility in deciding what aspects of their life should take priority and when.

In 2015, World Triathlon Corporation rolled out its new Full Refund Plan on 140.6 and 70.3 entries.[4] Athletes can purchase insurance on full-distance events for $90 and on half-distance events for $40, paid at the time of event registration. The nature of the coverage is outlined on the WTC website: "You may receive a full refund of the registration fees you paid if you are unable to participate due to an injury, illness, pregnancy or childbirth, unanticipated active duty deployment, unexpected covered travel delays, a family member's pregnancy or childbirth, a family member's loss of life, injury or illness."[5] The combination of the transfer program and refund plan offers WTC athletes much-needed flexibility with their race registration. Competitors seeking withdrawal are no longer stuck with swallowing all but $150 of their registration fee. This is an excellent evolution in registration policy. With that said, there are additional improvements that can make these registration refund and transfer policies even more athlete-friendly.[6]

1. Make the Transfer Program Valid for Twelve Calendar Months As mentioned, as the program currently stands, individuals registered for a late-season 140.6 may be left with no open races to transfer to. The program's policy specifies that in order to be eligible for a transfer, athletes must contact WTC no less than forty-five days before their event. For competitors registered for IRONMAN Florida, an event that takes place on the first Saturday of November, transfers must be requested by mid-September. Individuals registered for IRONMAN Arizona, an event that takes place later in November, must contact WTC by early October. At present, there are no mid-to-late November or December options for athletes seeking a later-season transfer. One way to address this limitation would be to make the transfer window valid for a full twelve months from the event withdrawal deadline. Instead of going by the calendar year—an approach that distinctly disadvantages athletes registered for late-season races—such a change would increase the flexibility that the program offers to athletes.

2. Expand the Transfer Program to Include 70.3 Registrants and Allow Upgrades The current program only provides opportunities for athletes seeking to transfer out of a full-distance event. These athletes can either transition to a different 140.6 race or to an open 70.3 event. Transfer from one 70.3 to another 70.3 should be permitted. Transfer from a 70.3 to a 140.6 would also be a welcomed enhancement. It is possible that an athlete's training could go better than expected. Such an individual may decide in the middle of the season, after race entry fees have already been committed, to take on a more substantial distance. The Rock 'n' Roll Marathon Series and the Baltimore Marathon offer strong models in this regard. By paying the difference in price between the shorter and longer events, plus an upgrade fee (for Rock 'n' Roll only), athletes can move from the half to the full marathon.[7] The fact that these events are road races should not preclude organizers of long-course triathlons from considering such policies. As it applies to WTC's North American Transfer Program, as long as slots are available, the opportunity to upgrade would provide athletes with more racing options. From a business perspective, it would also be more lucrative for the company. Athletes looking to upgrade would be filling slots at more expensive race entry points. Notably, for a processing fee of $25, Baltimore Marathon and Half Marathon competitors can defer their entry to the subsequent year. Their transfer and deferral options represent an extremely athlete-friendly combination—one that should be considered by all endurance sport event organizers.

3. Allow Transfers between Athletes Allowing athletes to defer their registration to the following year is a policy move that would give athletes the ultimate flexibility in making choices about their participation in sport. Practically speaking, instituting such a policy is undoubtedly easier said than done. The number of entrants into an IRONMAN-branded race is very tightly controlled—and with good reason. From an organizational perspective, having a highly fluctuating number of participants in a race with such challenging logistics and costs is undesirable. For this reason, allowing transfers between athletes presents a healthy middle ground for all parties. The Marine Corps Marathon (MCM) has an outstanding model in this regard. In 2015, athletes currently registered for the MCM could transfer their spot to another individual for a $50 administrative fee. The onus is on the registered athlete to find someone to complete the transfer with. The marathon does not issue a refund on the original entry fee, nor does it play a role in the monetary negotiation between the transferor and transferee. Instead, the marathon keeps the original entry fee and lets the transferring runners figure out the financial transaction themselves. Such a program does not result in a fluctuating number of participants, a major organizational positive. Instituting this type of program is a strong middle ground between allowing athlete deferrals and having no such policy at all.

4. Make the Insurance More Affordable While the introduction of WTC's insurance policy was welcomed by many athletes, the $90 price point may be financially limiting for some. Registration for WTC events are subject to additional fees. As an example, competitors registering for IRONMAN Chattanooga 2015 paid $685.00 for general entry, $41.10 in Active (the online registration management system) fees, and $12 for a one-day USA Triathlon license (assuming they did not have an annual membership to the organization). With a grand total of $738.10 staring them in the face, they could find the idea of shelling out an additional $90, or 12 percent, to be unpalatable. For those saving every penny to have the opportunity to compete, the $90 fee may simply not be an option at the time of event registration. Perhaps the current price is the most competitive one that WTC could identify among select insurance providers. I recognize that event organizers are dealing with a third party, and for that reason, cannot control pricing. With that said, I suggest that, to the fullest extent possible, this policy price point be reviewed and shopped among other insurance companies.

A good model for race insurance is currently offered by Sun Multisport Events (SME), a triathlon event production team from New England. It hosts events such as the Patriot Half Iron, the Cranberry Trifest, and the New England Trifest. At one point, SME offered a 100 percent reimbursement on race registration fees if a competitor could not start due to sickness or injury. As an incentive to attract early registration to its events, it offered this feature as a complimentary perk for those signing up for the race at least six months in advance. As SME concluded, such a generous policy can be prohibitively expensive for a smaller race management organization. In 2014, SME transitioned to a slightly different yet still generous registration policy.[8] If a refund is requested sixty days or more prior to the event, the athlete is issued a full refund minus a $25 processing fee. Within a forty-five-day window, for a $25 administrative fee, competitors can defer to the next year. Within a thirty-day window, they can transfer to another SME event.

It goes without saying that the ability to receive close to a full refund, without the need to file an insurance claim, is extremely athlete-centered. Challenge Penticton offers such a policy, refunding participants their registration payment, minus a $75 administration fee, if withdrawal happens at least sixty days prior to the event. This policy is sensitive to the idea that the world keeps turning after someone has registered for a race. Such a refund policy is hard to find in the triathlon market. For this reason, I suggest that consumers consider the importance of such a policy before registering for a 140.6 event. While most race organizers do not offer generous refund terms, a small minority do.[9]

Including Family-Centered Expo Events

Sporting events of all types should be sensitive to competitors with families. There are numerous examples of family-friendly races in the United States. Race directors looking to expand their offerings would do well to reflect on these more progressive family-centered models. One outstanding template for expo activities can be found at the Philadelphia Marathon. In the past, its two-day Health and Fitness Expo featured a "kids' fun zone." Programming for the pre-race festivities included storytelling, kids' yoga, and fitness fun. The events are all conducted by owners of local businesses. For example, in 2012, Monica Kriso of Monica Kriso Yoga conducted a yoga session. Martha Cooney of StoryUp offered a storytelling workshop. This type of family-centered expo model has multiple benefits. First, it gets the children involved in the race experience. Second, it also allows local businesses to have a unique presence in the pre-race festivities. It welcomes businesses that may not typically cater to marathoners to share the same stage as those in the running industry. The Philadelphia Marathon serves as an excellent model for another reason: the race festivities also included a kids' fun run. Race directors should think beyond their main event and consider peripheral family entertainment and events. This leads to a happy clientele, positive word of mouth, and the potential shaping of future competitors—the kids!

As another example of having an enhanced family-friendly expo, race directors should be sensitive to surrounding holidays. In the past, Rev3's event in Florida took place just before Halloween. In 2014, the event was moved to later in the calendar year. With its original late October date, the event management team provided trick-or-treating opportunities. Here is an excerpt from the athlete guide:

> Happy Halloween everyone!! We all know Halloween is not until the 31st but we want to celebrate early and give the kiddies an extra chance to sport their costumes. On Saturday October 27 we will be doing an expo TRICK OR TREAT. We want to encourage all kids (and adults) to dress up in your costumes and trick or treat in our expo. Every single tent will be a stopping point where they will be handing out candy and other fun goodies. Come out and have some fun before your race. We will do prizes for the best and most original costumes, bring the kids for some Halloween fun!!

That same year, WTC got into the action by adding a trick-or-treat component to its IRONKIDS Panama City Fun Run. While triathlon race directors are primarily focused on executing a safe and successful event, integrating surrounding holidays and/or cultural events enhances the race experience for families. A few of my study participants talked about how disappointed their kids were when they learned that travel plans to IRONMAN Florida would disrupt family trick-or-treating rituals. In other words, to kids, opportunities to trick-or-treat are not peripheral.

Finish-Line Chute Policy

With IRONMAN race popularity growing, WTC officials made the difficult choice of revisiting their finish-line policy in 2009. In years past, athletes and their families were allowed to cross the finish line together. Volunteers would also hold tape across the finish line, allowing each individual athlete (and family) to feel like a champion as they "cut the tape." As events grew in size, the organization determined that such a policy no longer was in the best interest of the competitors. The finish line became a congested place. Parents collecting their children and entering the race course in the final yards not only impeded the progress of other athletes but also caused safety concerns. Altering the finish-line policy is always a sensitive topic. This goes with the territory—the finish line represents a cherished place. Given the current size of finish-line chutes at WTC events, and the size of the competition field, the changes in policy make sense. We see that more than 3,000 bibs are now being issued for some branded events. For example, the bib list for IRONMAN Florida 2014, issued one month prior to the event, reflected 3,064 athlete slots issued. It is dangerous to have families interrupting a constant stream of athletes crossing the finish line. While eliminating families from the finish chute may not have been a universally popular choice for WTC, it was certainly a practical one.

Finish-line chute policy is an area where smaller events have more flexibility. Some independent 140.6 races may feature a competition field of 800 to 1,000 people, if that. The HITS Series, as an example, has numbers in the low double-digits for some of their full-distance races. Smaller fields mean less congestion in key areas. Whereas WTC designates many spaces as being off-limits to families (such as transition zones and post-race food tents), smaller independent races should feel empowered to expand on the concept of family space. The Challenge Family's races do just that. They allow families and friends to cross the finish line together.

Events with smaller fields can integrate families into the racing experience in other creative ways. When Rev3 was an independent entity, to highlight its family-friendly approach, it hosted an annual "Finisher Photo Contest." Here, Rev3 staff selected their two favorite finish-line photographs—one of an individual and one of a family. The website discussed the contest:

> Rev3 staff will choose a selection of our favorite FAMILY finisher photos and a selection of our favorite individual athlete finisher photos. Once we have chosen the top pictures, we will post these to our Facebook account and have our fan base vote on their top pick. The winning family and winning individual will receive free

entry into a Rev3 race of their choice and potentially a leading role in one of our magazine ads. So get creative—bring your pets, friends, family, or random strangers you meet along the course and cheese it up!!

From its inception, the Finisher Photo Contest was a hit. Athletes uploaded their photos to the Rev3 Facebook page, creating an album that could be shared. In one submission from the 70.3 event in Williamsburg, Virginia, a man posed at the finish line with his two boys. One boy was dressed as Superman, the other as Batman (capes and all). Another photograph featured a soon-to-be Iron Dad kissing the belly of his pregnant partner. This contest was a creative way to enhance the family experience. Families planned finish-line poses, dances, and costumes. The fact that each athlete received a free finish-line photograph promoted a culture of sharing this accomplishment with others. The photo contest has not been offered since 2013. Revival of this contest is recommended.

Advice for Iron Parents

As an athlete, one should take the time to consider details such as finish-line chute and refund policies. My research shows that Iron Dads put a lot of consideration into picking a race venue. They consider factors such as the event's time of year and attractiveness as a destination. With that, however, I suggest that competitors also consider the family-centered nature of the event. Some competitors already do this to a degree, but smaller details may elude first-time athletes. Events with larger competition fields require stricter policies when it comes to traffic control. WTC events, by necessity, exemplify this. Only athletes are allowed in the bib pick-up tent, transition (both before and on race day), the finish-line chute, and the finish-line tents. These traffic-control policies can be disruptive to the family experience. As numerous study participants pointed out, bigger events offer many luxuries. Having more volunteers and athletes to interact with is appealing to many. However, this increased volume of people comes with consequences. Athletes should feel empowered to pick events that best suit their desired experience.

In this vein, the world of iron-distance triathlon has benefited from the emergence of market competition. As previously mentioned, HITS Endurance and the TOUGHMAN series of races now share in that market. Prior to its brief one-year merger with the Challenge Family of races in 2015, Rev3 situated itself in the triathlon market as the "Family Friendly Experience." The business's website had a section specifically dedicated to family. This digital area featured a photograph of a father and his three young children crossing the finish line at one of their events. The caption read, "Family friendly events for everyone! Pros and age groupers." For those with concerns about the family experience, Rev3 demonstrated a progressive business model. Time will reveal if, upon returning to its own independent brand in 2016, Rev3 will elect to advance this model.

Digital technology is making it easier than ever for competitors to express their desires to race organizers. Recent groundswells that started in online environments have led to offline corporate action. One example is an op-ed written by Slowtwitch.com owner Dan Empfield. Dan, also a prominent player in the bike industry, wrote a blog entry called "A Civil Transfer Policy" (Empfield 2012). The op-ed was written in response to a blog post in which a fellow forum member discussed the illegal transfer of a bib. Empfield suggests that we have reached a point in the industry where bib transfers are no longer the "administrative nightmare" that they once were. "A happy ending" to the illegal bib transfer quandary, Empfield suggests, "would be a civilized transfer policy" (Empfield 2012). Just after the op-ed was published, Active.com, an event registration company that World Triathlon Corporation works with, announced the introduction of a new race registration insurance policy. Two years later, WTC announced the implementation of its own refund and transfer policy programs. While we will never know the real extent to which this online debate, specifically, prompted reform, the timing of such policy changes certainly raises an eyebrow. Iron Parents should feel empowered to shape their triathlon community by vocalizing their needs. Race production companies, including the larger players in the industry, are listening.

APPENDIX
Methodological Reflections

Being Reflective

Every year, I talk to my sophomore-level research methods class about the joys of social science research. The students enjoy when I share my experiences in the field for various projects. Among other populations, I have interviewed presidential campaign staff members, faculty at Research I institutions, female professional cyclists, and, of course, Iron Dads. My students inevitably get excited at the idea of popping out of their chairs and interviewing members of our university community. "Not so fast," I caution them. I liken research methodology to inflating a balloon. The air must be injected judiciously. Hasty enthusiasm does not lend itself well to good methodological practice. After all, nobody likes a popped balloon.

As social scientists, we have the rewarding task of studying fellow human beings. We observe, question, and measure behavior in a wide variety of social settings. I love my job for this exact reason. However, the joys of the job can also serve as the source of great pause. Studying fellow human beings is a complicated endeavor. In so doing, to varying degrees, we are studying the self. This is especially true when we attempt to study communities to which we currently belong. This phenomenon leads us to an interesting methodological puzzle. How can we, as objectively as possible, study the self? Is objectivity even possible? These are the questions that I asked myself as I entered the throes of iron-distance triathlon as a researcher. I decided that, while the challenge this puzzle presented was real, it was one worth taking on for both personal and professional reasons.

Identifying the Question

Through my experience with endurance sport, I learned just how closely iron-distance training resembles work. Training feels like a full-time job. At various points in my athletic career, I have paid for a professional coach to tell me how to train on a daily basis, communicating through an online training program called TrainingPeaks. The coach outlines training distance and intensity, and after executing the session, I write about my workout in the program. He holds me accountable if I miss a session. I have to explain why the workout did not happen. Having to justify athletic non-performance seems to transcend the boundary between "play" and "work." Executing workouts when you would rather be in bed or spending time with family also seems to speak to this blurred boundary.

I have also trained for iron-distance racing as a self-coached athlete, following a twenty-week plan that I located online. Even though a coach was no longer in the equation, I still felt a strong sense of obligation to complete each workout. Even when my daily activities seemed to consume every waking moment, I challenged myself to make time to complete my training. This could have meant getting up earlier than usual, pushing myself to be more time efficient in my other activities, or staying up late to accomplish my training. Again I noticed how much, and how easily, iron-distance "play" became iron-distance "work." Based on a combination of informal conversations and pilot interviews with other competitors, I have learned that most athletes who train for this distance either hire a coach or follow a pre-constructed training plan. Workouts seemed to become mandatory. Regardless of weather, desire, or personal conflicts, one constant remained—the training plan. I found this sense of "mandatory" activity caused a constant tension between training and other priorities in my life, particularly family and work.

Since my first 140.6-distance race in 2009, I have come to feel that the greatest difficulty in my iron-distance training is negotiating my relationship with my husband. There are numerous weekends where I go out for an all-day training session. I leave well before my husband gets out of bed and feel guilty knowing that he will wake up to an empty house. Additionally, I feel guilty knowing that he is constantly worrying about my safety. I have been involved in two cycling accidents since starting my career in endurance athletics. Despite being extremely cautious about how, where, and when I ride, accidents happen. While training for a long-course triathlon in 2010, I went down on uneven pavement just a few weeks before the event. On another occasion, while in graduate school, I was hit by a turning vehicle. Telling my husband, who happened to be 1,100 miles away from me at the time, was one of the hardest things I had to do. I subsequently came to wonder how other athletes dealt with this safety issue, particularly parents who know that they have children waiting at home. One of my study participants suggested that there are two types of cyclists—those who have been in a crash and those who will. I began to wonder if parents alter the way they train, knowing that the risk of injury is a real one.

My interest in studying Iron Parents grew as I wondered how mothers and fathers wrestled with these types of concerns. In my circumstance, daily negotiations with my husband involve two adults. Adding a dependent into the mix changes the equation. How do parents do it? Why do they do it, given the complexity and dependence of a child? How does the experience of training for a 140.6 event shape their identity as parents? How does being a parent shape their relationship with sport? In what ways do spouses support their partners during endurance triathlon training? Up until the publication of this work, sociologists had yet to address these questions.

In considering what type of parents I wanted to study, I decided to narrow my scope to fathers. There is a dire need for further scholarship in the field of fatherhood. I felt that this work represented a substantial contribution in that regard. Further, I felt that the narratives offered by Iron Dads may differ—likely substantially—from those presented by Iron Moms. I wanted to dedicate this work to exploring fathers' voices. Future work can focus on Iron Moms and Iron couples, respectively.[1]

As someone who made it to the iron-distance finish line numerous times, I understand the challenges that come with the race distance. My preparation for my first 140.6 race took more than a year, sacrificing my relationships, work, and a sizable amount of money. This and other experiences positioned me in a unique place as a researcher. I have perspective on what it takes to reach this goal. I also maintain an active presence on numerous triathlon blogs. These forums provided a rich recruiting pool for this study. My racing background supplied me with an understanding of the language participants may use when discussing the sport. Finally, being an active triathlete offered me perspective on the type of questions to ask participants in my attempt to better understand the relationship between fatherhood and sport. Due to my own training experience, I am intimately familiar with the details of preparing for a race of this magnitude. These intricacies could potentially be overlooked by someone not intimately familiar with the sport. I found it incredibly exciting to research something about which I was knowledgeable and passionate (endurance triathlon), but to which I was an outsider in many regards (parenting and fatherhood).

Recruitment Strategies

This research employed two main recruitment strategies. To begin, participants were recruited via two popular triathlon blog sites, Slowtwitch.com (ST) and Beginnertriathlete.com (BT). Second, participants were recruited at the 2012 IRONMAN Texas Exposition. I also interviewed one race director and one endurance triathlon industry employee, Mike Reilly. One final participant, Dick Hoyt, was interviewed because of his status as a pioneering Iron Dad. Dick and Rick Hoyt are a father-and-son team who compete to share their inspirational "Yes You Can!" message around the world. Dick and his son, a quadriplegic, have competed in more than 1,000 endurance events, including a remarkable six iron-distance triathlons. I met Dick unexpectedly in a hotel hallway while at the 2012 Disney Marathon. This chance encounter inspired me to reach out to him regarding my book. After telling him about my study, he agreed to participate in this research. In all, fifty men participated in this research. Thirty-two men were recruited via the Internet, fifteen from my booth at IRONMAN Texas, and three for their unique positions in the endurance sport industry—one of whom was an Iron Dad that who did not meet all of the study parameters.

Blogosphere Recruitment

The ST and BT blog sites complement each other because, generally speaking, they cater to different groups of long-course athletes. ST is typically geared toward more seasoned competitors, including elite age-group athletes and professionals. This is evident in the fact that the blog threads often focus on more nuanced training and racing questions. By comparison, BT is an attractive blog outlet for triathletes who are just getting into long-course triathlon. This is evident with website features such as training support groups and forums for beginners. Collectively, these sites attract participants competing at different stages in their endurance triathlon career.

Seven pilot-study participants were recruited via ST during the winter of 2009. My call for participants on this site yielded an overwhelming response, with more than fifty men expressing interest in the study. An additional twenty-six Iron Dads were recruited via BT in the fall of 2011 and spring of 2012. Due to this overwhelming response, I felt no need to return to ST for further recruitment.

Both BT and ST receive a sizable amount of web traffic, making them ideal places to recruit study participants. These websites are also growing exponentially, pointing to the booming interest in triathlon. Take ST as an example. On May 28, 2012, the main triathlon forum on the website featured 2,830,782 posts in 204,997 threads. Fast-forward just over three years. On July 2, 2015, ST featured 3,830,962 posts in 262,532 threads in just the main triathlon forum—a post increase of over 35 percent and thread increase of slightly more than 28 percent.[2] Additional forums, such as the women's and classified sections, further add to the vibrancy of this website.

As a measure of relative digital influence, we can see where each of these pages fall on Google's PageRank site-ranking system. On both May 28, 2012, and October 5, 2013, Slowtwitch.com scored a Google ranking of five out of ten. Beginnertriathlete.com scored a ranking of four out of ten on May 28, 2012, then it increased to a five out of ten on October 5, 2013. This means that while Beginnertriathlete.com may have been slightly less traveled than Slowtwitch a few years ago, it has come closer to parity as of late. The USA Triathlon website has also seen an uptick in popularity over the past few years. That site's rankings jumped from a six out of ten in 2012 to a seven out of ten in 2014. These trends point to two things. First, an increasing number of people are visiting triathlon-related websites. Second, both recruitment blog sites are less traveled than triathlon's governing body site. This serves as an important methodological indication that not all individuals interested in triathlon visit blogs related to the sport, a concern that will be elaborated on later in this appendix.

To alert bloggers to my research, a study recruitment posting was issued on both BT and ST. Potential participants expressed their interest in the study by either sending me a personal message (PM) on the blog or by posting a response in the call for participants thread. Most individuals contacted me directly via personal message through the site. I already had an established presence on these online forums.

Ironman Location Recruitment

As a second recruitment strategy, I met study participants at the 2012 Memorial Hermann IRONMAN Texas exposition. This annual event takes place in The Woodlands, a suburb of Houston. My experience at the exposition is discussed below.

In-Person Interviews

In-person interviews took place on site during the exposition dates prior to the race. I secured a booth with a small research grant awarded from what has since been renamed as the Carol A. Ammon College of Liberal Arts and Sciences at Central Connecticut State University (CCSU). The booth was open from May 16 through May 18, 9:00 A.M. to 4:00 P.M. each day. All race participants were required to attend the expo in order to pick up their race materials. Competitors would then spend time browsing the various booths, a pre-race highlight for many athletes. Approximately 2,700 athletes registered for IRONMAN Texas that year, with men making up approximately 70 percent of the field. The race attracted a diverse blend of first-time competitors and more-seasoned veterans.

I submitted a successful application for a CCSU Dean's Research Initiative Grant in the spring of 2012. The funds were awarded in March 2012 and expired on June 15 of the same year. This gave me a very limited window of opportunity to travel. Looking at the domestic full-distance triathlon circuit, this money only allowed me to attend one of two WTC races: IRONMAN St. George or IRONMAN Texas. I elected to go to Texas because of its deeper field (2,700 athletes as compared with 1,400). Due to its difficulty level, the event in St. George also attracted a more seasoned competitor base. I felt that Texas would offer a more diverse blend of athlete experience levels.

Having a presence at the expo booth provided a number of unanticipated advantages for this research. When the Iron Dads came up to talk with me, sometimes their families would join them. This allowed me to view family dynamics in action. I could read the body language of the family members as the father replied to my questions. Sometimes the wife jumped into the conversation. One very memorable instance of this exact scenario stands out. I was finishing up an interview with a first-time 140.6 competitor. I asked the Iron Dad if he anticipated competing in an iron-distance triathlon again after Texas. The man hesitated as he reflected on my question. Without missing a beat, the wife jumped in and answered, "No way. This is it for him." The father looked at me with a smirk. Managing the booth also allowed me to see how the race exposition can become part of the overall family experience.

I looked for visual clues to help with my question prioritization. For example, a father approached my booth with his wife and two sons. I noticed that his older son was wearing a T-shirt bearing a logo from a religious group. The wife was wearing a necklace with a cross. These artifacts both hinted at the idea that religion likely played a prominent role in the life of this particular family. I decided to pursue a line of questioning surrounding religion and training with the Iron Dad, a decision that turned out to be very rewarding. The father went on to speak extensively about his relationship with a Christian athletic training group.

There were a few challenges that were unique to the exposition setting. The expo took place just before the IRONMAN event itself. I was sensitive to the idea that competitors would want to get off of their feet and out of the ninety-degree heat. I offered participants a chair under an awning, but all of the competitors with family present declined to sit down. Given these factors, the interviews were considerably shorter than those conducted over the telephone. Additionally, it was challenging to administer Institutional Review Board consent. Some men came up to me and just started talking, effectively ignoring the clipboards containing consent forms, as did some mothers. In these instances, I had to find an opportunity to interrupt and ask for consent. Finally, some fathers were clearly overwhelmed with attempting to manage their kids at the expo. A few individuals stopped to talk with me but were obviously distracted by their young children. In these instances, I kept the interview very brief.

Interview Protocol

While it was difficult at times to accomplish, all participants were administered informed consent. Given the geographical diversity of bloggers, all interviews with men recruited online took place over the phone. For these interviews, I read the informed consent statement prior to proceeding with my questions. For the interviews that took place in Texas, participants were given a hard copy to read and sign. All study participants gave me permission to tape-record the conversation. I used a Sony ICD-MX20 with Dragon Speaking Naturally voice recognition software. With the aid of this software, I transcribed the first twenty interviews verbatim. A professional transcriptionist, as well as a student research assistant, transcribed the remainder.

Prior to the start of each interview, I reminded the participant about the purpose of this research. Based on language from the online recruitment posting, many of the participants from triathlon blogs were already somewhat familiar with this purpose. I wrote interview notes at the conclusion of each conversation. Memos are a key part of grounded theory analysis (Strauss and Corbin 1998). They challenge the researcher to consider the data on a theoretical level and aid in the construction of categories. The memoing process included details such as the setting in which the interview took place (if done in person), how I felt conducting the interview, and major theoretical and substantive themes that arose from the participant's answers. Those themes were used to help improve my interview guide as I went along. For example, after the first seven pilot interviews, I realized that religion played an important role in the lives of some participants. I then added questions relating to training and religion. This theme turned out to hold major significance for my project.

Memos were broken down into three categories—theoretical, methodological, and personal. Theoretical notes attempted to make theoretical connections from the raw data. In the memos for my pilot interviews, my notes were quite unrefined. My theoretical connections became more refined as I went along. Methodological memos reflected my thinking about the actual procedure of conducting this study. This is where the concept of memos providing an "audit trail" becomes extremely important (Lincoln and Guba 1985; Bowen 2009). In this regard, the memos served as a written memory, documenting where I have been. They reminded me of my logic as to why I made a particular project design change. Finally, personal memos detailed my reflections on topics not specific to theoretical or methodological issues. Personal memos helped me generate insights, often in combination with my own experience, that led to new angles for interviewing and analysis.

Selecting Participants

Interested participants had to meet a few requirements in order to be included in the study. While training for their iron-distance race, a participant had to:

1. Be a father, either biological or adoptive.
2. Have at least one child under the age of twelve. Participants could be either resident or non-resident fathers.
3. Have a full-time job, either self-employed or employed with a company, while iron-distance training and racing was occurring.
4. Be currently training for a 140.6-mile triathlon, or have completed one within the past year.

Each participant requirement was based on careful consideration of who would best be able to inform this study. Integrating training with parenting young children is a complex scenario. Twelve was selected as a threshold for the child's age because at or around this age, kids start to become more self-sufficient. When children are young, negotiating childcare becomes more of a central consideration in planning out one's training. Participants included both resident and non-resident fathers. Given the growing number of non-resident fathers in the United States, studying this group of men was important. A modified interview guide was used for them.

The call for Iron Dads also asked for potential participants to have been working a full-time job while training for their 140.6-mile race. If an individual took a job after completing the race, and did not have one while training, he was not qualified to participate in this study. Interviewing triathletes with full-time jobs helped to shed light on how endurance athletes negotiate their schedules while under substantial time constraints.

Study participants did not need to be married. Two Iron Dads were separated from their wives. I asked a separate set of questions to these individuals. A number of participants spoke about how their obsessive training almost resulted in divorce. It is not unheard of that a couple has divorced over iron-distance participation. This is evident in the fact that even while married, wives of long-course triathletes will often refer to themselves as "Iron Widows." As mentioned in chapter 4, one notable discussion thread offered readers both humor and truth on the topic. Writing from the standpoint of an Iron Widow, an anonymous blogger suggested that she had become overshadowed by her spouse's training.

There was a degree of time sensitivity associated with this research. I felt early on in the project that if more than one year has lapsed since the participant's race, the father may be too far removed from the process to recall certain details accurately. I wanted to capture the emotions associated with training for the distance—emotions that can become less vivid in one's memory as time passes. For this reason, I elected to focus on athletes who were currently or recently engaged in the iron-distance training process. As it turned out, virtually all of the interview participants were current 140.6 competitors.

Creating the Interview Guide

My interview guide was structured around sensitivities to certain issues and processes specific to identity construction, masculinity, parenting, and endurance sport. Considering these "sensitizing concepts" (Van den Hoonard 1997) allowed me to focus my interview guide in a way that would be most beneficial to my research. The development of these sensitizing concepts stemmed primarily from my life experiences as an endurance athlete. Having numerous marathons and full-distance events under my belt was extremely helpful in setting this project in motion. I was even training for a 140.6 event as I wrote this manuscript. These experiences gave me first-hand knowledge of some of the issues that Iron Dads could be facing. In that sense, my background as a competitor served as a great advantage for this project. Additionally, my interview guide was shaped by my academic training in both sociology and political science. I have taken courses on gender, class, and other topics of relevance to this research. My academic background in these topics led me to consider specific academic questions or themes. The interview guide focused on three major areas:

1. Identity: How Iron Dads construct their identity as a man, father, and athlete.
2. Sport: How endurance triathlon serves as a context for identity construction.
3. Resource Management: How Iron Dads make decisions about time, money, and space.

The interview guide used in this project was not designed to be rigid. Following the grounded theory approach of Anselm Leonard Strauss and Juliet M. Corbin (1998), the guide allowed for a free-flowing dialogue to occur. Similarly, my sensitizing concepts were not firm either. As Herbert Blumer noted, scholars should use "sensitizing" concepts, not "definitive" ones (Blumer 1954; van den Hoonaard 1997). The flexibility of both the sensitizing concepts and the interview guide allowed participants to discuss topics, emotions, and experiences that were most salient to them. As such, the guide constantly evolved. It changed in response to preliminary interviews and continued to develop as participants brought up new themes that I had not anticipated. The guide was also adjusted as new sensitizing concepts arose due to my own personal experiences with endurance sport. Such flexibility aids in avoiding the closure of ideas (Blumer 1954; van den Hoonaard 1997).

In 2009, I explored the usage of these sensitizing concepts in a pilot study with seven Iron Dads. A call for participants was posted on a triathlon blog site in January 2009. Telephone interviews took place from February through late June of that year. The pilot study allowed me to assess my sensitizing concepts' suitability, consider new concepts, and refine my interview guide. A few themes that I had not previously considered came out of these interviews. These included new dimensions of personal safety and the concept of an "athlete-friendly" work environment. While I had considered the issue of safety in terms of how Iron Dads protect themselves while training and racing, I did not initially include questions about how these men communicate about their safety to their family. Some fathers noted that they trained exclusively on stationary machines, specifically trainers and treadmills, to keep themselves safe during their workouts. Fathers training out in the elements often brought cell phones with them, had designated check-in call times, or wore athlete GPS tracking devices. The discussion of an athlete-friendly workplace focused on the degree to which Iron Dads felt comfortable disclosing their identity as an endurance athlete within their work environment. This also included things like a father's willingness to take extended lunches to maximize midday training opportunities. I amended my interview guide to ask about these issues.

The pilot study also quelled my fear about the possibility of participants not talking. From my own experience as an athlete, I know how difficult it can be to manage training and a marriage. The subject is not necessarily a pleasant one to talk about, especially when it comes to reflecting on the guilt that sport may cause. I was fearful that participants would be hesitant to disclose personal details about their lives. Thankfully, to the contrary, I found that participants were eager to talk to me. Couching the conversation in the context of iron-distance triathlon seemed to spark great interest from the men. This is exemplified by a comment from my first study participant. When he answered the phone, I thanked him for his participation in the interview. He immediately responded by saying, "We are talking about triathlon. I could talk for hours."

Analytic Strategy for the In-depth Interviews

Analysis of the in-depth interviews utilized a grounded theory approach (Strauss and Corbin 1998). Grounded theory allows researchers to investigate topics without any preconceptions or hypotheses (Glaser 1992; Strauss and Corbin 1994). Given that I am neither a man nor a parent, I could only speculate about some of the topics that could be of relevance to my study participants. Through the use of constant comparisons between indicators of concepts, as well as between concepts, researchers can extract major themes that appear repeatedly (Glaser 1992). Key themes were identified through this coding process.

Following Charmaz (2006) and Strauss and Corbin (1998), I completed rounds of initial, focused, and axial coding. The construction of initial codes represented a relatively low-level analysis that was the beginning of grounded theory (Charmaz 2006).

This stage is referred to as "open coding" by a number of scholars (Glaser 1978; Strauss and Corbin 1990; 1998). It is from this stage that more sophisticated analysis is generated. This required coding the transcripts line by line (Glaser 1978). I compared incident with incident, all the while being reflexive about my research decisions (Strauss and Corbin 1990).

I believe that the general coding process for this project started on September 8, 2008—the day that I signed up for my first iron-distance triathlon. Strauss and Corbin (1998) suggest that, if used correctly, our personal experiences can help us develop sensitivity toward the research topic. My background as an endurance athlete allowed me to develop a preliminary list of open codes, the first step in the coding process. As noted by Stauss and Corbin (1998), open coding allows one to "uncover, name, and develop concepts" (102). Through this coding process, I was able to move to the conceptualization process (103).

As an example, based on my pilot interviews, one of the first open codes that I developed was managing sporting guilt—the process of managing moments where guilt due to training and racing were expressed in numerous ways. One Iron Dad, Jordan, stated, "You only get to watch them [two daughters] grow up once. I am calling it quits after IRONMAN Arizona because I have just missed way too much. I feel horrible, so I will go back to IRONMAN after they have grown up." Continuing with Strauss and Corbin's constant comparison method, this and other open codes became important sources for the emergence of categories. For example, I came to understand that the guilt management described by Jordan became evident at very specific junctures: places where sport and other spheres of life merged. The theme of sporting guilt came from a labor-intensive data-coding process. For all seven pilot interviews, each paragraph of the transcription was coded with important notations, including what the respondent was talking about and adjectives that describe the phenomenon. As I moved beyond the pilot study phase of this research, open coding of the interview transcripts became more crucial for identifying additional concepts. The language and scope of the themes I identified in my initial interviews became more sophisticated as the project went along.

Using the coding notes and memos together, findings were sorted into common themes and concepts. Many similarities between interview and blog posting data became evident as I attempted to develop a grounded theory about how men construct an Iron Dad identity.

Reflecting on My Data While Training

From the very beginning of this project I began walking, running, and biking with a tape recorder. Athletic time became thinking time. I found myself continually reflecting on my data, even when the transcripts were not in front of me. This idea was inspired by a photograph of Boston Marathon race director David McGillivray. In addition to being the race director for one of the most prestigious marathons in the world, McGillivray is also an avid triathlete, eight-time iron-distance finisher, and long-course runner. I was looking through his book a few years back (McGillivray and Fechter 2006). One of the photographs that appears in the work is of him crossing a finish line, arms raised in cheerful bliss, with a tape recorder in his left hand. A lightbulb went off in my head. I agree with Melanie Birks and Jane Mills (2011), who suggest that "analytical breakthroughs are most likely to occur when pen and computer keyboards are inaccessible"

(39). For me, these inaccessible periods included the large volume of time that I spent biking and running. Periods that I also initially viewed as inaccessible ones included driving and resting. With creativity and the help of the recorder, I was able to turn some of these inaccessible moments into accessible ones. Ultimately, having a recorder on me at all times was one of the best decisions I made during the course of this research. It meant that I was able to advance the project, even while on the go.

Connecting Teaching and Scholarship

One of the most valuable professional lessons to emerge from this project came as I reflected on how teaching and scholarly pursuits can be more fully integrated. Specifically, I considered how I could more readily bring the lessons that I learned from this project into my classroom. This was an interesting challenge. The question that I had to contend with was gauging the tolerance that my students had for hearing about my work. The answer, I concluded, rests in how the information is presented.

For professors, talking about our research with students serves as a great avenue to make various methodological challenges come alive. I often tell my research methods classes that we must practice by doing. We must be fearless in getting our hands dirty and making mistakes. What better way to lessen the anxiety of this approach than by sharing our own mistakes in the field? I came to learn that humility and humor are powerful teaching tools. A memorable moment came when I shared a brief interview exchange with my class. This interview was part of my pilot project back in 2009. A clearly nervous researcher is talking with one of her very first study participants, a man assigned the name of Mark. I ask Mark if, given all of the time that he spends training, he is able to be the father that he wants to be. "No," he replies. In a moment of indecision, I turn the interview in a different direction. Oops! Everyone in the class shares a chuckle.

While that particular classroom moment provided some laughter, conducting social science research is serious business. As academics, we are trusted with confidential information. We are then tasked with accurately and honestly reporting our findings. It is important to remember that the seriousness of these tasks does not preclude us from responsibly using this material in the classroom. We make mistakes in the field. If we are doing our job judiciously, we should be continually reflecting on these errors. My take-home lesson in this regard is that it is a rewarding venture to expose our weaknesses to our students. To this end, I encourage faculty situated at all types of institutions to reflect on how teaching and scholarship can be better connected.

Interview Guides

Guide for Married, Cohabitating Fathers

Section A: Triathlon Identity Questions

> Tell me about your background in sport. How did you get started in triathlon? Iron-distance racing?
> What does being a triathlete mean to you?
> How important is being a triathlete to you?
> What iron-distance races have you competed in?
> Why do you compete in iron-distance races?

Section B: Family Questions

Tell me about your family.

To what extent does your wife support your triathlon lifestyle?

How do you involve your family in your training and racing?

Do you feel guilty when you train and race? How do you deal with this guilt?

Are you concerned about injury? Is your family? How do you manage this concern?

Have you spoken with your family about how you can stay safe while training?

How difficult has iron-distance training been on your family life? Why has it been difficult?

How do you negotiate the expenses of iron-distance racing?

Have you ever been in a fight with your wife concerning training or racing? If so, what was the fight about?

Section C: Employment Questions

What do you do for a living? Describe your work environment.

Do you ever feel hesitant to discuss your identity as a triathlete in the workplace? Why or why not?

Does your training ever get in the way of your work? If so, how? What do you do when this conflict happens?

Section D: The Nexus of Sport, Family, and Work

When you have conflicts between work, family, and your training, how you decide what should take first priority?

How hard is it to accommodate your daily training regiment?

Do you feel that you have had to compromise something in your life in order to accommodate your training schedule? If so, what have you compromised, and how much?

Overall, how has your participation in iron-distance racing changed your relationship with your children? Your wife? Your employer?

How has your identity as a triathlete evolved over time?

Do you compete in iron-distance racing as a means of setting a good example for your family? If so, tell me about this.

What advice would you give to a father considering participating in an iron-distance race?

Does faith play a role in your life? (If yes) What is the relationship between your faith and your training?

Section E: Demographic Questions

How old are you?

What is your highest level of education? What field is your degree in?

What is your approximate annual household income?

What religious denomination are you?

Do you affiliate with a political party? If so, which one?

Do you know of any other Iron Dads that may be interested in participating in this research?

Guide for Unmarried Fathers (Questions were adapted as fathers described their family situation)

Section A: Triathlon Identity Questions

> Tell me about your background in sport. How did you get started in triathlon? Iron-distance racing?
> What does being a triathlete mean to you?
> How important is being a triathlete to you?
> What iron-distance races have you competed in?
> Why do you compete in iron-distance races?

Section B: Family Questions

> Tell me about your family. (If divorced, probe about custody arrangement.)
> (If custody is shared) How often do you see your children?
> (If custody is shared) Describe how you typically spend your time when your children are with you.
> (If custody is shared) To what extent do you bring multi-sport activity into your visits?
> How do you involve your family in your training and racing?
> Do you feel guilty when you train and race? How do you deal with this guilt?
> Are you concerned about injury? Is your family? How do you manage this concern?
> Have you spoken with your family about how you can stay safe while training?
> (If father has sole custody) Given that you are the sole caretaker of your child/children, do you feel an added responsibility to train and race safely?
> How difficult has training been on your family life? Why has it been difficult?
> How do you negotiate the expenses of the iron-distance?
> (If divorced) Have you ever been in a fight with your ex-wife concerning training or racing? If so, what was the fight about? Were you married at the time?

Section C: Employment Questions

> What do you do for a living? Describe your work environment.
> Do you ever feel hesitant to discuss your identity as a triathlete in the workplace? Why or why not?
> Does your training ever get in the way of your work? If so, how? What do you do when this conflict happens?

Section D: The Nexus of Sport, Family, and Work

> When you have conflicts between work, family, and your training, how do you decide what should take first priority?
> How hard is it to accommodate your daily training regimen?
> Do you feel that you have had to compromise something in your life in order to accommodate your training schedule? If so, what have you compromised, and how much?
> Overall, how has your participation in iron-distance racing changed your relationship with your children? Your partner (if applicable)? Your employer?
> How has your identity as a triathlete evolved over time?

TABLE 3. Participant Recruitment Sources

Interview	Name	Source
1	Greg	ST
2	Frank	ST
3	Ryan	ST
4	Bill	ST
5	Mark	ST
6	Don	BT
7	Gary	BT
8	Larry	BT
9	Keith	BT
10	Sean	BT
11	Dan	BT
12	Mitch	BT
13	Adrian	BT
14	Dylan	BT
15	Tyler	BT
16	Ian	BT
17	Isaac	BT
18	Carter	BT
19	Kevin	BT
20	Parker	BT
21	Lance	BT
22	Cooper	BT
23	Aaron	BT
24	Brandon	BT
25	Arnold	BT
26	Tristan	BT
27	Josh	BT
28	Jackson	BT
29	Jordan	BT
30	Logan	BT
31	Leo	BT
32	Chase	BT
33	Samuel	IMTX
34	Jayden	IMTX
35	Alex	IMTX
36	Mike	IMTX
37	Justin	IMTX
38	Mitch	IMTX
39	Eli	IMTX
40	Jeff	IMTX
41	Peyton	IMTX
42	Max	IMTX
43	John	IMTX
44	Bryson	IMTX
45	Jeremy	IMTX
46	Colton	IMTX
47	Adam	IMTX
48	Dick	Other
49	Sean	Other
50	Mike	Other

KEY: ST = Slowtwitch.com; IMTX = Ironman Texas Expo (May 2012); BT = Beginnertriathlete.com
NOTE: Of 50 total study participants, 47 Iron Dads conformed to the study parameters, 1 Iron Dad did not conform to all of the study parameters (son was too old), and 2 men were not Iron Dads but held unique positions in the endurance sport industry.

Do you compete in iron-distance racing as a means of setting a good example for your family? If so, tell me about this.

What advice would you give to a father considering participating in an iron-distance race?

Does faith play a role in your life? (If yes) What is the relationship between your faith and your training?

Section E: Demographic Questions

How old are you?

What is your highest level of education? What field is your degree in?

What is your approximate annual household income?

What religious denomination are you?

Do you affiliate with a political party? If so, which one?

Do you know of any other Iron Dads that may be interested in participating in this research?

The Ironman Executive Challenge Debate

The Executive Challenge (XC) is a unique program within World Triathlon Corporation's offerings. It exists because, most centrally, the demographic profile of people competing in its events is not lost on the company. In addition to event entry and hotel accommodations, XC participants are awarded more exclusive perks such as a low bib number, optimal bike rack placement, and VIP seating at banquet functions. The program also allows competitors to identify one another by signature XC apparel, as well as in-person functions with program members.

The Executive Challenge program started with a rather humble beginning. Initiated in 2009, it only offered entry to five full-distance IRONMAN events and the World Championship. The program has now expanded to include 70.3 events. In a question-and-answer section on its website, WTC addresses the question, "Why participate in the IRONMAN XC Program?" The response emphasizes the value of the experience: "The IRONMAN Executive Challenge, also referred to as XC, offers business leaders exclusive privileges to the world's most challenging endurance event, the IRONMAN Triathlon. The turn-key program simplifies the race planning process, allowing you time to enjoy the IRONMAN journey and focus on other priorities such as work, family and training. Participation within IRONMAN XC provides a one-of a kind, unique race weekend experience for both athlete and family."[3]

Competitors operating within the ranks of the XC represent a collection of society's elite. Program competitors have included Phil Newbold, CEO of Memorial Health Systems; Juan Andrade, president of The Hartford; and Andrew Kosove, CEO of Alcon Entertainment (*Life of Luxury* 2010). Sam Peterson, senior vice president of technology at Overstock.com, was publicly acknowledged on his company's website after completing his IRONMAN event (Overstock.com 2010). As one would expect, WTC is not forthcoming in sharing information about the demographics of the XC, so it is hard to offer firm data on the program's clientele.

The *Bloomberg* article discussed in chapter 5 portrays XC athletes as men who will spend unlimited amounts of money on their status. Based on this research, which included two XC participants, I do not believe that it is fair to depict these men as selfishly and thoughtlessly throwing their money away. Is IRONMAN the "ultimate status feat," as Elizabeth Weil suggests in the title of her article? To some, yes. However, to many, it's a lifestyle. Being an IRONMAN means figuring out the identity puzzle on a daily basis. Sami Inkinen, an Executive Challenge triathlete interviewed for the *Bloomberg* article, says "Triathlons appeal to people who like puzzles. Running a race is easy. It's very, very simple. An IRONMAN is complicated." This puzzle is not simply about the race itself—it's about putting a lifestyle together. For many, as in the case of my study participants, this puzzle includes family. One father, an XC participant, described his reasoning for entering the program on an online forum:

> I have a variety of reasons that IM/XC makes sense for me. I suspect that it would not make sense for many folks who are on this forum. For example, it doesn't make sense for my son, even though he is a much better triathlete than I am. It would not make sense for him to do XC (he doesn't have a wife and 4 kids, and 4 friends, and a Mom who all want to come see him do his race). I'm a very critical buyer of things. If it's not worth the money I won't spend it. If it is, I do. The XC thing is worth it to me. I have a lot more wealthy friends who would never buy this product—and I agree with them. But for me, it is hands down one of the best things I spend my money on.

Jordan Rapp, a professional triathlete, father, and Princeton University graduate, also weighed in on the Executive Challenge criticism. Rapp blogged:

> The majority of XC athletes are repeat IRONMAN athletes. There are few "bucket listers" [individuals who seek to cross the activity off of their "must do" list], who simply use the program as a way to check another item off of their list, to collect, as Weil calls it, "the ultimate status bauble." In my experience, most XC athletes are diehard triathletes who pay the extra money for XC not because of the perks it provides for them but for those it provides to their family members, especially their wives who may feel like they are losing their spouse to both work and play. When you run a big company and race multiple IRONMANS in a year, well, there are still only twenty-four hours in a day. In talking with the XC athletes, many of whom I have been enjoying seeing at race after race, XC makes IRONMAN—admittedly one of the world's most boring spectator sports—more palatable to the "support crew." XC is not like the programs that have sprung up to escort unprepared executives to the top of Everest so they could claim to have conquered the high peak. It's a program designed for hyper-prepared executives to help their families, who were unprepared for just how all-consuming triathlon can be. (Rapp 2012)

So where does this debate leave us? While I believe that Weil's article missed a large part of why men sign up for the Executive Challenge, her piece is not without value. The program is emblematic of the issues, ironies, and challenges that face competitors in all age and gender divisions. Iron-distance athletes tend to be successful in their occupations. They take on a lot of responsibility in the workplace. As Weil correctly points out, and studies commissioned by USA Triathlon confirm, many competitors have access to sizable disposable incomes. That said, the article is noteworthy because it draws our attention to important realities about both 140.6 racing and sporting environments more generally. As elaborated on in chapter 5, iron-distance racing is engulfed in a culture of consumption. While not every competitor goes out and purchases VIP packages, basic event entry is expensive. More broadly, class can be—and is—used to create a more enjoyable family experience at race events.

Is the *Bloomberg* article a fair depiction of Executive Challenge athletes? Based on my interviews for this project, I suggest that Weil did not write the piece with full information. My research leads to the proposition that she missed a huge part of the equation for Iron Dads—their sensitivity toward balancing multiple identities. When Executive Challenge athletes purchase a VIP package, they are not simply considering personal perks that appear on race day. They are purchasing a family experience. They are also, in effect, purchasing time. Executives have busy schedules. The XC program allows for many details to be taken care of in advance by a WTC employee. This includes booking a hotel, ground transportation, arranging for food, and other critical details. Attending to these details is very time consuming. The narratives of my XC Iron Dads, as well as those posting online, remind us that before being critical of such a program, we had best learn from the scope of subtle yet important motivations of its participants.

NOTES

Chapter 1. Taking the First Step

1 Not all discussion threads were started by Iron Dads. However, as threads flourished, Iron Dads contributed to the conversations.

2 Part of the controversy surrounding Venkatesh's work stems from the fact that many believe that standard institutional review board protocol was not followed. Still, this title made the *New York Times* best sellers list. This reflects a deep popular interest in work utilizing cutting-edge "insider" approaches.

3 A comprehensive summary of this literature can be found at http://faculty .washington.edu/crowther/Misc/RBC/gender.shtml.

Chapter 2. Inside Triathlon Culture

1 The IRONMAN brand is a powerful force in the formation of such an identity. With its injection into popular culture, the brand fundamentally shapes perceptions of the 140.6 identity. For this reason, I use the phrase "IRONMAN identity" and not "iron-distance identity."

2 A video of this emotional event can be viewed at http://www.youtube.com/ watch?v=ndY9xptZI9w.

Chapter 3. To Tri or Not to Try

1 Additional information about Dan's story can be found at http://www.trimywill .com/home.

2 Marsiglio (2008) presents a thorough account of how men serve future generations through work in their local communities.

3 More information on the broadcast can be found at http://www.ironman.com/ triathlon/news/articles/2015/04/emmy-nomination.aspx#axzz3eMdk4cu8.

4 This information was provided by the IM Foundation in July 2015 in response to an e-mail inquiry.

5 See Bridel (2010) for a thorough literature review on the interconnectedness of pleasure and pain.

Chapter 4. The Juggling Act

1 The full Iron Widow discussion thread can be viewed at http://forum.slowtwitch .com/cgi-bin/gforum.cgi?do=post_view_flat;post=1911055;page=1;sb=post_ latest_reply;so=ASC;mh=-1.

2 I used the "word tree" function in the NVivo 9 platform. The word tree analysis was limited to online discussion threads where Iron Dads solicited advice from fellow forum members.

3 The Asics promotional video can be found at https://www.youtube.com/watch?v=3snUpvau044.

4 More information on the IRONKIDS series can be found at http://www.ironkids.com/#news.

5 More information on the Jeff's Running Partners program can be found at http://www.hartfordmarathon.com/Events/Eversource_Hartford_Marathon/Youth_Running/Jeff_s_Running_Partners.htm.

Chapter 5. Why Class Matters

1 For more on the Executive Challenge debate, see the appendix.

2 The study does not specify if this figure is for the individual or for the family.

3 Study figures are reported in http://www.nytimes.com/2010/10/24/fashion/24triathlon.html?pagewanted=2and_r=3.

4 The "Real Cost" series can be viewed at http://www.bloomberg.com/personal-finance/consumer-spending/.

5 The words "time trial" and "triathlon" are interchangeable in this context.

6 For an interesting piece on the relationship between citizenship and consumption, see http://rre.sagepub.com/content/36/1/139.extract.

7 The entirety of this thread can be viewed at http://forum.slowtwitch.com/Slowtwitch_Forums_C1/Triathlon_Forum_F1/What_career/job_do_you_have . . . _P2244589/.

8 The entirety of this thread can be viewed at http://forum.slowtwitch.com/cgi-bin/gforum.cgi?post=3809962%3Bsearch_string%3Dironman%20workplace%3B%233809962.

9 The entirety of this thread can be viewed at http://forum.slowtwitch.com/gforum.cgi?post=2155510;search_string=tell%20boss;guest=56894708 andt=search_engi%20one#2155510.

10 In prior years, WTC also designated a 140.6 race as well (IM Wisconsin). However, this program was pulled—likely due to small participation numbers. This suggests that the 140.6 distance is still quite inaccessible for those currently enrolled as a full-time college student.

11 Additional information on the Emerging Sport Grant program can be found at http://www.usatriathlon.org/about-multisport/ncaa.aspx.

Chapter 6. Faith Meets 140.6

1 More information on the FCA's mission can be found at http://www.fca.org/aboutus/who-we-are/mission-vision.

2 The most up-to-date listing of FCA huddles can be found at http://fcaendurance.com/huddles.

3 More information on Multisport Ministries' mission can be found at http://www.multisportministries.com/about.html.

Chapter 7. Throwing in the Towel

1 Further discussion comparing select event DNF rates can be found at http://forum.slowtwitch.com/gforum.cgi?do=post_view_flat;post=4309132;page=1;sb=post_latest_reply;so=ASC;m%20h=-1.

2 An interesting analysis of WTC's recent DNF rates at the 140.6 distance can be found at http://www.runtri.com/2013/09/ironman-triathlon-dnf-did-not-finish.html.

3 Additional details on Dick and Rick Hoyt can be found at http://www.teamhoyt.com.

Chapter 8. The Road Ahead

1 Readers seeking more detailed information on my methodology should consult the appendix.

2 For more details on the state of professional payouts, see Hichens (2015).

3 Early reactions to the race transfer program announcement can be viewed in this February 14, 2014, Slowtwitch thread: http://forum.slowtwitch.com/cgi-bin/gforum.cgi?do=post_view_flat;post=4972338;page=1;sb=post_latest_reply;so=ASC;mh=-1.

4 Further details of the plan can be viewed at http://www.ironman.com/full-refund-plan.aspx#axzz3ELIuooG6.

5 From http://www.ironman.com/full-refund-plan.aspx#axzz3eliuoog6.

6 These suggestions were made as of June 2015. The WTC Transfer Program is a living entity, and as such, may have evolved to adopt some of these concepts since publication.

7 In addition to the difference in registration price, the Rock 'n' Roll Marathon Series charges a $10 transfer fee. The Baltimore Marathon does not charge this fee.

8 Further discussion of the SME reimbursement policy can be found at http://www.sunmultisportevents.com/Patriot_Half/events.htm.

9 It is worth considering that the endurance triathlon context is constantly evolving. Some of the policies discussed in this book may have been modified since the time of publication.

Appendix

1 Ideas for how this scholarship can be approached are offered in chapter 8.

2 The most recent visit totals can be viewed at http://www.beginnertriathlete.com and http://www.slowtwitch.com, respectively.

3 From the IRONMAN XC program FAQ at http://www.ironman.com/triathlon/organizations/ironman-xc/benefits/faq-and-answers.aspx#faq1.

REFERENCES

Adams, Adi, Eric Anderson, and Mark McCormack. 2010. "Establishing and Challenging Masculinity: The Influence of Gendered Discourses in Organized Sport." *Journal of Language and Social Psychology* 29 (3): 278–300.

Adams, Mary Louise. 2011. *Artistic Impressions: Figure Skating, Masculinity, and the Limits of Sport.* Toronto: University of Toronto Press.

Ahlander, Nancy, and Kathleen Slaugh Bahr. 1995. "Beyond Drudgery, Power, and Equity: Toward an Expanded Discourse on the Moral Dimensions of Housework in Families." *Journal of Marriage and the Family* 57: 54–68.

Amato, Paul R., Alan Booth, David R. Johnson, and Stacey J. Rogers. 2007. *Alone Together: How Marriage in America Is Changing.* Cambridge, MA: Harvard University Press.

Amis, John. 2005. "Interviewing for Case Study Research." In *Qualitative Methods in Sports Studies*, edited by David L. Andrews, Daniel S. Mason, and Michael L. Silk, 103–138. Oxford: Berg.

Anderson, Eric. 2005. *In the Game: Gay Athletes and the Cult of Masculinity.* Albany: State University of New York Press.

———. 2011. Masculinities and Sexualities in Sport and Physical Cultures: Three Decades of Evolving Research. *Journal of Homosexuality* 58 (5), 565–578.

Anderson, Eric, and Rhidian McGuire. 2010. "Inclusive Masculinity and the Gendered Politics of Men's Rugby." *Journal of Gender Studies* 19 (3): 249–261.

Atencio, Matthew, Becky Beal, and Charlene Wilson. 2009. "The Distinction of Risk: Urban Skateboarding, Street Habitus, and the Construction of Hierarchical Gender Relations." *Qualitative Research in Sport and Exercise* 1: 3–20.

Atencio, M., and J. Wright. 2009. "Ballet it's too whitey: discursive hierarchies of high school dance spaces and the constitution of embodied feminine subjectivities." *Gender and Education* 21 (1), 31–46.

Atkinson, Michael. 2008. "Triathlon, Suffering, and Exciting Significance." *Leisure Studies* 27 (2): 165–180.

Atkinson, Michael, and Kevin Young. 2008. *Deviance and Social Control in Sport.* Champaign, IL: Human Kinetics.

Baker, William J. 2007. *Playing with God: Religion and Modern Sport.* Cambridge, MA: Harvard University Press.

Bale, John. 1993. *Sport, Space, and the City.* London: Routledge.

———. 1994. *Landscapes of Modern Sport.* Leicester: Leicester University Press.

_____. 2004. *Running Cultures: Racing in Time and Space*. London: Routledge.

_____. 2006. "The Place of Pain in Running." In *Pain and Injury in Sport: Social and Ethical Analysis*, edited by Sigmund Loland, Berit Skirstad, and Ivan Waddington, 65–75. New York: Routledge.

Barry, Dan. 2012. "He's a Quarterback, He's a Winner, He's a TV Draw, He's a Verb." *New York Times*, January 14, A1. Accessed January 20, 2012. http://www.nytimes.com/2012/01/14/sports/football/fascinated-by-tim-tebow-on-more-than-sundays.html?_r=0.

Baudrillard, Jean. 2001. "The System of Objects." In *Jean Baudrillard: Selected Writings*, edited by Mark Poster, 13–31. Stanford, CA: Stanford University Press.

Beal, Becky, and Charlene Wilson. 2004. "Chicks Dig Scars: Commercialization and the Transformations of Skateboarders' Identities." In *Understanding Lifestyle Sports*, edited by Belinda Wheaton, 31–54. London: Routledge.

Bianchi, Suzanne M. 2011. "Family Change and Time Allocation in American Families." *Annals of the American Academy of Political and Social Science* 638: 21–44.

Birks, Melanie, and Jane Mills. 2011. *Grounded Theory: A Practical Guide*. Thousand Oaks, CA: Sage.

Birrell, Susan. 2007. "Approaching Mt. Everest: On Intertextuality and the Past as Narrative." *Journal of Sport History* 34: 1–22.

Blaydon, Michelle J., and Koenraad J. Linder. 2002. "Eating Disorders and Exercise Dependence in Triathletes." *Eating Disorders* 10: 49–50.

Bloomberg Rankings and Nikhil Hutheesing. 2012. "The Real Cost of Completing a Triathlon." *Bloomberg.com*, November 10. http://www.bloomberg.com/consumer-spending/2012-11-05/the-real-cost-of-completing-a-triathlon.html.

Blumer, Herbert. 1954. "What Is Wrong with Social Theory?" *American Sociological Review* 19 (1): 3–10.

Bond, Katherine, and Jo Batey. 2005. "Running for Their Lives: A Qualitative Analysis of the Exercise Experience of Female Recreational Runners." *Women in Sport and Physical Activity Journal* 14 (2): 69–82.

Bourdieu, Pierre. 1984. *Distinction: A Social Critique of the Judgment of Taste*. Cambridge, MA: Harvard University Press.

_____. 1985. "The Social Space and the Genesis of Groups." *Theory and Society* 14 (6): 723–744.

_____. 1989. "Social Space and Symbolic Power." *Sociological Theory* 19 (1): 14–25.

Bowen, Glenn A. 2009. "Supporting a Grounded Theory with an Audit Trail: An Illustration." *International Journal of Social Research Methodology* 12 (4): 205–216.

Brah, Avtar, and Ann Phoenix. 2004. "Ain't I a Woman? Revisiting Intersectionality." *Journal of International Women's Studies* 5 (3): 75–86.

Bridel, William Francis. 2010. "Finish . . . Whatever It Takes: Considering Pain and Pleasure in the Ironman Triathlon; A Socio-cultural Analysis." PhD diss., Queen's University.

_____. 2013. "Not Fat, Not Skinny, Functional Enough to Finish: Interrogating Constructions of Health in the Ironman Triathlon." *Leisure/Loisir* 37 (1): 37–56.

Brotherson, Sean E., David C. Dollahite, and Alan J. Hawkins. 2005. "Generative Fathering and the Dynamics of Connection between Fathers and Their Children." *Fathering* 3 (1): 1–28.

Brown, Gary. 2012. "Triathlon Poised to Be the Next Emerging Sport for Women." National Collegiate Athletic Association, August 29. Retrieved January 20, 2012. http://www.ncaa.org/about/resources/media-center/news/triathlon-poised-be-next-emerging-sport-women.

Brown, Mary Ellen. 1987. "The Dialectic of the Feminine: Melodrama and Commodity in the Ferraro Pepsi Commercial." *Communication* 9: 335–354.

Brown, Trent D., Justen P. O'Connor, and Anastasios N. Barkatsas. 2009. "Instrumentation and Motivations for Organized Cycling: The Development of the Cyclists Motivation Instrument (CMI)." *Journal of Sports Science and Medicine* 8: 211–218.

Brymer, Eric. 2010. "Risk Taking in Extreme Sports: A Phenomenological Perspective." *Annals of Leisure Research* 13 (1–2): 218–238.

Bryson, Lois. 2002. "Sport and the Maintenance of Masculine Hegemony." *Women's Studies International Forum* 10 (4): 349–360.

Burke, Kenneth, and Joseph R. Gusfield, eds. 1989. *On Symbols and Society.* Chicago: University of Chicago Press.

Burke, Peter J., and Donald C. Reitzes. 1981. "The Link between Identity and Role Performance." *Social Psychology Quarterly* 44 (2): 83–92.

Butterworth, Michael L. 2013. "The Passion of the Tebow: Sports Media and Heroic Language in the Tragic Frame." *Critical Studies in Media Communication* 30 (1): 17–33.

Chambliss, Daniel F. 1989. "The Mundanity of Excellence: An Ethnographic Report on Stratification and Olympic Swimmers." *Sociological Theory* 7: 70–86.

Charlesworth, Hannah, and Kevin Young. 2004. "Why English Female University Athletes Play with Pain: Motivations and Rationalizations." In *Sporting Bodies, Damaged Selves: Sociological Studies of Sports-Related Injury*, edited by Kevin Young, 163–180. Oxford: Elsevier.

Charmaz, Kathy. 1994. "Identity Dilemmas of Chronically Ill Men." *Sociological Quarterly* 35 (2): 269–288.

———. 2006. *Constructing Grounded Theory: A Practical Guide through Qualitative Analysis.* Thousand Oaks, CA: Sage.

Christiansen, Shawn L., and Rob Palkovitz. 2001. "Why the 'Good Provider' Role Still Matters: Providing as a Form of Paternal Involvement." *Journal of Family Issues* 22 (1): 84–106.

Clarke, Alan, and John Clarke. 1982. "Highlights and Action Replays—Ideologies, Sport, and the Media." In *Sport, Culture, and Ideology*, edited by Jennifer Hargreaves, 62–87. London: Routledge.

Coakley, Jay. 2006. "The Good Father: Parental Expectations and Youth Sports." *Leisure Studies* 25: 153–163.

———. 2009. *Sports in Society: Issues and Controversies.* 10th ed. New York: McGraw-Hill.

Cole, C. L., M. D. Giardina, and D. L. Andrews. 2004. "Michel Foucault: Studies of Power and Sport." In *Sport and Modern Social Theorists*, edited by Richard Giulianotti, 207–223. New York: Palgrave Macmillan.

Connell, R. W. 1987. *Gender and Power: Society, the Person, and Sexual Politics.* Stanford, CA: Stanford University Press.

_____. 1995. *Masculinities.* Berkeley: University of California Press.

_____. 2000. *The Men and the Boys.* Berkeley: University of California Press.

Cooley, Charles Horton. 1902. *Human Nature and the Social Order.* New York: Scribner's.

Crenshaw, Kimberlé. 1989. "Demarginalizing the Intersection of Race and Sex: A Black Feminist Critique of Antidiscrimination Doctrine, Feminist Theory, and Antiracist Politics." *University of Chicago Legal Forum* 140: 139–167.

Cronan, Megan Kelly, and David Scott. 2008. "Triathlon and Women's Narratives of Bodies and Sport." *Leisure Sciences: An Interdisciplinary Journal* 30 (1): 17–34.

Crosset, Todd W. 1995. *Outsiders in the Clubhouse: The World of Women's Professional Golf.* Albany: State University of New York Press.

Crosset, Todd W., and Becky Beal. 1997. "The Use of 'Subculture' and 'Subworld' in Ethnographic Works on Sport: A Discussion of Definitional Distinctions." *Sociology of Sport Journal* 14 (1): 73–85.

Daniels, Pamela, and Kathy Weingarten. 1982. *Sooner or Later: The Timing of Parenthood in Adult Lives.* New York: W. W. Norton.

Denzin, Norman K., and Yvonna S. Lincoln. 2000. *Handbook of Qualitative Research.* Thousand Oaks, CA: Sage.

Dermott, Esther. 2008. *Intimate Fatherhood: A Sociological Analysis.* London: Routledge.

de St. Aubin, Ed, Dan P. McAdams, and Tae-Chang Kim. 2004. *The Generative Society: Caring for Future Generations.* Washington, DC: American Psychological Association.

Dienhart, Anna. 1998. *Reshaping Fatherhood: The Social Construction of Shared Parenting.* Thousand Oaks, CA: Sage.

Dollahite, David C. 1998. "Fathering, Faith, and Spirituality." *Journal of Men's Studies* 7 (1); 3–15.

Dollahite, David C., and Alan J. Hawkins. 1998. "A Conceptual Ethic of Generative Fathering." *Journal of Men's Studies* 7 (1):132–190.

Dollahite, David C., Alan J. Hawkins, and Sean E. Brotherson. 1997. "Fatherwork: A Conceptual Ethic of Fathering as Generative Work." In *Generative Fathering: Beyond Deficit Perspectives*, edited by Alan J. Hawkins and David C. Dollahite, 17–35. Thousand Oaks, CA: Sage.

Doucet, Andrea. 2006. *Do Men Mother? Fathering, Care, and Domestic Responsibility.* Toronto: University of Toronto Press.

Drummond, Murray. 2010. "The Natural: An Autoethnography of a Masculinized Body in Sport." *Men and Masculinities* 12: 374–389.

Dworkin, Shari Lee, and Faye Linda Wachs. 2000. "The Morality/Manhood Paradox: Masculinity, Sport, and the Media." In *Masculinities, Gender Relations, and Sport*, edited by Michael A. Messner, Don Sabo, and Jim McKay. Thousand Oaks, CA: Sage. Reprinted in Michael S. Kimmel and Michael A. Messner, eds. 2003. *Men's Lives*, 507–521. Boston: Allyn and Bacon.

Dzikus, Lars, Robin Hardin, and Steven N. Waller. 2012. "Case Studies of Collegiate Sport Chaplains." *Journal of Sport and Social Issues* 36 (3): 268–294.

Eggebeen, David J., and Chris Knoester. 2001. "Does Fatherhood Matter for Men?" *Journal of Marriage and Family* 63: 381–393.

Eitzen, D. Stanley. 2009. *Sport in Contemporary Society: An Anthology*, 8th ed. New York: Paradigm Publishers.

Eitzen, D. Stanley, and George H. Sage. 2003. *Sociology of North American Sport.* New York: McGraw-Hill.

_____. 2009. *Sociology of North American Sport*, 8th ed. Boulder, CO: Paradigm Publishers.

Empfield, Dan. 2012. "A Civil Transfer Policy." Slowtwitch.com. Retrieved November 21, 2012. http://www.slowtwitch.com/Opinion/A_Civil_Transfer_Policy_3236.html.

Erickson, Bonnie H. 1996. "Culture, Class, and Connections." *American Journal of Sociology* 102 (1): 217–251.

Erikson, Erik H. 1950. *Childhood and Society.* New York: W. W. Norton.

ESPN. 2012. "Tim Tebow Trademarking 'Tebowing.'" *ESPN News Service*, October 20. Retrieved January 20, 2013. http://espn.go.com/new-york/nfl/story/_/id/8525097/tim-tebow-new-york-jets-trademarks-tebowing.

Falkenrath, Ryan. 2013. "2014 Ironman Chattanooga Sells Out in 3 Minutes." *Examiner.com*. Retrieved November 1, 2013. http://www.examiner.com/article/2014-ironman-chattanooga-sells-out-3-minutes.

Fineman, Joshua, and Michael Buteau. 2011. "New York Ironman Triathlon Competition Sells Out $895 Slots in 11 Minutes." *Bloomberg.com*. Retrieved November 1, 2013. http://www.bloomberg.com/news/articles/2011–06–15/new-york-ironman-triathlon-sells-out-895-slots-online-in-11-minutes.

Fink, Don. 2004. *Be Iron Fit: Time-Efficient Training Secrets for Ultimate Fitness.* Guilford, CT: Lyons Press.

Fitzclarence, Lindsay, and Christopher Hickey 2001. "Real Footballers Don't Eat Quiche: Old Narratives in New Times." *Men and Masculinities* 4: 118–139.

Fletcher, Robert. 2008. "Living on the Edge: The Appeal of Risk Sports for the Professional Middle Class." *Sociology of Sport Journal* 25: 310–330.

Flouri, Eirini. 2005. *Fathering and Child Outcomes.* Chichester: John Wiley.

Ford, Nick, and David Brown. 2006. *Surfing and Social Theory: Experience, Embodiment, and Narrative of the Dream Glide.* London: Routledge.

Foucault, Michel. 1977. *Discipline and Punish: The Birth of the Prison.* Translated by Alan Sheridan. Harmondsworth: Penguin.

Furst, David M., Thomas Ferr, and Nancy Megginson. 1993. "Motivation of Disabled Athletes to Participate in Triathlons." *Psychological Reports* 72: 403–406.

Fusco, Caroline. 2005. "Cultural Landscapes of Purification: Sports Spaces and Discourses of Whiteness." *Sociology of Sport Journal* 22: 283–310.

Galinsky, Ellen, Kerstin Aumann, and James T. Bond. 2009. *Times Are Changing: Gender and Generation at Work and at Home.* New York: Families and Work Institute.

Gard, Michael, and Robert Meyenn. 2000. "Boys, Bodies, Pleasure, and Pain: Interrogating Contact Sports in Schools." *Sport, Education, and Society* 5 (1): 19–34.

Gardner, Ann Marie. 2010. "Triathletes, 40-Somethings, Going for Youth." *New York Times*, October 22. Retrieved November 25, 2010. http://www.nytimes.com/2010/10/24/fashion/24triathlon.html?pagewanted=all.

Giddens, Anthony. 1991. *Modernity and Self-identity: Self and Society in the Late Modern Age*. Stanford, CA: Stanford University Press.

Glaser, Barney G. 1978. *Theoretical Sensitivity: Advances in the Methodology of Grounded Theory*. Mill Valley, CA: Sociology Press.

———. 1992. *Emergence vs. Forcing: Basics of Grounded Theory Analysis*. Mill Valley, CA: Sociology Press.

Glaser, Barney G., and Anselm L. Strauss. 1967. *The Discovery of Grounded Theory: Strategies for Qualitative Research*. Chicago: Aldine.

Goffman, Erving. 1959. *The Presentation of Self in Everyday Life*. Garden City, NY: Doubleday Anchor.

Goldman, Robert, Deborah Heath, and Sharon L. Smith. 1991. "Commodity Feminism." *Critical Studies in Mass Communication* 8:333–351.

Granberg, Ellen. 2006. "Is That All There Is? Possible Selves, Self-Change, and Weight Loss." *Social Psychology Quarterly* 69 (2): 109–126.

Grand'Maison, Karine. 2004. "What Mental Skills Ironman Triathletes Need and Want." *Journal of Excellence* 10: 86–94.

Hadzipetros, Peter. 2009. "Triathlon: Multi-Event Sport Surges in Popularity." *CBCNews.com*, April 3. Retrieved May 21, 2012. http://www.cbc.ca/news/health/story/2009/04/03/f-triathlon.html.

Hall, Donald E., ed. 1994. *Muscular Christianity: Embodying the Victorian Age*. New York: Cambridge University Press.

Hanold, Maylon. 2010. "Beyond the Marathon: (De)Construction of Female Ultrarunning Bodies." *Sociology of Sport Journal* 27 (2): 160–177.

Hardman, Charlotte. 1973. "Can There Be an Anthropology of Children?" *Journal of the Anthropological Society of Oxford* 4 (2): 85–99.

Harris, John, and Andrew Parker. 2009. "Introduction: Sport and Social Identities." In *Sport and Social Identities*, edited by John Harris and Andrew Parker, 1–14. New York: Palgrave Macmillan.

Hartmann, Douglas. 2015. "The Sanctity of Sunday Football: Why Men Love Sports." In *Sociological Perspectives on Sport: The Games Outside the Games*, edited by David Karen and Robert E. Washington, 123–129. New York: Routledge.

Helliker, Kevin. 2012. "One Running Shoe in the Grave: New Studies on Older Endurance Athletes Suggest the Fittest Reap Few Health Benefits." *Wall Street Journal*, November 27, D6. Retrieved November 27, 2012. http://online.wsj.com/article/SB10001424127887323330604578145462264024472.html.

Hichens, Liz. 2015. "Challenge Americas Eliminates Pro Prize Purse from 5 Races." *Triathlete.com*, May 11. http://triathlon.competitor.com/2015/05/news/challenge-americas-eliminates-pro-prize-purse-from-5-races_116075.

Hochschild, Arlie, with Anne Machung. 2012. *The Second Shift: Working Families and the Revolution at Home*. New York: Penguin.

Holstein, James A., and Jaber F. Gubrium. 2000. *The Self We Live By: Narrative Identity in a Postmodern World*. New York: Oxford University Press.

Horne, John. 2005. *Sport in Consumer Culture*. New York: Palgrave Macmillan.

Huizinga, Johan. 1950. *Homo Ludens: A Study of the Play-Element in Culture*. Boston: Beacon Press.

Jenkins, John. 2009. "With One Eye on the Clock: Non-resident Dads' Time Use, Work, and Leisure with Their Children." In *Fathering through Sport and Leisure*, edited by Tess Kay, 88–105. New York: Routledge.

Karen, David, and Robert E. Washington. 2015. "Section 1: Sport and Sociology: Meanings and Dimensions." In *Sociological Perspectives on Sport: The Games Outside the Games*, edited by David Karen and Robert E. Washington, 1–18. New York: Routledge.

Kaufman, Gayle. 2013. *Superdads: How Fathers Balance Work and Family in the 21st Century*. New York: NYU Press.

Kay, Tess. 2006. "Where's Dad? Fatherhood in Leisure Studies." *Leisure Studies* 25 (2): 133–152.

_____, ed. 2009. *Fathering through Sport and Leisure*. New York: Routledge.

Kiecolt, K. Jill. 1994. "Stress and the Decision to Change Oneself: A Theoretical Model." *Social Psychology Quarterly* 57: 49–63.

Kimmel, Michael S. 1992. "Reading Men: Men, Masculinity, and Publishing." *Contemporary Sociology* 21 (2): 162–171.

_____. 2004. "Masculinities." In *Men and Masculinities: A Social, Cultural, and Historical Encyclopedia*, vol. 2, edited by Michael S. Kimmel and Amy B. Aronson, 503–507. Santa Barbara, CA: ABC Clio.

Ladd, Tony, and James A. Mathisen. 1999. *Muscular Christianity: Evangelical Protestants and the Development of American Sport*. Grand Rapids, MI: Baker Publishing Group.

Lamb, Michael E., ed. 2010. *The Role of the Father in Child Development*, 5th ed. Hoboken, NJ: Wiley.

Lamont, Matthew, and Millicent Kennelly. 2011. "I Can't Do Everything! Competing Priorities as Constraints in Triathlon Event Travel Careers." *Tourism Review International* 14 (2): 85–97.

_____. 2012. "A Qualitative Exploration of Participant Motives among Committed Amateur Triathletes." *Leisure Sciences* 34 (3): 236–255.

Lamont, Matthew, Millicent Kennelly, and Erica Wilson. 2011. "Selfish Leisure? Competing Priorities and Constraints in Triathlon Event Travel Careers." Paper presented at the annual meeting of the Council for Australian University Tourism and Hospitality Education (CAUTHE) Conference, University of South Australia, City West Campus, Adelaide, South Australia, February 8–11.

LaRossa, Ralph. 1997. *The Modernization of Fatherhood: A Social and Political History*. Chicago: University of Chicago Press.

_____. 2005. "Grounded Theory Methods and Qualitative Family Research." *Journal of Marriage and Family* 67: 837–857.

_____. 2009. "Until the Twilight Glows: Fatherhood, Baseball, and the Game of Playing Catch." In *Fathering through Sport and Leisure*, edited by Tess Kay, 23–39. New York: Routledge.

LaRossa, Ralph, and Maureen Mulligan LaRossa. 1981. *Transition to Parenthood: How Infants Change Families*. Beverly Hills, CA: Sage.

Laurendeau, Jason. 2008. "Gendered Risk Regimes: A Theoretical Consideration of Edgework and Gender." *Sociology of Sport Journal* 25: 293–309.

Laurendeau, Jason, and Nancy Sharara. 2008. "Women Could Be Every Bit as Good as Guys: Reproductive and Resistant Agency in Two 'Action' Sports." *Journal of Sport and Social Issues* 32: 24–47.

Lesser, Eric L. 2000. *Knowledge and Social Capital: Foundations and Applications.* Woburn, MA: Butterworth-Heinemann.

Life of Luxury. 2010. "Ironman Executive Challenge (XC)." *Life of Luxury,* June 1. Retrieved November 25, 2012. http://www.thelifeofluxury.com/ironman-executive-challenge-xc/.

Lincoln, Y. S. and E. G. Guba. 1985. *Naturalistic Inquiry.* Beverly Hills, CA: Sage.

Loland, Sigmund. 2006. "Three Approaches to the Study of Pain in Sport." In *Pain and Injury in Sport: Social and Ethical Analysis*, edited by Sigmund Loland, Berit Skirstad, and Ivan Waddington, 49–62. New York: Routledge.

Mackinnon, Kevin. 2011. "Ironmanlife: Performances of the Year." *Ironman.com.* Retrieved January 3, 2012. http://m.ironman.com/triathlon-news/articles/2011/12/ironmanlife-performances-of-the-year.aspx#axzz3m2ICuWHC.

Markus, Hazel, and Paula S. Nurius. 1986. "Possible Selves." *American Psychologist* 41: 954–969.

Markus, Hazel, and Ann Ruvolo. 1989. "Possible Selves: Personalized Representations of Goals." In *Global Concepts in Personality and Social Psychology*, edited by Lawrence A. Pervin, 211–241. Hillsdale, NJ: Erlbaum.

Marshall, Catherine, and Gretchen B. Rossman. 1999. *Designing Qualitative Research.* 3rd ed. Thousand Oaks, CA: Sage.

Marsiglio, William. 2008. *Men on a Mission: Valuing Youth Work in Our Communities.* Baltimore, MD: The Johns Hopkins University Press.

Marsiglio, William, and Mark Cohan. 1997. "Young Fathers and Child Development." In *The Role of the Father in Child Development*, 3rd ed., edited by Michael R. Lamb, 227–244, 373–376. New York: Wiley.

Marsiglio, William, and Sally Hutchinson. 2002. *Sex, Men, and Babies: Stories of Awareness and Responsibility.* New York: NYU Press.

Marsiglio, William, and Joseph H. Pleck. 2005. "Fatherhood and Masculinities." In *The Handbook of Studies on Men and Masculinities*, edited by Robert W. Connell, Jeff R. Hearn, and Michael S. Kimmel, 249–269. Thousand Oaks, CA: Sage.

Marsiglio, William, and Kevin Roy. 2012. *Nurturing Dads: Social Initiatives for Contemporary Fatherhood.* ASA Rose Monograph Series. New York: Russell Sage Foundation.

Marsiglio, William, Kevin Roy, and Greer Litton Fox. 2005. *Situated Fathering: A Focus on Physical and Social Places.* Lanham, MD: Rowman and Littlefield.

McCarville, Ron. 2007. "From a Fall in the Mall to a Run in the Sun: One Journey to Ironman Triathlon." *Leisure Sciences* 29 (2): 159–173.

McGillivray, David J., and Linda Glass Fechter. 2006. *The Last Pick: The Boston Marathon Race Director's Road to Success.* Foreword by Joan Benoit Samuelson. Emmaus, PA: Rodale.

McNees, Mark. 2011. *Immersion: Live the Life God Envisioned for You.* CreateSpace Independent Publishing Platform.

Mead, George Herbert. 1934. *Mind, Self, and Society.* Chicago: University of Chicago Press.

Messner, Michael A. 1995. *Power at Play: Sports and the Problem of Masculinity.* Boston, MA: Beacon.

_____. 1997. *Politics of Masculinities: Men in Movements.* Thousand Oaks, CA: Sage.

Messner, Michael A., Michele D. Dunbar, and Darnell M. Hunt. 2012. "The Televised Sports Manhood Formula." In *Sport in Contemporary Society*, 9th ed., edited by D. Stanley Eitzen, 59–72. Boulder, CO: Paradigm.

Messner, Michael A., and Michela Musto. 2014. "Where Are the Kids?" *Sociology of Sport Journal* 31: 102–122.

Midol, Nancy, and Gerard Broyer. 1995. "Towards an Anthropological Analysis of New Sport Cultures: The Case of Whiz Sports in France." *Sociology of Sport Journal* 12: 204–212.

Milestone, Katie, and Anneke Meyer. 2012. *Gender and Popular Culture.* Cambridge: Polity.

Milkie, Melissa A., Marybeth J. Mattingly, Kei M. Nomaguchi, Suzanne M. Bianchi, and John P. Robinson. 2004. "The Time Squeeze: Parental Statuses and Feelings about Time with Children." *Journal of Marriage and Family* 66: 739–761.

Miller, Toby. 1998. "Commodifying the Male Body, Problematizing 'Hegemonic Masculinity?'" *Journal of Sport and Social Issues* 22 (4): 431–446.

Moore, Mark E., Chris Keller, and James E. Zemanek Jr. 2011. "The Marketing Revolution of Tim Tebow: A Celebrity Endorsement Case Study." *Innovative Marketing* 7 (1): 17–25.

Murphy, Ben. 2010. "The Transformer: Ironman Dan Benintendi." *Thefatherlife.com*, October 22. Retrieved January 20, 2013. http://thefatherlife.com/mag/2010/10/22/the-transformer-ironman-dan-benintendi/.

Nash, Jennifer C. 2008. "Re-thinking Intersectionality." *Feminist Review* 89: 1–15.

Nixon, Howard L. II. 1996. "The Relationship of Friendship Networks, Sport Experiences, and Gender to Expressed Pain Thresholds." *Sociology of Sport Journal* 13: 340–355.

Norris, Pippa. 2001. *Digital Divide: Civic Engagement, Information Poverty and the Internet Worldwide.* Cambridge: Cambridge University Press.

Norris, Trevor. 2006. "Hannah Arendt and Jean Baudrillard: Pedagogy in the Consumer Society." *Studies in Philosophy and Education* 25: 457–477.

Novak, Michael. 2013. "Foreword." In *Sports and Christianity: Historical and Contemporary Perspectives*, edited by Nick J. Watson and Andrew Parker, xi–xiii. New York: Routledge.

Ogles, Benjamin M., and Kevin S. Masters. 2000. "Older vs. Younger Adult Male Marathon Runners: Participative Motives and Training Habits." *Journal of Sport Behavior* 23 (2): 130–143.

_____. 2003. "A Typology of Marathon Runners Based on Cluster Analysis of Motivations." *Journal of Sport Behavior* 26 (11): 69–85.

Overstock.com. 2010. "There's an Ironman among Us." *Inside Overstock* (blog), October 14. Retrieved January 20, 2013. http://www.overstock.com/63326/static.html.

Pain, Matt T. G., and Matthew A. Pain. 2005. "Risk Taking in Sport." *Lancet* 366 (1): S33–S34.

Parry, Jim, Mark Nesti, Simon Robinson, and Nick Watson. *Sport and Spirituality: An Introduction.* New York: Routledge.

Pleck, Joseph H. 2004. "Two Dimensions of Fatherhood: A History of the Good Dad–Bad Dad Complex." In *The Role of the Father in Child Development*, 4th ed., edited by Michael E. Lamb, 32–57. Hoboken, NJ: Wiley.

Pleck, Joseph H., and Brian P. Masciadrelli. 2004. "Paternal Involvement by U.S. Residential Fathers: Levels, Sources, and Consequences." In *The Role of the Father in Child Development*, 3rd ed., edited by Michael E. Lamb, 222–271. New York: Wiley.

Pringle, Richard. 2005. "Masculinities, Sport, and Power: A Critical Comparison of Gramscian and Foucauldian Inspired Theoretical Tools." *Journal of Sport and Social Issues* 29 (3): 256–278.

_____. 2009. "Defamiliarizing Heavy-Contact Sports: A Critical Examination of Rugby, Discipline, and Pleasure." *Sociology of Sport Journal* 26: 211–234.

Pringle, Richard, Robert E. Rinehart, and Jayne Caudwell, eds. 2015. *Sport and the Social Significance of Pleasure*. New York: Routledge.

Pronger, Brian. 1990. *The Arena of Masculinity: Sports, Homosexuality, and the Meaning of Sex*. New York: St. Martin's.

Putnam, Robert. 1995. "Bowling Alone: America's Declining Social Capital." *Journal of Democracy* 6 (1): 65–78.

_____. 2000. *Bowling Alone: The Collapse and Revival of American Community*. New York: Simon & Schuster Paperbacks.

Putney, Clifford. 2001. *Muscular Christianity: Manhood and Sports in Protestant America, 1880–1920*. Cambridge, MA: Harvard University Press.

Rapoport, Rhona, and Robert N. Rapoport. 1975. "Leisure and the Family Life Cycle." In *Sociology of Leisure: A Reader*, edited by Chas Critcher, Peter Bramham, and Alan Tomlinson, 66–70. London: E. and F. N. Spoon.

Rapp, Jordan. 2012. "Status Bauble or Self Discovery." *Slowtwitch.com*, December 17. Retrieved December 17, 2012. http://www.slowtwitch.com/Opinion/Status_Bauble_or_Self_Discovery_3281.html.

Rinehart, Robert E., and Synthia Syndor, eds. 2003. *To the Extreme: Alternative Sports, Inside and Out*. Albany: State University of New York Press.

Roderick, Martin. 2006. "The Sociology of Pain and Injury in Sport: Main Perspectives and Problems." In *Pain and Injury in Sport: Social and Ethical Analysis*, edited by Sigmund Loland, Berit Skirstad, and Ivan Waddington, 17–33. New York: Routledge.

Rosecrance, John. 1985. "The Invisible Horseman: The Social World of the Backstretch." *Qualitative Sociology* 8 (3): 248–265.

Ryle, Robyn. 2015. *Questioning Gender: A Sociological Exploration*, 2nd ed. Thousand Oaks, CA: Sage.

Schrock, Douglas, and Michael Schwalbe. 2009. "Men, Masculinity, and Manhood Acts." *Annual Review of Sociology* 35: 277–295.

Seippel, Ørnulf. 2006. "Sport and Social Capital." *Acta Sociologica* 49 (2): 169–183.

_____ 2008. "Sports in Civil Society: Networks, Social Capital, and Influence." *European Sociological Review* 24 (1): 69–80.

Shaw, Susan M., and Don Dawson. 2001. "Purposive Leisure: Examining Parental Discourses on Family Activities." *Leisure Sciences* 23 (4): 217–231.

Snarey, John. 1993. *How Fathers Care for the Next Generation: A Four Decade Study*. Foreword by George E. Vaillant. Cambridge, MA: Harvard University Press.

Speechly, David P., Sheila R. Taylor, and Geoffrey G. Rogers. 1996. "Differences in Ultra-Endurance Exercise in Performance-Matched Male and Female Runners." *Medicine & Science in Sports & Exercise* 28 (3): 359–365.

Stebbins, Robert A. 1992. *Amateurs, Professionals, and Serious Leisure*. Montreal and Kingston: McGill-Queen's University Press.

_____. 2007. *Serious Leisure: A Perspective for Our Time*. New Brunswick, NJ: Transaction Publishers.

Stoddart, Mark C. J. 2011. "Constructing Masculinized Sportscapes: Skiing, Gender, and Nature in British Columbia." *International Review for the Sociology of Sport* 46 (1): 108–124.

Strauss, Anselm Leonard. 1969. "Turning Points in Identity." In *Mirrors and Masks: Transformations of Identity*, 92–100. New York: Macmillan.

Strauss, Anselm Leonard, and Juliet M. Corbin. 1990. *Basics of Qualitative Research: Grounded Theory Procedures and Techniques*. Thousand Oaks, CA: Sage.

_____. 1994. "Grounded Theory Methodology—An Overview." In *Handbook of Qualitative Research*, edited by Norman K. Denzin and Yvonna S. Lincoln, 273–285. Thousand Oaks, CA: Sage.

_____. 1998. *Basics of Qualitative Research: Techniques and Procedures for Developing Grounded Theory*. 2nd ed. Thousand Oaks, CA: Sage.

Stryker, Sheldon. 1968. "Identity Salience and Role Performance: The Relevance of Symbolic Interaction Theory for Family Research." *Journal of Marriage and the Family* 4: 558–564.

_____. 1980. *Symbolic Interactionism: A Social Structural Version*. Menlo Park, CA: Benjamin/Cummings Publishing Co.

Stryker, Sheldon, and Peter J. Burke. 2000. "The Past, Present, and Future of an Identity Theory." *Social Psychology Quarterly* 63 (4): 284–297.

Thorpe, Holly. 2005. "Jibbing the Gender Order: Females in the Snowboarding Culture." *Sport in Society* 8: 76–100.

_____. 2008. "Foucault, Technologies of Self, and the Media: Discourses of Femininity in Snowboarding Culture." *Journal of Sport and Social Issues* 32: 199–229.

Tomlinson, Alan. 1998. "Power: Domination, Negotiation, and Resistance in Sports Cultures." *Journal of Sport and Social Issues* 22: 235–240.

Tomlinson, Alan, Neil Ravenscroft, Belinda Wheaton, and Paul Gilchrist. 2005. "Lifestyle Sports and National Sport Policy: An Agenda for Research." *Report to Sport England*. Chelsea School Research Centre, UK.

TribeGroup. 2009. "The Mind of the Triathlete: Executive Summary." *USAtriathlon.org*. Retrieved January 20, 2010. www.usatriathlon.org/~/media/7b4ece9adaaa4c18804fa90571997a90.ashx.

Trujillo, Nick. 1991. "Hegemonic Masculinity on the Mound: Media Representations of Nolan Ryan and American Sports Culture." *Critical Studies in Mass Communication* 8: 290–308. http://www.uky.edu/~addesa01/documents/Trujillo_Baseball.pdf.

USA Triathlon. 2011. "SGMA Report: U.S. Triathlon Participation Reaches 2.3 Million in 2010." *USAtriathlon.org*, August 2011. Retrieved January 2014. http://www.usatriathlon.org/news/articles/2011/08/sgma-report-us-triathlon-participation-reaches-23-million-in-2010.aspx.

_____. 2014a. "NCAA Triathlon News." *USAtriathlon.org*, January 2014. Retrieved June 9, 2014. http://www.usatriathlon.org/about-multisport/ncaa.aspx.

_____. 2014b. "USA Triathlon Annual Membership Hits Record High in 2013." *USAtriathlon.org*, June 2014. Retrieved September 1, 2014. http://www.usatriathlon.org/about-multisport/demographics.aspx.

_____. 2015. "USA Triathlon Annual Membership Report." *USAtriathlon.org*, August 2015. Retrieved September 11, 2015. http://www.usatriathlon.org/about-multisport/demographics.aspx.

U.S. Census Bureau. 2010. *Statistical Abstract of the United States: 2010*. Washington, DC: U.S. Department of Commerce.

van den Hoonaard, Will C. 1997. *Working with Sensitizing Concepts: Analytical Field Research*. Thousand Oaks, CA: Sage.

van Ingen, Cathy. 2003. "Geographies of Gender, Sexuality, and Race: Reframing the Focus on Space in Sport Sociology." *International Review for the Sociology of Sport* 38: 201–216.

Varner, Monica K., and J. David Knottnerus. 2002. "Civility, Rituals, and Exclusion: The Emergence of American Golf during the Late 19th and Early 20th Centuries." *Sociological Inquiry* 72: 426–441.

Venkatesh, Sudhir. 2008. *Gang Leader for a Day: A Rogue Sociologist Takes to the Streets*. New York: Penguin Press.

Vertinsky, Patricia. 2004. "Locating a 'Sense of Place': Space, Place, and Gender in the Gymnasium." In *Sites of Sport: Space, Place, Experience*, edited by Patricia Vertinsky and John Bale, 8–24. London: Routledge.

Voydanoff, Patricia. 2004. "The Effects of Work Demands and Resources on Work-to-Family Conflict and Facilitation." *Journal of Marriage and Family* 66: 398–412.

Waitt, Gordon. 2008. "Killing Waves: Surfing, Space, and Gender." *Social and Cultural Geography* 9: 75–94.

Wang, Wendy, Kim Parker, and Paul Taylor. 2013. *Breadwinner Moms*. Pew Research Center. Retrieved on June 3, 2015. http://www.pewsocialtrends.org/2013/05/29/breadwinner-moms/.

Watson, J. 2000. *Male Bodies: Health, Culture and Identity*. Buckingham: Open University Press.

Watson, Jonathan, and Sarah Nettleton, eds. 2000. "The Male Body in Everyday Life." In *Male Bodies: Health, Culture, and Identity*, 89–108. Buckingham: Open University Press.

Watson, Nick J., and Andrew Parker, eds. 2013. *Sports and Christianity: Historical and Contemporary Perspectives*. New York: Routledge.

Weber, Max. 1978. *Economy and Society: An Outline of Interpretive Sociology*. Edited by Guenther Roth and Claus Wittich. Los Angeles: University of California Press.

Weil, Elizabeth. 2012. "The Ironman: Triathlete Executives' Ultimate Status Feat." *Bloomberg Businessweek*, December 13. Retrieved December 13, 2012. http://www.bloomberg.com/bw/articles/2012–12–13/the-ironman-triathlete-executives-ultimate-status-feat.

Wheaton, Belinda. 2004. *Understanding Lifestyle Sports: Consumption, Identity, and Difference*. New York: Routledge.

Willer, Robb, Christabel L. Rogalin, Bridget Conlon, and Michael T. Wojnowicz. 2013. "Overdoing Gender: A Test of the Masculine Overcompensation Thesis." *American Journal of Sociology* 118: 980–1022.

Williams, D. J. 2009. "Deviant Leisure: Rethinking 'The Good, the Bad, and the Ugly.'" *Leisure Sciences* 31 (2): 207–213.

Willms, Nicole. 2009. "Fathers and Daughters: Negotiating Gendered Relationships in Sport." In *Fathering through Sport and Leisure*, edited by Tess Kay, 124–144. New York: Routledge.

World Triathlon Corporation. 2009. "Universal Sports and WTC Sign Multi-Year Deal." *Ironman.com*, September 10. Retrieved September 11, 2009. http://www.ironman.com/triathlon-news/articles/2009/09/universal-sports-and-wtc-sign-multi-year-deal.aspx#axzz203ZSx8oo.

———. 2012. "IRONMAN Coeur d'Alene 2012—Full Circle." *YouTube.com*, June 29. Retrieved July 1, 2012. http://www.youtube.com/watch?v=JgzM5wVErbo.

———. 2013. "IRONMAN Florida Sells Out in Record Time." *Ironman.com*, November 5. Retrieved November 7, 2013. http://www.ironman.com/triathlon-news/articles/2012/11/ironman-florida-sells-out-in-record-time.aspx#axzz203ZSx8oo.

———. N.d. "The IRONMAN Foundation: Everyone's Non-Profit." *Ironman.com*. Retrieved June 3, 2015. http://www.ironman.com/triathlon/organizations/ironman-foundation/programs/your-journey-your-cause.aspx#ixzz3eNMHZOqt.

Yeung, W. Jean, John F. Sandberg, Pamela E. Davis-Kean, and Sandra L. Hofferth. 2001. "Children's Time with Fathers in Intact Families." *Journal of Marriage and the Family* 63: 136–154.

Young, Kevin. 2004. "Sports-Related Pain and Injury: Sociological Notes." In *Sporting Bodies, Damaged Selves: Sociological Studies of Sports-Related*, edited by Kevin Young, 1–25. Bingley, UK: Emerald Group Publishing Limited.

Youngman, Jason D. 2007. "Risk for Exercise Addiction: A Comparison of Triathletes Training for Sprint-, Olympic-, Half-Ironman-, and Ironman-distance Triathlons." PhD diss., University of Miami.

INDEX

abuse, 21
Adams, Adi, 63
Adams, Mary Louise, 34
advice for parents, 150–151
Alvarez, Luis, 90
Anderson, Eric, 63
Andrade, Juan, 166
athletic invisibility, 68, 70–71, 73–74, 78, 86
athletic visibility continuum, 14, 24–25, 61,
    68–74, 133, 142; faith and, 111, 114–115, 117;
    invisible training, 68, 70–71, 73–74,
    78, 86
Augusta National Golf Club, 14
authenticity, 89, 94–100

balancing mechanisms, 14, 74–86, 133;
    compromise with family, 75–80; faith as,
    119–120; technology as, 102–103; in
    two-athlete families, 79–80
Barry, Dan, 112
Beginnertriathlete.com, 10–11, 155–156
bike stickers, 96–97
Birks, Melanie, 161
Blaydon, Michelle J., 67
blogs, 8–11, 88, 101, 135–137, 155–157; quitting
    training and, 125–127, 131. See also
    Beginnertriathlete.com;
    Slowtwitch.com
body marking, 117, 125
body transition, 44–49
Bourdieu, Pierre, 15, 90
Brah, Avtar, 62
Bridel, William, 30, 123

Cafrae, Marinda, 39
Charmaz, Kathy, 134, 160

class, economic and social, 15–16, 24, 87–95,
    100; conflict negotiation and, 103–104;
    economic costs of triathlon, 36, 57, 92–94,
    104–107, 137, 141; intersectionality and,
    61–62; Iron Dad identity and, 89, 100;
    IRONMAN culture and, 35–36, 87, 90,
    98; occupational flexibility and, 90,
    100–103; sporting guilt and, 142; sports
    participation and, 15–16, 47, 61, 88–91;
    triathlon and, 16, 35, 87, 91–95,
    104–107
collegiate sports, 107–108
commercialization, 35–36, 98–99; IRONMAN
    brand and, 22, 96, 98, 100
competitive aspirations, 86
conflict negotiation, 89, 103–104
Connell, R. W., 33, 131–132
consumption, 16–17, 89, 92–94,
    98–100, 168
context, 68, 72–74
Cooney, Martha, 148
Corbin, Juliet M., 159–161
Crenshaw, Kimberlé, 61
Crosset, Todd, 15
cycling, 95, 141; bike stickers, 96–97;
    costs of bicycles, 16, 35, 94, 95–97;
    triathlon bike as symbol of authenticity,
    37, 95–96

Doucet, Andrea, 6

economic costs of triathlon, 36, 57, 92–94,
    104–107, 137, 141
Empfield, Dan, 151
endurance sport. See also sport; triathlon
exercise addiction, 67, 71–72

faith, 25, 109–120; athletic visibility continuum and, 111, 114–115, 117; as balancing mechanism, 119–120; Fellowship of Christian Athletes (FCA), 57–58, 109, 113–114, 117, 119; masculinity and, 113; as motivation for participation in triathlon, 57–58, 118; religious gatherings at IRONMAN events, 109–111; sport and, 25, 111–113; training and, 58
family-friendly races, 80–82, 147–148, 150–151
fatherhood, 4–7, 39–40, 138–139; athletic visibility and, 71; compromise with family, 75–80; fathers as role models, 49–53; generative fathering, 50–51; Iron Dad identity and, 24, 28–30, 40, 50, 80; narratives of masculinity, 6; self-image of fathers, 6; societal expectations of, 4–6, 39–40; sport and, 20–21, 51; superdads, 5; training and, 6–7, 64–65, 64–66, 70, 73, 75, 83–86, 125–126, 139; work-family conflict and, 6, 39–40. See also Iron Dad identity
Fellowship of Christian Athletes (FCA), 57–58, 109, 113–114, 117, 119
feminism, 99–100
finish-line chute policy, 149–150
fitness, 14, 22–23, 50, 102; as motivation for participation, 44, 46, 48. See also health
front/back stage performance, 72, 94, 127, 129
fundraising, 58–59

generativity, 50, 52, 140–141
Giddens, Anthony, 37
Goffman, Erving, 37, 72
Goldman, Robert, 99–100
golf, 14–15, 90
grounded theory approach, 8–14, 43, 61–62, 68, 90, 158–161

Hanold, Maylon, 16
health, 22–23; as motivation for participation in triathlon, 44–50
Heath, Deborah, 99–100
hegemonic masculinity, 6, 33–35, 39, 100, 124–125, 131–132
HITS Endurance series, 137, 150
Hollander, Lew, 45–46
Hoyt, Dick and Rick, 10, 131–132, 155
Huizinga, Johan, 44
Hutchinson, Sally, 47, 127

ice skating, 34
identity, 28–32, 140; athletic visibility continuum model and, 68; cycling and, 95; faith and, 114; Iron Dad identity, 24, 27, 50; iron-distance triathlon and, 30–32; IRONMAN identity, 30–32, 38, 123, 153n1; multiple identities, 28–30; reflexive biography and, 37; sporting identity, 14, 32–33, 68, 74–75, 114, 139–140; symbolism and, 36–37. See also Iron Dad identity; IRONMAN identity
inclusive masculinity, 127, 131–132
Ingraham, Wendy, 34
Inkinen, Sami, 167
integration, 68, 71–72, 75, 86
intentionality, 68, 70–71
intersectionality, 61–62, 67, 82
interview process, 9–10, 133–135, 138–139, 156–160, 162–164, 166
invisible training, 68, 70–71, 73–74, 78, 86
Iron Couples, 138–139
Iron Dad identity, 24, 27, 37, 50, 77; authenticity and, 94–95; balancing mechanisms and, 74–75, 80; class and, 89; commercialism and, 35–37; Executive Challenge (XC) and, 168; expectations of athletes, 39; faith and, 111, 115; fathers as role models, 50–52; quitting and, 123–124; role of women in, 7; sporting guilt and, 62–65; symbolism and, 94–95. See also fatherhood; identity; IRONMAN identity
iron-distance events. See triathlon
IRONKIDS events, 80–81, 148
IRONMAN brand, 11, 18, 22, 34, 38, 153n1; commodification of, 22, 96, 98, 100; media coverage and, 55
IRONMAN culture, 27; author's personal experience of, 3, 41–42; body transformation and, 47; commercialization and, 35–36; faith and, 110–111; identity formation and, 28–32; manliness and, 34; pain and, 59–60; quitting training and, 125–127; symbolism and, 94–100
IRONMAN Foundation, 58–59
IRONMAN identity, 30–32, 38, 123, 153n1; commercialization of, 35–36; expectations accompanying, 38–39. See also identity; Iron Dad identity

IRONMAN races, 9, 57; age-grouping in, 45–46; author's personal experience of, 26–27, 41–42, 109–110, 156–157; children's involvement in, 81; cost of, 36, 57, 92–94, 104–107, 137, 141; demographics of, 20; faith and, 116; IRONMAN Arizona, 82; IRONMAN 70.3 Austin, 108; IRONMAN Chattanooga, 19; IRONMAN Coeur d'Alene, 13, 31, 54; IRONMAN Executive Challenge program, 87–88, 90, 166–168; IRONMAN Florida, 3, 8, 19, 82, 93; IRONMAN Lake Placid, 44; IRONMAN St. George, 34, 124; IRONMAN Timberman, 1–2; IRONMAN U.S. Championship, 19; IRONMAN Wisconsin, 3, 124; IRONMAN World Championship, 15, 34, 39; media broadcast of, 54–55; religious gatherings at, 110. *See also* triathlon

Iron Moms, 4, 7, 23, 45, 138

Iron Prayer meetings, 109–111, 119

"Iron Widows," 65–66, 159

Kaufman, Gayle, 5

Kay, Tess, 21, 40

Kennelly, Millicent, 18, 43–44, 138

Kimmel, Michael, 33

Kosove, Andrew, 166

Kriso, Monica, 148

Lamont, Matthew, 18, 43–44, 138

LaRossa, Ralph, 6

Laurendeau, Jason, 35

Lieto, Matt, 53

Linder, Koenraad J., 67

the long ride, 77–80

Marine Corps Marathon (MCM), 146

marriage, 7–8, 45, 129–130; "Iron Widows," 65–66, 159; job stress and, 40; training and spouses, 7–8, 65–67, 70, 78–80, 121–122, 129–130, 154, 159

Marsiglio, William, 47, 127

masculinity, 33–35, 123, 131–132; commodification of, 36, 89, 100; faith and, 113; hegemonic masculinity, 6, 33–35, 39, 100, 124–125, 131–132; inclusive masculinity, 127, 131–132; income earning and, 6, 67, 131; Iron Dad identity and, 37, 39; sport and, 6, 32–35, 39, 46, 63, 67, 124–125, 131

materialism, 16, 35, 92–94, 98. *See also* commercialization; consumption

McCarville, Ron, 44

McCormack, Mark, 63

McGillivray, David, 161

McNees, Mark, 110–111

Mead, George Herbert, 36

Messner, Michael, 139

Mills, Jane, 161

motherhood, 4–6, 138, 142; Iron Moms, 4, 7, 23, 45, 138; societal expectations of, 4; women's workforce participation and, 5–6

Multisport Ministries, 114

Muscular Christianity framework, 113

Musto, Michela, 139

Newbold, Phil, 166

obtrusiveness, 68–70

occupational flexibility, 67, 89, 90, 100–103, 107

pain, 32, 59–60; endurance sport and, 34–35, 141; masculinity and, 39; pleasure and, 23–24, 44; quitting training and, 34, 122, 124

Philadelphia Marathon, 148

Phoenix, Ann, 62

pleasure, 23–24, 44, 59–60, 141

policy advice for race directors, 143–150; child-friendly races, 147–148; finish-line chute policy, 149–150; refund and transfer policies, 143–147

pre-race ritual, 29, 125, 127

privilege, 15, 61–62, 107; gender and, 33, 46; Iron Dads as privileged, 24, 33–34, 61, 101; triathlon and, 4, 32–34, 137

progressive masculinity, 127, 131–132

race-cation, 7–8, 82, 103–104

Raelert, Andreas, 39

Rapoport, Rhona and Robert, 20

Rapp, Jordan, 97, 167

reflexive biography, 37

refund and transfer policies, 123, 143–147, 151

Reilly, Mike, 10, 26, 47, 51–52, 143

religion. *See* faith

research methodology, 8–14, 133–138, 153–161;
interviews, 9–10, 133–135, 138–139, 156–160,
162–164, 166; participant selection, 158–159;
personal observations, 11–12; recruitment
strategies, 155–156; textual analysis, 10–11;
use of Internet, 8–11, 135–136, 155–156,
170n2
Rev3 series, 11, 148–151
Rhodes, Jeff, 34
role salience, 22, 29

selfishness, 3, 7, 57, 59, 84, 102, 127–129, 167
Slowtwitch.com, 10–11, 155–156
Smith, Sharon L., 99–100
social class, 24
sport, 14–20; children's involvement in, 80–82,
139–140, 147–148; class and, 15–16, 47, 61,
88–91; collegiate sports, 107–108; faith
and, 25, 111–113; fatherhood and, 20–21,
51; gender and, 33–35; growing popularity
of endurance sport, 18–20; health and,
22–23; masculinity and, 6, 32–35, 39, 46,
63, 67, 124–125, 131; materialism and, 16–17;
middle-class values and, 15–16; motivations
for participation, 43–44; physically
challenged athletes and, 131–132; privilege
in, 15, 137; societal vs. individual views of,
63–64; sporting failure, 123; sporting guilt,
14, 24, 62–65, 73, 133, 142, 161; sporting
identity, 14, 32–33, 68, 74–75, 114, 139–140;
work and, 22. See also training; triathlon
sporting failure, 123
sporting guilt, 14, 24, 62–65, 133, 142, 161;
training and, 73
sporting identity, 14, 32–33, 68, 74–75, 114,
139–140; consumption and, 98; faith and,
111, 115
spouses. See marriage
Stephens, Cathy, 31
Strauss, Anselm Leonard, 159–161
structural overlap, 29
Stryker, Sheldon, 29
superdads, 5
symbolic interactionist (SI) perspective, 20,
36–37
symbolism, 94–100; consumption and, 98–100

Tebow, Tim, 112
Thom, Kara Douglass, 55

training, 3, 24; author's personal experience
of, 153–154; compromise and, 75–80;
concept of time and, 77; dropping down
in distance, 130–131; emotional impact
of quitting, 125–127; exercise addiction,
67, 71–72; faith and, 58, 115–116; invisible
training, 68, 70–71, 73–74, 86; location of,
75–76; the long ride and, 77–80; obsession
and, 65–67; obtrusiveness and, 69–70;
pain and, 34, 76, 122, 124; parenting and,
6–7, 9, 64–66, 73, 75, 83–86, 125–126, 139;
perceptions of training programs, 64–65;
reasons for ending, 25, 122–124, 127–130;
selfishness and, 3, 7, 57, 59, 84, 102, 127–129;
sporting guilt and, 73; spouses and, 7–8,
65–67, 69–70, 78–80, 121–122, 129–130, 154,
159; workplace conflicts and, 73–74, 101–103
triathlon, 1, 17–21, 23; age-grouping in, 45–46,
107–108; author's personal experience of,
12–14, 26–27, 41, 153–155; bodily transition
and, 44–49; children's involvement in,
80–82, 139–140; class and, 16, 35, 87, 89,
91–95, 104–107; at collegiate level, 107–108;
consumption and, 16–17, 92–94, 98–100,
168; demographics of participants, 20–22,
91–92, 107; dropping down in distance,
130–131; economic costs of, 36, 57, 92–94,
104–107, 137, 141; Executive Challenge
(XC) program, 87–88, 90, 166–168; faith
and, 57–58, 109–111, 115–116; gender and,
15, 33–35; health as motivation, 44–50;
identity formation and, 30–32; inclusive
masculinity and, 131–132; insurance
and, 123, 145, 146–147, 151; iron-distance
contrasted with standard, 3, 18, 43, 77, 141;
as means for doing the extraordinary,
53–54; media as motivation, 54–55;
obsession and, 65–67; occupations of
participants, 40; pain and, 34–35; as
participation in something larger than self,
57–59, 118; physically challenged athletes
and, 131–132; policy advice for, 143–150;
popular conceptions of competitors, 38–39;
privilege and, 4, 32–34, 137; proximity as
motivation, 56–57, 144; refund and transfer
policies, 123, 143–147, 151; role modeling as
motivation, 49–52; selfishness and, 3, 7, 57,
59, 84, 102, 128–129, 167; as status symbol,
87–88, 166–167; training for, 3; types of,

17–18; ultra-distance, 140–141; weather conditions and, 123–124; women in, 39. *See also* IRONMAN races; sport

Tri Dads, 139

turning points, 49, 123, 127–128; ending of training and, 127–128; IRONMAN identity and, 30–31

ultra-distance triathlon, 140–141

Ultraman race series, 140–141

United States Triathlon Association, 18

Urbach, Rob, 54

USA Triathlon (USAT), 19, 156

Venkatesh, Sudhir, 12, 153n2

Watson, Jonathan, 45

Weber, Max, 89

weight loss, 46–50

Weil, Elizabeth, 87–88, 167–168

Welch, Sian, 34

Wellington, Chrissy, 15, 39

Wheaton, Belinda, 30

Wide World of Sports (television program), 54–55

Wilson, Erica, 138

World Triathlon Corporation (WTC), 18, 22; Executive Challenge program, 87–88, 90, 166–168; fundraising and, 58–59; refund and transfer policies, 143–145, 151; youth races and, 80–81. *See also* IRONMAN races

Youngman, Jason D., 67

ABOUT THE AUTHOR

DIANA TRACY COHEN currently serves as an associate professor of political science at Central Connecticut State University (CCSU). A sport ethnographer, she writes on marathon and multi-sport cultures. She has authored multiple pieces on teaching qualitative methods through active learning. Additionally, she has published works on the topic of new media integration into political campaigns. Her current work in progress, *Invisible Pelotons: The Gendered Politics of Cycling,* investigates the lived experiences of professional female cyclists. Diana works as a faculty expert for CCSU's Center for Public Policy and Analysis, where she has served as the principal investigator for numerous survey research projects.

Diana is an avid endurance athlete. She has finished nine IRONMAN events, fifteen 70.3s, and more than forty marathons. She has a particular fondness for multi-day running challenges. A certified third-degree black belt with the World Tae Kwon Do Federation, she trains under the tutelage of Grandmaster Moo Yong Lee. While an undergraduate at the University of Connecticut, Diana had the honor of serving as the starting goaltender for the Huskies' inaugural Division I women's ice hockey team. From 2001 through 2015, she held the school record for number of saves in a single game (55). Diana resides in northeastern Connecticut with her husband, Dan, and two cats, Nemo and Busker.

CPSIA information can be obtained
at www.ICGtesting.com
Printed in the USA
BVOW11s0214090416

443451BV00006B/18/P

9 780813 570945